From P...

... To Prosperity

Blueprint
For a
Democratic
Humanistic
Economy

By Darwen Cook

Going to the Economic

"Moon"

Text Copyright © 2014 Darwen Cook
All Rights Reserved

Published by Amazon.com July 4, 2014

2nd Update October 31, 2016

3rd Update November 15, 2017

4th Update December 10, 2018

To my wife and kids for their love and support:

You can chase after the truth in your mind,

But you can only capture it in your heart,

And savor it in your soul!

Dedicated to a Brave New Breed

This book envisions a new frontier of Economic Engineering based on axiomatic principles and human rights intended to achieve maximum economic prosperity for the vast majority of all humanity sustained indefinitely. We will build this new discipline with little risk on the sound foundation of the conventional theories of macroeconomics and microeconomics by embedding them inside a new metaeconomic shell based on these humanistic first principles. So this book begins where *Small is beautiful; economics as if people mattered* left off in 1973.

Schumacher introduced the idea that metaeconomics should establish "the place and role of man in the economy". I have expanded and completed that idea to include the converse proactive idea that metaeconomics should also define the role of economics in human life. This idea mandates that human life came first and foremost and that economics must be subservient not just the other way around! It also implies that metaeconomics should be proactive not passive. So humanity should **define and assert** the proper role of economics in human life as a true "human science" rather than just studying how "wealth economics" affects human life as a passive economic victim.

For the first time in history the field of Economics will be harnessed using the superstructure of human rights and axiomatic first principles to modern engineering technology and methodology that proactively produce and optimize democratic economic prosperity for all mankind. Consequently the field of Economics will become proactive for all humanity as **principals of our economy** instead of being passive for humanity as victims. This new metaeconomic idea represents a true **renaissance** in economic thinking making Capitalism humane based on a new prosperity paradigm instead of Capitalism's profit paradigm.

We will no longer need to try to live high-tech "smartphone" lives in a medieval economic world. Soon these new ideas may become part of the curriculum in the School of Engineering, the School of Political Science, or the School of Economics and it will produce either a new breed of Engineer, a new breed of Economist, or new breed of Political Reformist who can professionally and scientifically lead humanity out of our medieval economic darkness with little or no economic risk!

Table of Contents

Preface: Economic Democracy 6
Prologue: Going to the Economic "Moon" 8
Introduction 9
The Economic Bill of Rights 11
Summary of Key Ideas 13
Summary of the Goals 23
The Humanistic Economic Reform Act (HERA) 26
Title 1: The Greater Good of the Majority 27
Title 2: Formation of the Economic Control Authority 28
Title 3: A Scientific Economy Facilitates Economic Engineering 37
Title 4: Pollution and Depletion of Natural Resources 38
Title 5: Freedom from the Economic Privileged Class 42
Title 6: Equal Value Pay for Equal Valued Productivity 45
Title 7: Equal Currencies Buy Equal Goods and Services 52
Title 8: Minimum Wage Equals Minimum Cost of Living 55
Title 9: The National Fund and Public Capital Formation 57
Title 10: The Responsibility for Worker/Consumer Rights 67
Title 11: Management of National Income and Wealth 68
Title 12: Equal Access to Available Employment 75
Title 13: Business Competition on a Level Playing Field 81
Title 14: The Prosperity Mandate Guides Business Optimization 81
Title 15: Streamline Businesses for Efficiency 86
Title 16: Streamline Business Taxation for Maximum Prosperity 92
Title 17: Eliminate Dividends and Stock Buybacks 95
Title 18: Tax Excessive Sales, Marketing, and Advertising 96
Title 19: Eliminate the Burden of Consumer Credit 101
Title 20: Tax Excessive Legal Costs 103
Title 21: Restrict Management Pay at a 40:1 Ratio 104
Title 22: Scientific Tax Methodologies 109

Title 23: Wealth Tax to Encourage Economic Investment	112
Title 24: Economic Investment and Capital Gains Tax	119
Title 25: Speculation is Threatening Financial Stability	123
Discussion Topics:	125
Is a Humanist a Democrat, Republican, or an Independent?	125
The Wealth Concentration Issue	130
The Invisible Economic Slavery	133
Fair Competition vs Foul Exploitation	137
Capitalism vs Humanism	139
Humanistic Economic Axioms and Guiding Principles	147
Avoiding Class Warfare	158
Crisis Responsibilities and Liabilities	160
The Role of Profits in Humanism	163
The Role of Professional Economists	175
The Role of "Free" Markets in Humanism	180
The Role of Old Wealth vs. New Wealth	194
Perpetual Wealth is Perpetual Power and Perpetual Corruption	198
The Renaissance of Economics as a Science	202
The Academic and Professional Challenge	206
The Role of Labor Efficiency	210
Beware! Economists, Greed & Productivity	217
Nobody is in Charge!	221
It is Time for Economic Law and Order	224
Trickle Down "Magic"	225
It is Time for a New World Order!	229
Near Term Global Economic Outlook	244
What Would Adam Smith Have Thought?	250
Justice in Economics	256
The Unification of Business and Labor	264
Understanding the Power of Design	271

A Legislative Road Map 275
Understanding the Political Challenge 281
Epilogue Discussions: 291
Ok, What Can You Do To Help? 291
Political Strategy and Membership Goal Analysis 293
A Call to Action 296
Phase I: ECA Formation Legislation 298
Bibliography 301

Preface: Economic Democracy

This book is directed to the middle 80% of all humanity and in particular to the middle 80% of humanity in the USA. You have been extorted, exploited, cheated, and lied to for far too long. It is time for an economic renaissance to enlighten you as to your circumstance and to show you a simple path to much greater prosperity. This solution will make you principals of the economy instead of its subjects. It is based on a simple idea that the economy is democratically yours!

Why should you be exploited like a victim of your own economy? The economy should serve the middle 80% instead of the middle 80% serving the economy! This would make our economy democratic: of the people, by the people, and for the people! I hope to empower you and embolden you to seek a more prosperous economy for you and your children. Moreover I hope to highlight a vision by which you can achieve it, simply and easily within your economic and political grasp.

To achieve this goal we will need to think "outside the box". Instead conventional wealth economists, politicians, and financial experts are stuck inside a profit paradigm that is doomed to failure. In this stuck condition they are useless as a resource to achieve our goals. They are capable of contributing much more to the problem than to the solution. They are not just "blind"; rather they are blind to their own blindness!

So we will have to rely more on "outside" expertise and leadership of a "new breed". Luckily we are a nation full of high quality scientific, mathematical, engineering, and technical expertise that can quickly adapt to a new paradigm with new ideas and new solutions. These "outsiders" are not stuck in the old paradigm; therefore it is easy for them to see solutions where the insiders only see unsolvable issues.

The issues facing us and the benefits of greater prosperity are not based on complex mathematics or esoteric economic theories. Instead they are based on common sense and simple arithmetic that anyone can understand. If you find some aspects of this book to be too complex it is my failure to simplify not your inadequacy or the complexity of the idea. Please read on; it will probably be explained better again later on or it is just a detail not worth any more confusion.

Most of all do not give up because you think this is just another "pie in the sky" fantasy that will never materialize. It is attainable and the effort required by you and your fellow man is very small and doable. Furthermore the effort will be successful even if only a fraction of you have the courage to stand and participate! Only 56 people risked their lives by signing our Declaration of Independence. Like our forefathers, a brave minority can achieve democracy for the vast majority of all!

You don't need a savior and you don't need permission! Your strength is in your numbers and your political democracy already entitles you to economic democracy! Once you are done reading ask yourself the key feasibility question: when we vote on these economic reforms will we have the most votes or will they? We outnumber them a hundred to one! How could we not have the most votes? Even if a savior did arrive, she or he would likely succumb to a disease or an accident soon thereafter. So don't get caught up waiting for personalities and saviors!

Ideas are much more powerful because they empower all mankind so they last forever! This economic blueprint will make our economic destination perfectly clear. The path *from profits* for the privileged, *to prosperity* for all mankind will be brightly lit with mathematical clarity, certainty, and simplicity. Our situation is perfect for a worldwide grassroots movement from the bottom-up rather than the top-down. A call for action is at hand. It is time for you to stand and be counted. Together we can achieve a metaeconomic miracle that will provide us with "**economics as if people mattered**" (Schumacher, 1973). This vision is easy to understand and it is yours for the wishing!

Prologue: Going to the Economic "Moon"

We, our children, and grandchildren live at a special time. I belong to a generation that went to the moon and ended the cold war. Yet I belong to a generation that recklessly expanded debt, invented smog, and squandered our natural resources producing pollution that left our children and grandchildren with less economic hope than our parents left us. Shame on my generation! Now we and our families stand at a precipice with two equally possible visions for our future facing us.

For the first time that I can remember, we are immobilized with fear and confusion; we are lost without a clear direction without a clear goal to rally around. I can remember clearly when JFK spoke to our nation and told us we were going to the moon and we would be there within the decade. I was not sure what it all meant. But I was sure we could do it and I was anxious to get started with such an exciting goal. Now once again I feel that same feeling but this time I know what it all means. Yet I still know we can do it and I am anxious to get started.

On one hand we are at the dawn of a new golden age, an exciting age of unprecedented prosperity for all: rich, middle class, and poor, generation after generation. We will achieve fair prosperity not just for the USA but prosperity for the whole world! Prosperity here will precipitate prosperity there. Prosperity there will reinforce prosperity here. Our prosperity goal will produce a global win-win situation that will unify the entire world with a common goal of prosperity for all!

Prosperity will be locked in a positive feedback loop in which all humanity is the clear winner! We will enter a "fourth dimension" of prosperity never before imagined! This new golden age of prosperity will be accomplished with an economic renaissance. This renaissance will shift from a profit paradigm into a prosperity paradigm, from Capitalism into Humanism. We will change our economics into the science of democratic and sustainable prosperity with metaeconomics!

On the other hand we are at the dawn of worldwide economic collapse. The profit paradigm has exhausted itself with mindless and heartless greedy exploitation. It has now turned inward in a desperate quest for more exploitation. It has started the process of exploiting itself like an ugly dog-eat-dog nightmare. How could the "dogs" possibly win? The "gloom and doom" warnings are everywhere on a scale never seen before. The first wave of our crisis began in 2008 and we are still under unprecedented worldwide central bank stimulus in hopes of a recovery that has not yet fully developed 10 years later. Interest rates are still near zero worldwide and excess central bank balance sheet capital is still flooding our global economy with excess capital.

I certainly hope we do recover and soon. Unfortunately even if we do recover, this will not be the last wave of the crisis. This crisis will be like an economic tsunami consisting of wave after wave. So we have an unknown and possibly short window of opportunity between waves during which to implement the new prosperity paradigm. If we wait until the next wave of the crisis, we risk not having the time or the resources to make the transition that will likely take a decade or more.

I think the reason we are lost as a nation and as a world is because we do not have a clear and understandable vision of what to do and how to do it? We are waiting for a savior like JFK but this is not a "savior" kind of problem. It is a "grassroots" kind of problem. I do not think we are lacking in ability or enthusiasm. Instead we need a guiding vision.

We want to go to the economic "moon" but we are not sure how to formulate the goal and our professional economists are **not** leading us. So I have dedicated this book to painting a clear picture of what we must **do** and how we can **do** it. I hope you will join me in my quest for a democratic economy based on a prosperity paradigm that will change economics into the science of democratic and sustainable prosperity!

Introduction

It is our intention to implement major economic reforms that will translate Capitalism into Humanism. This economic transition will be accomplished with the guidance of first principles including a constitutionally compatible Economic Bill of Rights and an axiomatic mathematical system. Together these political and scientific guiding principles will ensure a stable and safe transition from a profit paradigm to a prosperity paradigm, from wealth to prosperity. The majority of this book is a blueprint that will concentrate on the detail application of these first principles to the economic reforms implied and the resultant humane consequences for all mankind indefinitely.

To organize, manage, and achieve these goals it is our intention to start a new party called the Economic Humanist Party (EHP). This will be an unusual party because it will not take any political position outside the implementation of the Humanistic Economic Reform Act (HERA) discussed below. We will be careful to take **no** position on issues like "abortion", "immigration", "gay marriage" or "no child left behind". Furthermore it will be a non-electoral party with no candidates.

We will have a political platform with only one plank. However, this one plank is more important to humanity than all of the other political issues combined! Moreover this one plank will not be available in the Democrat or the Republican platforms because it is too big and too ambitious for them to absorb the risks without upsetting their parties. This ambitious path forward must be navigated by a new organization that is designed to absorb the initial risks. It will take about a decade to implement the reforms and then attain the benefits that we intend.

In many ways the Economic Humanist Party is more of a democratic economic movement than a political party. Consequently most of us will simply think of it as the **Prosperity Party** and we will think of ourselves as economic humanists rather than capitalists, or socialists. The goals of this movement are so large in scope as to require a new prosperity paradigm to replace the old profit and wealth paradigm.

This scope is too large to address without a dedicated party to sponsor it. Yet it is also too large to address without support from constituents of the Democrat and Republican parties. For this reason the Prosperity Party (EHP) will need to be different. If the Democrat and Republican parties are thought of as vertical in alignment then the Prosperity Party must be horizontal in nature crossing party lines in a unifying manner.

The Republican and Democrat parties are political parties but the Economic Humanist Party is an economic party with an economic agenda that is equally attractive to Democrats, Republicans, Independents, and specialized parties. The EHP is sponsoring prosperity and we know of no political party that is against prosperity!

Furthermore our two party system is more than capable of facilitating the ongoing political process once the movement is initially successful with formation and absorption of risks. So you should continue as a member of any of these political parties that suit your political beliefs and simultaneously join the Economic Humanist Party so we can help achieve that initial formation success. See the "Epilogue Discussions" for more discussion on the Prosperity Party and its formation plans. In addition see the discussion "Is a Humanist a Democrat, Republican, or an Independent?" for more discussion on political considerations.

The Economic Bill of Rights

Our proposed economic reforms are based on the following Economic Bill of Rights. Our first step towards an economic democracy is to make a strong and direct connection with our political democracy based on these rights. These rights provide direct support and guidance from our political democracy and its Constitution. Some of these rights were first proposed by FDR in the 1940's and I have expanded the list.

I believe that these specific rights are already included, implied, or inferred by the general rights already contained in our existing Constitution. Therefore I believe that we can proceed forward with our economic reforms without any need to first amend our Constitution. This easy approach supports the idea that "we don't need permission" to have a democratic economy! So we will present our Economic Bill of Rights in the same spirit as our Declaration of Independence. We hold these fundamental economic human rights to be self-evident:

Inalienable Implied Rights Already Supported by our Constitution

1. The right to equal valued pay for equal valued work

2. The freedom from the oppression of an economic privileged class based on race, creed, gender, inheritance, or other unearned or perpetual economic privileges

3. The freedom from economic exploitation especially unfair wages, unfair competition, unfair trade, unfair currency values, and other unfair or unequal economic treatments

4. The right to equal access to employment based on equal qualifications and abilities

5. The right to a living wage sufficient to achieve life, liberty, and the pursuit of happiness

6. The democratic collective right and responsibility to pursue and achieve economic prosperity for the common good of the majority

7. The right to sustainable life free from pollution and the right to share equally in the nation's natural resources with the responsibility to sustain them so all generations will preserve the same right

8. The freedom from taxation without representation achieved by financial or contractual burden passed forward perpetually from generation to generation

9. The right to affordable medical care and the opportunity to achieve and maintain good health

10. The right to an affordable education so that every human has the opportunity to develop to their full abilities

These economic rights provide us with the legal guidance we need to institute economic reforms that are consistent with and guided by our Constitution. Notice how these rights are simple, clear, intuitive, and ring true to any citizen so that they can quickly conclude with absolute certainty: "Yes! I wish to live, work, and do business in a fair world where economics must support these rights". So our inalienable rights are inherently unifying, exactly what a grassroots movement needs.

Who could or would argue against any of these rights? They are not controversial in any way; they do not divide us in any way. They exclude no one except those who wish to be excluded. Instead they unify us! Furthermore they help identify the "opposition". Only a paid representative for the enemies of democracy would waste their time or reputation arguing against these rights. So bring on your self-incriminating arguments! They will only prove the inalienable power of these economic human rights and our Constitution that sponsors them. The majority of humanity will support and demand these rights!

Summary of Key Ideas

I hope you find many worthwhile ideas in this book. I will not try to summarize them all because the most important ideas are the ones that trigger your imagination not necessarily the ones I think are most important. However I will begin by explaining one general concept that is integral for understanding the ideological basis for the reforms in HERA. In addition to the legal guidance of the Economic Bill of Rights, we will use mathematics and science as analogs to provide the proactive engineering guidance needed to institute a democratic economy in a safe, secure, and stable fashion using economic axioms.

So I have reformulated Capitalism as a mathematical, axiomatic, democratic system. I call this reformulation of Capitalism **Humanism** and this book is at most a mere beginning to challenge Capitalism. The closest common idea that is similar would be the Euclidean Geometry that we all studied in high school. It was an axiomatic system and all of its power came from 5 axioms. You will probably remember one of those axioms was: "a straight line can be drawn between any two points". Who would argue that you can't draw a straight line between any two points? These axioms are postulates that are so fundamental, simple, and self-evident that they were unarguable! The result has been a timeless, irrefutable system of geometric thought that has been beneficial to humanity for thousands of years ever since Euclid.

What if economics could be organized into such a powerful democratic, axiomatic system of economic thought? I believe it can! Many axiomatic principles are discussed in this book. Moreover the most important axiomatic ideas are summarized in the following five key axioms. As with our Economic Bill of Rights we present these axioms in the same spirit as our Declaration of Independence. We hold these fundamental economic human truths to be self-evident:

1. **The fundamental reason our economy exists is to serve humanity in facilitating the worker/consumer duality by achieving maximum prosperity for the vast majority of mankind.** This axiom makes our economy democratic because all humanity is a principal of the economy. So we become democratic "citizens" of our economy rather than its "subjects". Similar to the way we are democratic citizens of our political system rather than its subjects. This axiom clearly establishes an economic difference between humanity and commodities such as zinc or soybeans or other products or resources. This is a profound difference that Capitalism fails to distinguish. This axiom ends the possibility of economic slavery once and for all! It sets the stage for economics of the people, by the people, and for the people on a worldwide scale by establishing economics as the science of democratic prosperity based on the axioms and their metaeconomic theory.

2. **Equal value wages must be paid for equal productivity of equal quality.** This axiom tells us how to balance all wage rates nationally and internationally.

3. **Equal currencies can buy equal cost of living goods and services in their local economies.** This axiom tells us how to balance all currencies internationally.

4. **The minimum wage paid must be equal or greater than the minimum cost of living to achieve life, liberty, and the pursuit of happiness.** This axiom provides us with a quantitative initial condition or starting point that in turn can establish all quantitative wages using the balance equations of axioms 2) and 3) above, nationally. Each nation can choose its own minimum wage including none at all. This national axiom

provides a direct link with our political democracy. Our political democracy guarantees our right to "life, liberty, and the pursuit of happiness" and this axiom ensures the economic means to achieve it without interfering with other nations.

5. **Wages should increase at least to compensate for product price inflation, not caused by wage inflation, plus any increase in labor productivity.** This axiom tells us how to balance wages from year to year over time and how to increase prosperity over time nationally and internationally. Together with the other axioms this axiom implements the "prosperity mandate" identified in axiom 1 and item 6 of the Economic Bill of Rights. An exact prosperity metric is proposed herein as well. See goals 4 & 5 in "Summary of the Goals" below.

We can summarize these five axioms in order as 1) the prosperity mandate, 2) the equal pay mandate, 3) the equal currency mandate, 4) the minimum wage mandate, and 5) the wage increase mandate. Notice how these axioms are also simple, clear, intuitive, and ring true to any citizen so that they can quickly conclude with absolute certainty: "Yes! I wish to live, work, and do business in a fair world where economics must comply with these axioms as human truths".

If your mind finds this conclusion easy to reach, your heart has just joined the spirit of a worldwide economic renaissance! Consequently your soul will not be denied because these axioms allow humanity to engineer our own **economic destiny**. The first axiom defines the mission statement and fundamental purpose of our global economy. Furthermore axioms 2 through 5 define the key mathematical requirements to achieve that purpose. I believe these five axioms are sufficient to form a logical, axiomatic **system of thought** for all of economics and they are based on simple arithmetic. Indeed they are as simple as $2 + 2 = 4$. So anyone can understand this system of thought.

Human Rights and Human Truths

Notice also how similar the axioms are with our Economic Bill of Rights; yet they are different. The Economic Bill of Rights establishes our constitutional rights as applied to our economic lives but they do not tell us what to **do** proactively in order to assert or achieve these economic rights. Unfortunately in traditional "wealth economics" humanity has had little or no representation like the political and legal representation we do have in other democratic matters. Consequently without economic representation it was impossible for humanity to assert, achieve, and maintain their economic rights even though these rights were always part of our constitutional political human rights!

Our economic rights were just brushed aside by wealth economists as economically inconvenient or impractical. This lack of democratic economic representation was never successfully challenged in the courts because economics was immune to any scientific, mathematical, or engineering critique or scrutiny. Furthermore in the legal realm there was no law and order in economics! Thus there was no professional scrutiny, analysis, or measurement that could support the challenge and no economic court in which to present the challenge. Economics was not required to be scientific. Indeed the field of Economics is a self-declared non-science so economists successfully claimed that economics could not be judged by those usual standards. Instead "fair is foul and foul is fair in economics" (Keynes, 1931).

Thus the field of economics was allowed to stand as a kind of inhumane alchemy where it was its own judge, jury, and sole plaintive while humanity was left with no "standing" in economic matters! So wealth power and corruption were allowed to determine and dominate the purpose, the goals, and the methodology of economics on a day-to-day basis as if it was their private privileged fiefdom. So humanity was left as a silent victim with no voice or representation in economics!

All issues in economics were determined by ad hoc opinions of the economic elite designed to match the conveniences and preferences of wealth power as embodied in the slogan "what is good for business is good for the economy". In other words "good economics is whatever wealth power finds convenient and profitable". This contradiction is at the heart of our democratic dichotomy; we are a political democracy that tries to coexist floating on a sea of economic aristocracy and privilege. Eventually we will be forced to abandon one idea or the other! Instead Humanism will propose and substantiate a humane system of "**economics as if people mattered**" (Schumacher, 1973).

Furthermore the axioms are quantitative, mathematical, and scientific in nature so they tell us exactly what to **do** to accomplish our economic rights! Each one of the axioms defines a specific action to accomplish an economic goal that can be quantitatively measured and analyzed scientifically. The axioms are compliance formulas for economic democracy! They guide, direct, and mandate that economics must comply proactively. So the axioms resolve the contradiction of our democratic dichotomy once and for all by making economics democratic and scientific giving an economic voice to all of humanity!

So we do not have to trust in the good faith of corrupt economics to produce the representation that we wish for, because we can verify it ourselves or hire engineers, mathematicians, and scientists to do it for us! Additionally we will add to this a "NASA" like, independent, professional **economic department** of government charged and chartered with representation and enforcement of these axioms, rights, measurements, analyses, and controls as "the economic law of the land". Finally we will have the complete democratic economic governance solution for the first time in our economic history!

Just like the Economic Bill of Rights, these axioms are inherently unifying. Who could or would argue against any of these axioms? They are not controversial in any way; they do not divide us in any way. They exclude no one except the self-declared elite who wish to stand above us. Instead the goal of common democratic prosperity unifies us worldwide even more than political democracy achieved!

Furthermore these first principles also help identify the "opposition" because only a paid representative for continuing economic corruption would waste their time or reputation presenting such arguments against prosperity! So bring on your self-incriminating arguments! They will only prove the power of these axioms! Thus for the first time in history fair and democratic economics becomes a choice within our economic and political grasp. Now is the time for the courage to make that choice for ourselves, our children, our grandchildren, and all future generations. We will be judged by posterity if we fail to stand!

It is worth noting that supply/demand markets are not even mentioned directly in these five axioms. These markets are included in axiom 1 as part of the terminology: "facilitating the worker/consumer duality".

Supply/demand markets are a powerful tool that can be used either to create vast economic prosperity or create vast economic exploitation and harm with equal ease and equal effectiveness! Unfortunately the supply/demand market mechanism did not come with directions for humane use! But the Economic Bill of Rights and the key axioms do!

According to axiom 1, what is good economics for zinc and soybeans is **not** necessarily good economics for humans! So the market is controlled by the most wealthy, privileged, and powerful of people to do what they wish. To correct this privileged abuse we must add a higher level of **axiomatic control above the market mechanism** to guide and mandate economics of the people, by the people, and for the people to do what we wish instead. After all it is our economy!

Furthermore since the Humanistic axioms are added as a layer on top of our existing economic system there is little opportunity for negative impact because the internal nature of our economic system is unchanged! Instead axiomatic level concepts are added that provide humane guidance to the system we already have. For example supply/demand markets could be used without modification for all commodities and other such products consistent with current theory.

Only two markets would have to be modified or enhanced to meet the axioms for a human labor market or for a currency market. This will be achieved by "hybridizing" those markets with embedded axiomatic guidance and control that do not interfere with or upset either of those markets! See further discussion in topics: "The Invisible Economic Slavery", "Capitalism vs Humanism", "Humanistic Economic Axioms and Guiding Principles", "The Role of "Free" Markets in Humanism" and "What Would Adam Smith Have Thought?" on hybrid concepts.

It is important to understand that many different axioms could have been chosen for Euclidean Geometry or for our new Economic Geometry as well. Axioms are chosen skillfully not logically deduced or discovered. The choice of these axioms is made at a level **outside and above** the system we want to create usually called the meta-physical level. If the axioms chosen are highly consistent with the reality in which we live or **wish to live in** then the resulting system is very useful for humanity to achieve and maintain that wish. Moreover if the axioms are also consistent with our Economic Bill of Rights we have a powerful combination of economic human truths and economic human rights we need as a foundation for our economic renaissance!

Unfortunately there are no known mathematical methods or science for choosing or conjecturing the axioms. A lot of perseverance and a good bit of luck are certainly desirable. So the process might seem arbitrary and capricious to you? However once the candidate axioms are proposed there is a very simple, scientific, and logical process by which the axioms can be evaluated by anyone of reasonable skill.

The way Euclidean Geometry was taught to us in high school, we students became the validators of this logical system. And we never found one contradiction in the system! We can do the same for these axioms. Even if you do not feel comfortable with mathematics or logic, you can be sure that once these proposed axioms reach the light of day they will be scrutinized extensively using the vast resources wealth power will buy. So surely there will be plenty of paid scrutiny!

In our physical sciences, the axioms are called "laws" and they can be derived by the Scientific Method. This method consists of trial and error conjectures followed by measuring our physical world to test and prove the conjectures. The law of gravity or Maxwell's equations would be common examples of such "laws". We are attempting to make the field of Economics into a similar human "science". So we must derive these human axioms from our human world in much the same way. We test and prove these axiomatic conjectures in our metaphysical human world by intellectual testing the human truth of them in the minds, hearts, and souls of humanity much the same way as we verify that "we can draw a straight line between any two points".

To avoid subjectivity we hold the truth test criteria to a very high standard associated with first principles. We require truth that is internally consistent, intrinsic, self-evident, fundamental, inalienable, and irrefutable much the same as the idea that "all men are created equal" is tested and proved in our political democracy. So it would be more correct to refer to these proposed axiomatic conjectures as human "truths" rather than scientific "laws". Except for this minor difference between the Scientific Method and the Logical Method all the other benefits of an axiomatic system including economic engineering can still be achieved with this new Economic Geometry.

Unfortunately economists and their corrupt patrons used this minor difference as justification for avoiding entirely any axiomatic or scientific system at all. Instead they self-declared economics as a non-science (religion) because they were afraid that such an axiomatic system could mandate results outside of their control, different than the wealth privilege and wealth corruption they wanted and intended.

The power of these axioms is that they cannot be successfully denied; they can only be defied. This defiance leaves the defiant in a most untenable position forced out into the open, unveiled for all to see the truth; "the economic Emperor has no clothes"! So bring on your self-incriminating arguments! They will only prove the inalienable power of these axioms to provide a system of humane economics for all!

One consequence of this metaphysical concept is that the credentials and expertise of the economic meta-physicists are likely outside and different from the economists themselves! The economic meta-physicists are more likely to be philosophers, mathematicians, scientists, or engineers than economists. Furthermore the world we wish to live in depends on who does the wishing! So the economic world that perpetually wealthy capitalists wish to live in is a very different and ugly economic world from the world humanity wishes to live in; it is time humanity did our economic wishing for a change!

We have excellent credentials. All humans are born experts on humanity and we don't need permission! Our political democracy already entitles us to economic democracy! These axioms form a new shell of metaeconomics encompassing the macroeconomics and the microeconomics we already have. Humanism's expanded concept for economics will provide humanity with the economic renaissance that we have been deprived of for so long! In turn this renaissance will provide humanity with the professional economic representation and voice that has been so lacking and wanting in economics until now.

If you are a mathematician, scientist, or engineer you will quickly grasp the power of such an axiomatic, mathematical systemization of economics. It would initiate a transition of economics from a "soft" corruptible study into a "hard" rigorous science of democratic prosperity. However this book was written primarily for the middle class of nurses, teachers, plumbers, small businessmen, and so many others like them. This talk of Economic Geometry probably sounds like the economic "mumbo jumbo" that you are used to hearing.

But it is not! This axiomatic approach is particularly advantageous to you because it empowers you especially. Once you decide that you want the democratic economy that these axioms mandate, you can go back to your regular lives with confidence! Because once you "do the wishing", the axioms do all the rest of the work for you and your children forever just like the axioms of Geometry did for Euclid and his successors! So economics can be enforced by our professionals!

The axioms mathematically guarantee that economics must comply with our democratic goals without you needing to watch out for every new scheme or scam that comes along; the axioms do the work for you as a watchdog. The axioms are to our economic democracy what our constitution is to our political democracy – an overriding protection! Yet this axiomatic power is even greater because these axioms are inalienable, unarguable, and self-evident for all humanity worldwide.

So there is no need for a national or international supreme court to interpret these axioms because they are mathematically interpretable by anyone and everyone! The power of mathematics is inherently democratic. So $2 + 2 = 4$, without needing any permission, worldwide, without a treaty, or an army, even for the week and most vulnerable, no matter what language you speak, or what alphabet you use, or what kind of government you have, or what religion you believe, or how much wealth you have. It is true even when it is *An Inconvenient Truth* and it is not negotiable even in the face of a threat by a nuclear power! That is powerful and it's yours for the wishing. No permission needed!

The Impact of Humanism

You may think that many ideas in this book are new but they are not. Euclid or his successors could have easily proposed these axioms for economics if the Greek's experiment with democracy had lasted longer but sadly it was short-lived. So to the best of my knowledge every idea in this book already exists or should exist by implication somewhere in the bowels of economic theory where it sits doing absolutely nothing for mankind without economic representation! What is new in this book is a vision of how to embed current economic theory and practice inside an axiomatic, mathematical shell or superstructure that would guide and mandate Capitalism in the direction of a humane and democratic economics open to all that I call Humanism.

What is truly amazing to me is that the prosperity economics of Humanism can be accomplished with only a **few minor changes in the wealth economics** of Capitalism and its markets. Yet there is a profound and overwhelming difference in the quality and sustainability of life for those on our planet, exactly what we need for a renaissance!

The axioms make this profound difference. Our quest to go to the real moon excited, empowered, and emboldened the whole world with a "we can do" attitude. Now let's apply that "si se puede" attitude to our economic "moon". Join with me in this powerful vision of prosperity for all! Let's give an economic voice to the vast majority of all mankind. And let's shout out our demand for a better world for all!

I believe that there is a strong worldwide "bubble" of frustration, anger, and outrage with wealth economics, its wealth inequality, and harmful exploitation that will eventually burst again. The last time it burst we ended up with a majority of the world's population under the economics of Communism and it took 100 years to recover! Yet this idea goes much further than just giving a voice to frustration. Anyone could express outrage and anger with our unfair system and many do.

Look at the "Occupy Wall Street" movement of a few years ago. It was made up of mostly college age youth. It expressed that same anger and that is what made it so popular so quickly. It touched a core issue already boiling inside all of us. But it fizzled just as quickly for two reasons. They just expressed anger; they did not explain, justify, and validate the anger in a technically sound, insightful, and compelling way that is empowering instead of just frustrating! Furthermore OWS just complained and protested. They did not follow through with a technically sound way to fix the broken, unfair, and corrupt system. So it left no place for the feelings they aroused and expressed to "go" except into even more frustration and an even bigger boiling "bubble"!

The anarchists waiting on the sidelines love bigger "bubbles" because "popping" them creates the chaos that gives anarchists temporary power that they believe will result in automatic improvements. But chaos and anarchy seldom result in anything other than automatic regression. No problems are solved and more problems are created so the situation only gets worse. Communism has become the icon for that kind of fantastical expectation and eventual disappointing failure.

What if the feelings boiling in the bubble could be validated and redirected into constructive empowerment instead? What if a blueprint for change were to be architected in advance that could be scrutinized carefully and was based on sound, scientific, and mathematical first principles that required minimal changes to the existing system? Then this constructive empowerment could be automatically directed to a constructive goal of creating more law and order not chaos! See the discussion: "It is Time for Economic Law and Order" for more details.

I soon realized that completion of the philosophical and mathematical systemization of economics was not necessary in order to proceed with the benefits and reforms implied. I am an engineer more than a mathematician and I am driven by a sense of impending urgency. Euclidean Geometry was used for generations mostly for construction engineering before it became fully systematized. The rest of this book deals with economic reforms and visions of our hopeful exciting future implied by these fundamental ideas. If you understand these simple ideas you already understand the mind, heart, and soul of this book!

Summary of the Goals

Here is a summary of the goals to be accomplished by our reforms herein called the Humanistic Economic Reform Act (HERA). These reforms were devised by engineering application of the Economic Bill of Rights and the key axioms to the capitalistic economy we already have. Consequently Humanism is an offshoot of Capitalism that replaces the profit paradigm with the prosperity paradigm instead. As such I refer to this body of ideas as "prosperity economics" instead of conventional "wealth (profit) economics". A method to achieve each of these goals will be discussed in the detail Titles that follow. We will conclude with further explanation of general topics and concepts followed by a political road map and legislative implementation plan.

1. Establish an independent department of proactive government responsible for the prosperity and management of our economy
2. Facilitate an economic renaissance from a profit paradigm to a prosperity paradigm
3. Institute Humanism: a form of Capitalism with a democratic focus
4. Define economic majority as the middle 80% (M80) of earners
5. Define a prosperity metric = average income of M80 / minimum cost of living
6. Stop further expansion of sovereign debt as taxation without representation
7. Pay off the existing Sovereign debt over the next 60 years or less
8. Eliminate budget deficits by law
9. Restructure Social Security and Medicare into a sustainable system with a significant increase of benefits
10. Reduce the national budget and regulate the budget at a fixed percentage of GDP
11. Reduce and drastically restructure taxation on businesses so that 50% pay no tax
12. Tax businesses so that they are encouraged to maximize national prosperity
13. Replace the 15% to 35% income tax on businesses with prosperity taxes
14. Eliminate the need for businesses to keep profits offshore
15. Eliminate the 6.2% matching Social Security tax for business
16. Eliminate business unemployment taxes and costs
17. Streamline businesses so that they are no longer involved in health care, pensions, and other fringe benefits
18. End the economic privileged class over the next 80 years with an inheritance tax that heavily taxes inheritances larger than 10 times the average inheritance
19. Eliminate the "curse" of unemployment and costly unemployment benefits

20. Establish a policy of equal pay for equal work that applies nationally
21. Establish a minimum wage that is at least equal to the minimum cost of living
22. Implement by international treaty a fair valuation system for all currencies worldwide
23. Implement by international treaty an equal value pay for equal work rule worldwide
24. Make sustainable life and natural resources the right and responsibility of all generations
25. Manage the national income so that there is no wage inflation and no wage erosion
26. Manage national income and national wealth to match a fixed percentage formula
27. Institute direct, demand driven capital formation using a public capital concept based on a national retirement fund
28. Integrate monetary policy, fiscal policy, investment policy, and tax policy into a cohesive unified economic control system
29. Establish the scientific truth that a prosperous economy cannot be achieved by profit or revenue optimization of each individual business
30. Implement economic cost valuations that will discourage pollution and natural resource depletion
31. Introduce the idea of scientific economic axioms and principles that support economic engineering solutions
32. Use scientific principles for expanding the use of formula controlled democracy
33. Use tax incentives to encourage economic investment and discourage speculation
34. Institute a two-tier wealth tax on Net Worth that encourages economic investing
35. Eventual elimination of the personal income tax on the lower 90% of earners

36. Institute civil rights laws that ensure that the representational voice of wealth power is kept proportional to the voice of the populace
37. Win the "war on democracy" by achieving a sustainable democratic economy

The Humanistic Economic Reform Act (HERA)

Once we have the guiding principles from our political system and the guiding principles from our scientific system we are then ready to implement the economic reforms needed to achieve our goal of a democratic sustainable economy. HERA specifically addresses these economic reforms for the USA. It should be possible to use the USA reforms as a template for economic reforms for the rest of the world's economies. Our economic ideas have more commonality than politics.

Humanism is easy and safe to globalize. All the world's economies have already adapted to Capitalism so it will be easy nation by nation to expand this current adaptation to include the reforms for Humanism as well. This act is based on our general constitution, the Economic Bill of Rights stated above, and our key axioms. Our key axioms are mathematical in nature and were intended to apply to all mankind. See discussion topic "Humanistic Economic Axioms and Guiding Principles" for a formula for each axiom. Only axiom 4 has national variance. Likewise the Economic Bill of Rights is mostly inalienable rights and protections for all mankind. So the international relevance of HERA is much broader than might be thought at first impression.

The intention of this act is to reform our economy and its management to a new idea of Humanism that is based on Capitalism but with a democratic prosperity focus. So it is our intention that this act will set up an independent department of government responsible for the implementation and proactive management of these economic goals.

It is further intended that this act will be passed as normal legislation approved by Congress and the President without needing an amendment to our Constitution. Each of the 25 Titles below are intended to be converted into legislation and taken together they form the template for HERA. At this time these Titles are more explanatory than legislative. However once we understand these ideas it will be easy to reduce them to legislation that is politically achievable now.

The proposed economic reforms mandated by the Economic Bill of Rights and the key axioms will be described Title by Title in detail. The 37 key goals will be accomplished with these 25 Titles. Then we will continue with various discussion topics on ideas, goals, and concepts that explain and support the reform act in general. Finally we will discuss a detailed action plan to implement these reform ideas.

These ideas may seem overwhelming and farfetched at first impression but when you are done reading you will realize that these basic ideas are very simple and easy to understand and to implement. Our most important goal is to use these details to understand the overall vision and how it applies to our economy and our lives. Once you understand this vision at that level, these details will no longer be as important.

Title 1: The Greater Good of the Majority

A Humanistic economic system is intended to serve the majority of humanity, rather than have the majority of humanity serve the economic system. Humanism intends to expand the conventional concept of democracy to include matters of the economy as well, as embodied in axiom 1 and item 6 of the Economic Bill of Rights.

Herein for the purpose of measurement, "majority" is defined as the middle 80% by income (M80) excluding the top and bottom 10% (T10, B10). This is a very broad statistical definition of majority well beyond the traditional democratic political concept of majority (51%). So this statistical measure focuses on a very broad scale definition of middle class including both lower middle and upper middle classes.

The exclusions used in this definition (T10, B10) are outliers intended to provide statistical focus and are based on the belief that the top 10% need little or no accommodation. While the bottom 10% need special attention and accommodation beyond that of the majority anyway.

Nevertheless, including only the middle 80% in this measurement method still results in significant prosperity benefits for at least 97% of earners! See discussion "Capitalism vs Humanism" for more analysis.

That 97% certainly justifies the use of the term "vast majority of mankind" in axiom 1. Our statistical definition of majority can then be used mathematically in defining prosperity as: M80 average income divided by the standardized cost of living basket of axiom 4. Thus this prosperity index is a currency-less number that measures the number of cost of living "baskets" in the average M80 earner's income. See Title 14 and "Capitalism vs Humanism" for more index discussion.

An alternate measurement for the preferred method defined above would be to use the national median income instead of the M80 average income. The median method has the characteristic of biasing the measurement somewhat in favor of the lower middle class without excluding any data points. I prefer the exclusion method because it favors the upper middle class which I believe has a more important impact on general prosperity because their incomes are larger. The median method could have an advantage for constitutional legal reasons because it excludes no data points. Either method can fully accomplish the goals and methodologies discussed herein.

Title 2: Formation of the Economic Control Authority

A humanistic economy would be best provided by adding a fourth, Economic branch of government equal to the Executive, Legislative, and Judicial branches. However this would require amending our Constitution. Instead most if not all of our goals can be achieved by simply expanding the scope of the current Federal Reserve System into an independent **E**conomic **C**ontrol **A**uthority referred to as the ECA.

The importance of our economy and its management certainly warrants having a dedicated and independent government department. We want to go to the economic "moon". So we need a "NASA" like department of government full of our best and brightest scientists, engineers, analysts, computer scientists, and economists to get us there using proactive methodology based on **economic first principles**.

The highly technical and objective nature of this task demands that the department be apolitical and independent from the other branches of government. This new department of government will incorporate and consolidate the traditional functions of the Central Bank (monetary policy) together with 5 new professional departments for Economic Management, Economic Taxation, Economic Labor, National Fund, and Economic Trade and most other financial and economic matters.

The constitutional authority for this legislation will come solely from Congress's general authority and they will have oversight. The Judicial and Executive branches are unchanged except for the Department of Labor. The Treasury will be left as is although it would have been beneficial to have incorporated it with the other financial functions. The Department of Labor will be transferred to the ECA and its responsibilities expanded by this act to reduce its political bias.

The ECA will absorb the Federal Reserve System and continue its current responsibilities and mandates unchanged, as a sub department of 12 existing Governors and a new department head. The Governors will be appointed and serve as they are currently. The new mandates are totally compatible and non-conflicting with the old mandates. The ECA will use most of the same structure and its authority will come from Congress which will have oversight as with the old Fed System.

As with the current system there will be one Chairman and 6 full-time board members. However the Chairman and board members will no longer be restricted to be a Federal Reserve Governor. Each pair of the 12 districts will have one board position open in addition to the national Chairman. Moreover there will be a new department head reporting to the board for each major function such as Central Bank, Economic Management, Economic Taxation, Economic Labor, National Fund, and Economic Trade. The new department heads will be appointed by the ECA board and confirmed by the President and then by Congress. Every effort will be made to depoliticize the ECA so that it can focus on its economic management responsibilities in a professional manor. So the ECA will only be guided by **economic and Constitutional first principles** not petty political haggling and bias.

Each ECA board member will serve 14 year staggered terms as currently, provided the central mandate and the sub mandates are met. However, the chairman and the board members will not be appointed politically. Rather our nation's Colleges and Universities will nominate and select the top three candidates for each board position open for the local district pair and for the national Chairman as well.

This selection will be based on technical qualifications and should be devoid of any political characteristics. A taskforce of universities can be charged with developing the nomination guidelines. Candidates that have taken a public political posture would be excluded. Consequently if we have public knowledge that a candidate is a Conservative or Liberal, Democrat or Republican the candidate should be excluded.

After the three candidates for each board position have been selected the mayors of all incorporated cities nationwide will vote to select their district pair representative and jointly to select the national chairman. City mayors were chosen because they are the most apolitical of any political position and they are most in touch with the populace and their economic issues. Furthermore since every mayor has an equal vote the smaller town voice will not be drowned out by the larger metropolitan areas. Once the final nominee has been selected by the mayors the President will approve or disapprove and then Congress will confirm the final nomination similar to the current system. If not confirmed the process will repeat with new nominees.

The ECA will draw from a wide variety of scientists, engineers, analysts, computer scientists, and economists rather than the narrow banking focus of the Federal Reserve. The ECA will be self-financed much the same as the current Federal Reserve. It will deliberately generate a significant surplus, much larger than currently, which will be used to retire the current national debt over the next 60 years or less and satisfy the liabilities of the current Social Security Retirement System including Medicare for retirement over the next 45 years.

The new National Fund payroll deduction plan will replace the Social Security deduction plan. The Social Security Administration will remain as is now and the retirement benefits will be improved drastically. The general goal for the next working generation will be approximately twice the benefit for half the cost! This would represent approximately a 4:1 (400%) benefit/cost ratio improvement over the current Social Security Retirement System. The National Fund will take over the current assets and liabilities of our Social Security.

Over the next 45 years there will be a gradual shift from a cash system to an accrual system. That is from a system where those who are now working pay for those who are retired. Converting instead to a system where those working now pay for their **own** retirement by investing their **own** savings in their **own** National Fund account. They will earn a significantly larger retirement annuity than the old Social Security System could hope to provide. So all workers will become capitalists!

The NF target retirement benefit for the minimum 6.2% deduction will be approximately 70% of a worker's average lifetime salary based on a modest estimate of 5% average real return over 65 years (45 working + 20 retired). Notice that this minimum benefit level would be about twice the current level. Note also, the 5% return is not wishful thinking because it is consistent with our national economic goal of 5% of GDP profits. See topic "The Role of Profits in Humanism" for more details.

During the 45 year transitional period the two benefit systems will coexist in a prorated manner. For example if one retired with 45 years of service, 25 of which were under the old deduction system then 25/45 of their total benefit would be the old benefit rate. In addition their new annuity would pay the rest provided it was larger than the old benefit rate. So the old benefit would be a minimum for the new.

Eventually in about 45 years the old benefit system will phase out completely except for the minimum. In the long run this new system would be self-sustaining but the old system's liabilities and promises must be paid off. So the one-time, non-recurring funding for paying off the old liabilities will come from the windfall proceeds of the inheritance tax of Title 5 and the Wealth tax of Title 23 which will phase in over this same period. Any residual balance of the proceeds will be added to the surplus (above) for paying down the national debt.

a) **National Budget**

The Legislative and Executive branches are still responsible for the national budget. The Legislative, Judicial, and Executive branches are provided budget funds by the ECA bank of not more than 14% of GDP for all federal expenditures including transfers but excluding the interest on the national debt. This fixed percentage of 14% is referred to herein as the "budget mandate" and it is a protection intended to protect against excessive future taxation and deficits. The interest and principal of the national debt together with the unfunded liabilities of Social Security retirement and Medicare retirement will become the responsibility of the ECA not paid out of the general 14% of GDP.

Over an approximately 40 to 60 year period the interest and principal of the national debt together with the unfunded liabilities of Social Security Retirement System will be reduced to zero by the ECA. To protect against economic crises such as a recession in which the GDP might drop, the national budget will have a minimum cap as well so the budget will not drop more than 1% of its current budget amount per year even if it exceeds its 14% of GDP temporarily. This plan represents a tax reduction and will be at least partially offset by savings in the need for unemployment benefits (see Title 12 below).

Budget deficits are no longer allowed and ECA bank deficits if any will be monetized **without** additional sovereign debt. Additional sovereign debt is not allowed unless recommended by the ECA and approved by all branches of government for each specific national emergency. It is our belief that sovereign debt is taxation on future generations without representation and that it is democratically unjustifiable unless the future existence of our country is at stake. The Supreme Court will have to rule that the situation is an acceptable emergency and the remaining branches will have to approve before further debt will be allowed. This will end unfair generational taxation.

Incurring sovereign debt that is never paid off by the generation that benefited from the debt proceeds, forces future generations to accept the interest cost (taxation ~ 1 trillion $/yr.) and then pass the burden of the principal and interest on to their children perpetually. This burden is exactly taxation without choice (representation) and it is clearly an unconstitutional transfer of burden forward! We can debate this constitutional issue later but we must fix this obvious problem now.

The ECA can monetize tax and withholding deficits and print money as needed provided the actual inflation rate is less than a 7%

maximum. The central bank inflation mandate target will be unchanged at its current 2% level initially. The idea of a formulaic budget mandate is that people want the best government services they can achieve within a fixed percent of GDP cost. We believe that the voting populace wants Congress to decide how the budget is spent but not decide how large the budget should be. Consequently the size of the federal budget will be mandated by referendum of the people in this reform legislation at 14% of GDP or less enforced by the ECA.

Thus the people mandate that Congress and the President provide the best government they can for a 14% of GDP cost. Every year the budget discipline is exactly the same: spend the 14% on those budget line items that in proportion give us the best government possible by political representation. Herein we refer to this as the "budget mandate". Notice that this is not a budget freeze but rather a **strategic economic formula** that shows how the budget will increase as the GDP increases. Consequently there is no economic reason that this formula would not be appropriate for the next 1,000 years or more!

Notice that the budget discipline is enforced by the ECA, a separate department of government according to a charter voluntarily legislated by the President and Congress. It might seem that they could just modify or abort the charter if they wanted to thwart the voluntary budget mandates just like they have already done with the debt limit. However once the charter has been established, the ECA has the power and responsibility to enforce its economic charter and its mandates by directly opposing Congress or the President when this is necessary.

Although the debt limit could not "talk back" in opposition, the ECA **must** "talk back" and take a public position against any modification that they think is economically inappropriate! For example the existing Central Bank has never been overruled by Congress so it is less likely that Congress will overrule the new ECA either! Likewise the ECA's opinion now weighs in on the public debate and this would make any modification come at a higher political cost to Congress and require a much higher political threshold. Eventually if Congress or the President refuses to comply with their self-discipline the people will be forced to amend our constitution as one constitutional alternative. Remember our political system has always been vulnerable to this kind of constitutional crisis forced by one branch conflicting with another.

Furthermore it is likely that the Supreme Court may very well weigh in on some or all of these matters because of the likely constitutionality of the Economic Bill of Rights and their supporting axioms. If some or all of these rights are confirmed by the court then court imposed restrictions and remedies may be required. For example if the court was required to rule on the constitutionality of perpetual debt, they would likely find it unconstitutional taxation without representation!

Moreover the court would require Congress to implement a remedy supervised by the court as well as future restrictions. These remedies and restrictions could very well be much less attractive to Congress than the 14% of GDP budget mandate proposed above combined with the minimal debt pay-down plan. So Congress may have a strong motive in self-discipline as a preemptive action to avoid even tougher court appointed restrictions and remedies! See further discussion in "Crisis Responsibilities and Liabilities" and "Justice in Economics".

The Treasury will continue as it is currently except that they will also respond to tax and revenue directives issued by the ECA under general Executive order approved by this legislation. If tax collection revenues exceed the 14% of GDP the balance will be transferred to the ECA bank as a surplus. If there is a revenue shortfall below the 14% of GDP, the differential will be transferred from the ECA bank to the Treasury. The nominal Social Security (NF) deduction and Medicare deduction will be transferred directly to the National Fund. The ECA bank will transfer operating funds directly to the Social Security Administration to pay prior benefit commitments and future annuities.

Medicare for retirement will be treated exactly as specified above for retirement annuity funding. There will continue to be a separate Medicare retirement payroll deduction as currently. However this deduction will be invested in the NF and benefit from the 400% benefit to cost ratio as discussed above. So the Medicare for retirement payroll deduction could be only 1/4th of the current deduction if the future benefit and cost is the same. The Medicare insurance plan benefits will be unchanged with the same benefits as now but the plan's funding will change. The excess deduction (3/4) could be used to increase the annuity, increase benefits, or offset some of the onetime 45 year transition costs required to finance this new retirement plan. All Medicare funding costs will be covered completely by premiums.

These Medicare retirement premiums will be paid by each retiree out of their NF savings account which includes contributions from both the annuity (6.2%) and Medicare deductions. Currently these premiums are being paid by the current working generation rather than paid from savings. Non-retirement uses of the Medicare plan will have to pay their own Medicare premiums out of the general tax proceeds **not** the retirement plan. Likewise disability, Aid for Dependent Children, and other welfare funding will be included in the 14% of GDP not the retirement plan. See further discussion in Title 9 below.

As discussed with the annuity, the benefits of compound return on investment would offset increases in future Medicare costs. Like retirement, Medicare would no longer be a current cash cost but rather funded with savings of each individual. Of course the current obligations and liabilities of Medicare would have to be paid off by wealth taxes just like Social Security Retirement. Once these liabilities are paid off Medicare retirement costs would no longer be a tax on future generations. Each citizen would pay for their **own** retirement annuity and their **own** Medicare premium out of their **own** NF savings investment accounts. This tax improvement for our children and all future generations would be an enormous economic achievement!

The ECA will be responsible for managing the taxations, debt paydown, interest costs, and unfunded liabilities of Social Security and Medicare retirement. This solution is a lot like the "good bank/bad bank" type of crisis scenario where all the problems are consolidated and addressed by one specialized authority to avoid contagion in normal operations. Because of its multifaceted partisan and political nature Congress could not solve these problems even though they had sufficient authority to do so. They were locked in a dysfunctional paralysis. This paralysis spread and inhibited them from even solving political and legislative problems that were very much in their forte.

In this scenario Congress realizes that contagion is causing gridlock and uses its authority to expand a proven independent professional department, the Central Bank, with new authority (ECA) to address the new "unsolvable" problems. This allows Congress (good bank) to be revitalized immediately with a manageable and sustainable long term budget structure that can be used to address a myriad of political problems it is well suited to solve for many generations into the future.

In turn the new ECA (bad bank) is staffed with our finest and brightest technical minds and the tools to solve the "unsolvable" problems with oversight of Congress. Once the systematic machinery is put in place and observed to be working, the whole world will regain its confidence in the USA, its reserve currency, and the worldwide financial system even though the solution takes many years to unfold completely. We will lead the way to debt reform. This is a win-win solution scenario that benefits everyone starting now! See additional discussion in Title 9, Title 22, and discussion "Crisis Responsibilities and Liabilities".

b) **ECA Charter**

The ECA will primarily act on formulaic rules and responsibilities contained in the Economic Bill of Rights, the key axioms, and the Humanistic Economic Reform Act. The central and most important of these goals is the responsibility of the ECA to achieve the maximum prosperity for the middle 80% of earners. Herein this key central goal is referred to as the "prosperity mandate" consistent with axiom 1.

Other responsibilities include acting as central bank, managing labor utilization, managing delegated taxation, managing the National Fund, managing national income and national wealth distributions, and managing the economic and financial aspects of international trade ratification. In particular the ECA should have new subordinate mandates for employment participation greater than 70%, underemployment less than or equal 0% (100% full employment), and productivity improvements greater than 2% per year. These three new sub mandates are in addition to the existing Central Bank inflation sub mandate because inflation will be under direct mathematical control.

In addition to the central prosperity mandate and the four sub mandates, the ECA will recommend approval from Congress to adopt non-conflicting national economic goals from time to time that further our nation's prosperity and achieve our national economic "moon". All these proactive mandates are complementary and compatible with one another and there will be no conflict of interest between them that the ECA cannot easily resolve within its authority and responsibility. The ECA will become our proactive department responsible for managing axiomatic metaeconomics. See discussion topic "Understanding the Power of Design" for a list of likely future national economic goals.

c) **Transparency**

Corruption is a major concern in forming the ECA. It is so important to keep the ECA apolitical, independent, and technically professional. For this reason we will institute stringent rules for lobbying and contact between ECA members individually or collectively and outsiders including the other branches of government. In general there should be minimal lobbying. If lobbying is needed, lobby Congress! Here are some suggested rules for lobbying and contact with the ECA.

- All proposals must be submitted in writing as part of the public topic record. There can be no private proposals!
- All other communications and contact must be recorded verbatim by a court certified stenographer and filed.
- All communication and contact on a topic will be recorded by time on a given topic. There can be no secret discussions.
- There will be a protocol for starting, stopping, and archiving topics.
- All proposals and other documents will be filed by reception date.
- All topics will be kept updated on a department website for transparent view by the public and watchdog groups.
- Matters of national security must comply but they can be protected and classified in the normal manner.
- Matters of national security must record the contact event in the record unless the matter is of the highest classification.
- Each topic will have a public blog associated with it for public comment.

Title 3: A Scientific Economy Facilitates Economic Engineering

Our proposed Humanistic system is different than traditional Capitalism. It is intended to be much more of a principle or axiom based system, more of a hard science than a soft science. The key axioms provide this scientific basis. One outstanding consequence of this approach is the use of economic engineering based solutions, much like our physical sciences act as a base for modern day physical engineering. For example capitalism's trickle-down approach to capital formation will be enhanced with direct public capital formation (NF).

Also Humanistic economics will rely much more on formulaic democracy where the voting populace establishes a formulaic goal. And the government is then responsible for executing that formulaic goal in a transparent, measurable manner rather than total reliance on the good faith of elected representatives to do the will of the voters. The national budget mandate of a fixed 14% of GDP is a good example of formulaic democracy. See Title 6 & 11 for more examples.

Humanism will also rely much more on formulaic rules and calculations combined with the markets that are the basis of Capitalism. Consequently Economic Engineering will play the same role in achieving our economic "moon" as physical Engineering did in achieving our real moon. Our prosperity can be engineered proactively guided by the mathematical axioms and the Economic Bill of Rights.

Look at the vast achievements mankind has enjoyed from physical engineering based on the physical sciences. Then you can imagine the vast prosperity improvements that can be achieved from economic engineering guided by the axioms! Titles 6 and Title 23 are good examples. See further discussion about "market hybridization" in Title 11 and the discussion "The Role of "Free" Markets in Humanism".

Title 4: Pollution and Depletion of Natural Resources

Our current economic system treats all natural resources the same. All natural resources are considered to be "free for the taking". Only the labor cost for the "taking" is considered cost. So the last ounce taken is the same cost as the first ounce taken – zero! Likewise our current economic system treats our planet as a "free dump" for pollutants. These "advanced" intellectual economic concepts are on a plane with the disgraceful medieval alchemy of times past. What a shameful flaw!

Clearly such a valuation system encourages reckless and excessive consumption of natural resources and reckless and excessive production of pollution with no regard to their real economic cost! This sad situation discourages recovery and recycling of our natural resources as well as increasing production of "no cost" pollution. Yet our economists cannot come up with a better idea for the valuation of natural resources and pollution! This conceptual situation is a travesty of economic failure on an epic scale that gravely threatens humanity and our planet. Item 7 of our Economic Bill of Rights clearly demands a better concept for all of humanity as does axiom 6 discussed below!

Notice that this book takes a somewhat different position on natural resources and pollution than the normal. Usually these issues are thought to be political issues and are treated that way. But here we are saying that they are clearly economic issues first and foremost. Furthermore the solutions must be achieved within our economic system with some specific economic mechanism. As political issues we have made little or no progress except with common awareness. There is no systematic economic plan or mechanism for a solution.

Without such an economic plan and a designed solution mechanism there can be **no** political solution. To make further progress we need an embedded economic mechanism that establishes **fair**, not **foul** economic valuations. Democratic axiomatic economics could provide this exact embedded mechanism much the same way as we will for the labor market and for the currency market. Wage discrimination is a parallel issue that is discussed further in topic: "Justice in Economics". All of these issues bring home the clear idea: economic failure is not just a political problem. It is an economic problem first and foremost. So we cannot achieve a **fair** political world based on **foul** economics!

Natural resources belong to all citizens and all generations. No one generation should use a disproportionate amount or use resources at a rate that is not sustainable for future generations. Likewise every generation is responsible for the elimination cost for its own pollutants without dumping them for future generations to eliminate at their expense. Consequently our government cannot encumber these resources by such legal contract for more than 20 years or so at a time.

Otherwise we would have another form of taxation without representation where the current generation makes a deal (with itself) beneficial to the current generation that obligates future generations to an unfair deal without their representation. For example suppose the current generation "agrees" that pollution and global warming are free, even though we know they are not, so that future generations will have the burden of paying for them! That is an unconstitutional transfer of tax burden forwards much like the sovereign debt transfer. I believe that a strong case can be made that the current generation is violating the Constitutional rights of their children and of all future generations.

This idea is suggested in item 7 of the Economic Bill of Rights and the depletion/pollution axiom 6 discussed below. In any case export of these resources can only be allowed with strict adherence to long term sustainability. The ECA should be charged by Congress to develop a natural resource depletion plan and a pollution elimination plan including depletion/pollution taxes nationally and internationally. Implementation of depletion and pollution management will be the primary responsibility of the Economic Trade Department of the ECA. Refer to discussion: "Humanistic Economic Axioms and Guiding Principles" and "The Role of "free" Markets in Humanism" for more discussion on depletion/pollution ideas and valuation tax solutions.

Worldwide overpopulation is a collateral issue that severely exacerbates our economic problems in general and our pollution/depletion problems specifically. Population represents the largest load on our ecosystems and on our economic resources. Overpopulation is a very difficult problem to deal with for many rather ugly reasons:

- Religions sponsor selective (me but not you) overpopulation as a means to dominate their religious competitors. If the birth rate of my religion exceeds yours, my religion will eventually dominate. Thus religious domination depends on a disastrous race to higher birth rates. Bad religion justifies bad economics!
- Nations sponsor selective overpopulation as a means to dominate their national competitors much like religions.
- Races and ethnicities sponsor selective overpopulation as a means to dominate their competitors in a similar manner.
- Governments sponsor selective overpopulation because it results in ever increasing tax revenues and political power.
- Wall Street, big business, big banking, and big wealth sponsor general overpopulation because it ensures ongoing growth in

- demand, increased unemployment, and general desperation that make profit exploitation easier and cheap labor more available.
- Organized retirement plans like our old Social Security System require selective overpopulation growth to be successful.
- Yet without organized retirement plans, poverty encourages big families and high birth rates as a disastrous substitute.
- International governance and leadership are totally lacking on this issue and this vacuum further encourages the petty rivalries and petty selfishness mentioned above.

Thus facing this issue will be a daunting, impossible task politically, leaving our planet in grave danger. This is a classic "Not-In-My-Backyard" problem where everyone agrees that someone else should solve the problem but not us! However there is hope if we look at the problem as an economic issue at the grassroots level. We know from experience that as prosperity increases, families automatically adjust their birth rates down to sustainable levels even without organization, governance, or leadership. So mutual prosperity can be our solution.

Furthermore citizens of nations with robust retirement systems are even less inclined to accept the burden of large families. Consequently axiomatic, prosperity economics can offer worldwide prosperity and a robust retirement as substitutes for the draconian impoverishment of Capitalism and solve the overpopulation problem as well. Therefore axiomatic, prosperity economics is our only hope for the future of mankind on this planet! See topic "The Planetary Risk" for more ideas.

In this regard let us try to project Capitalism and its paradigm of wealth economics out in time to its final conclusion with sustainable life on our planet. The final image is stark and ugly: a handful of extremely expensive "glass bubbles" instituted for the economic privileged class and their chosen agents supported by the economic slavery of the rest of humanity who are outside choking on pollution, starving of natural resources, and working exhaustedly to sustain the unsustainable bubbles with draconian poverty expanded endlessly!

Eventually the constantly degrading bubble system reaches its draconian limit, breaks the back of humanity, and precipitates the final collapse! Unfortunately painting this ugly picture is even more painful than reading it. I so prefer optimism and the positive over the negative.

I hope and believe that Humanism provides exactly that redeeming positive we need for faith and hope in our collective future forever!

Notice how Capitalism encourages the false belief that a "glass bubble" system of privilege will survive at the expense of humanity. So we have wealth economics for "the few" achieved at the expense of bad economics for "the many". The power of this delusion provides the path of tunnel vision all the way to the final foul disaster. So the elite think they are protected by privilege from our joint consequences. Instead our democratic humanistic system prohibits this delusion at the outset axiomatically, ideologically, and proactively as a first principle.

Consequently other options will still exist and we will still have time to turn away from this insanity of privilege and elitism. Humanism guides us away from privilege and towards prosperity for all humanity that our planet can afford to sustain indefinitely! So Humanism and its democratic science become inexorably joined with sustainable life into one axiomatic idea or "Ism" for humanity. For more discussion on how Humanism directs us to sustainable life, see Title 18 and axiom 6 discussion: "Humanistic Economic Axioms and Guiding Principles".

Title 5: Freedom from the Economic Privileged Class

Economic privilege based on race, creed, gender, inheritance, or any other unearned or perpetual privilege is not allowed in Humanism because of item 2 of the Economic Bill of Rights and axioms 1 and 2. Any inheritance in excess of ten times the average inheritance of the M80 group will be taxed to approximate the objective. The maximum will apply to the amount of the estate as well as the amount of any individual inheritance or gift. Any larger inheritance would defy the equal opportunity right of all humans. This is the most humane way to end perpetual wealth by simply letting it expire over one lifetime by design and intention as a national economic goal achieved by the ECA.

Current inheritance tax rates will remain as is up to the maximum. So there will be no new tax burden on the majority. Only the top 2% or so will be impacted. Notice that this 10 to 1 range is based on the average inheritance of the M80 group. The actual range from rich to poor is much larger. Using the expected distribution of wealth of Title 11b below, the ratio of the average of the top 1% to the average of the bottom 1% would still be a staggering 100,000 to one. Yet the current ratio is 10,000,000 to one or more. Let's end this huge ugly disparity!

It should be noted that we do not have any constitutional rationale for our proposal of a 10 to 1 ratio over average. We know of no plausible justification of why 10 times average should be so large! We chose the 10 to 1 because it was very much less harmful than the current disparity and yet still on the "unjustifiably large" side of reasonable. This represents a somewhat ugly compromise for an extremely ugly problem. So this compromise is practical yet within our human rights.

Practically speaking, we cannot just cap inheritances at 10 times the average. We need to provide some incentive to achieve tax cooperation. So we will modify the inheritance tax rate schedule with a sharp increase at 10 times average to approximate our goal. For $ values we will assume that average (A) is $100,000. To provide smooth continuity, the after tax estate is the maximum of the current schedule or the next lowest maximum schedule whichever is largest.

Taxable Estate (A = $100,000)	Tax Rates	% Estate	$ Range
Less than 10A	37%	63%	Up to $630K
Between 10A - 100A	80%	20%	$630K – $2M
Between 100A - 1000A	90%	10%	$2M - $10M
Between 1000A - 10,000A	95%	5%	$10M - $50M
Greater than 10,000A	98%	2%	$50M – 2%

Special provisions will exist for inheritance of small family owned businesses. These provisions will be restricted to apply only to family members who wish to continue operating the family business after their parents are deceased. This will apply only for business whose net worth is less than a specified maximum. As specified in the will or as agreed to by all family members, some or all of the family members may defer their inheritance in lieu of continuing to actively participate in operating the family business as an ongoing enterprise indefinitely.

The family members can continue to operate the business as restricted owners of record until they are deceased or they decide to abandon the business and take their original inheritance if the business net worth will allow. Any sale, transfer or deactivation of the business will be considered abandonment. If not abandoned, when they are deceased, their children in turn will have the same options for inheritance or for continuing operation in an ongoing fashion indefinitely.

Gift taxes and other wealth transfers will be restricted accordingly. Philanthropic contributions and trusts will be allowed that meet high humanitarian standards. But family members cannot participate or benefit. Keep in mind that this inheritance tax is targeted to support a transition to the greatest retirement system ever achieved for mankind. So this becomes the standard that philanthropic contributions must exceed to be tax deductible during the next 45 year working lifetime!

The tax status of other trusts that act as a conduit for perpetual inheritance will have to be reevaluated, modified, and taxed heavily. All other tax loopholes will need to be eliminated to accomplish our national goal of eliminating wealth perpetuation within one generational lifetime. Abandoning citizenship will prematurely trigger the inheritance event for resolution of the estate's inheritance tax and other tax liabilities. So there is no place to hide from this wealth tax.

If the inheritance tax falls short of the national goal of eliminating perpetual wealth, the net worth tax of Title 23 can be used to further comply with our national economic goal. We are likely to find that trillions of dollars will be spent to defeat this national goal by wealth power. Wealth power manifests itself primarily through big business, big banking, Wall Street, and perpetual wealth. So civil rights laws will be needed that make it a felony offense to use personal, corporate, or institutional wealth as a political privilege to advocate harm, obstruct, reduce, or interfere with, or exert unreasonable influence over the democratic rights of others especially "equal opportunity", "one man one vote", and the Economic Bill of Rights. We will refer to this new economic civil rights law as the "balanced voice mandate".

In addition to the general concept we need specific regulations limiting the annual sum of all local, state, and federal political contributions including specific lobbying and promotional costs. For institutions or businesses the sum of these costs cannot exceed the individual median contribution of the B90 group multiplied by the number of equivalent full-time employees or members. Thus the voice of an institution, corporation, or business is kept proportional to the voice of those citizens employed by or members of it as our constitution requires.

For wealthy individuals the total cannot exceed the median contribution of the T10 group multiplied by 10. Thus the voice of wealthy individuals is kept proportional to the median of other wealthy individuals in their wealth class magnified by ten. These restrictions ensure that the voice of the populace is kept in proportion to the voice of wealth power as constitutionally implied. See further discussion under Title 11b, Title 23, and discussions: "Crisis Responsibilities and Liabilities", "Trickle Down "Magic"", and "Justice in Economics".

Title 6: Equal Value Pay for Equal Valued Productivity

Equal value must be paid for equal work. If two people make the same product or service in the same time with the same quality, they **must** receive the same value of pay. This is an inalienable right of all humans worldwide as embodied in axiom 2 and item 1 of the Economic Bill of Rights which mandate proportional pay for proportional economic performance. As such our government must not trade with any nation unless they comply with this axiom or apply tariffs to compensate. Equal pay rate for equal productivity rate would be another way of stating the same axiom in terms of equal rates.

The equality formula would automatically compensate for productivity differences since time/value is linear. For example if you take twice the time to make the same product with the same quality you should be paid half the rate. Amortized automation capital costs should be included in productivity cost analysis. However trade/transportation costs such as export, lading, international shipping, import, unlading, national shipping differential, amortized trade startup costs, and other trade related costs should be measured and accounted separately as extra trade costs not as productivity costs. These costs add no value.

Reasonable variations are allowable for job experience, leadership, and other job related worker characteristics, provided the characteristics are treated equally. For example if job experience is the variation, then all those with the same experience should receive the same pay if their performance is the same. It is interesting that this general axiom directly addresses the gender bias and racial bias issues that perpetuate worldwide with a systematic economic solution that will eliminate these problems as well! See Title 11a and topic "Justice in Economics" for implementation details. What is truly amazing is that productivity is the most measured and analyzed quantity in economics. Yet we can only resolve fair wages with a power war between business and labor?

It is important to understand that axiom 2 specifies a relationship between total labor costs including wages, salaries, and other labor costs (W) and productivity (P) that applies at the macro and micro economic levels. However it will be much easier to apply controls and measurements for this concept at the macro level. As a formula this relationship would be: $W = M \times P$ as we learned in high school algebra. This simple formula says that labor wages must be directly proportional to productivity. If we graphed this relationship it would be a straight line starting at the origin (0,0) with a slope of "M".

Based on the analysis discussed in "The Role of Profits in Humanism" the value of M for total labor costs is about .95. All complying nations would conform to this same line using the same value of M within some specified tolerance. But they can operate over any range on the line that is appropriate for their situation. They do not need to have a minimum wage and they can choose any minimum wage that is appropriate for them provided it is a **point on the straight line**.

Developed nations would choose a high minimum wage and they would operate on the high end of the line. Recently emerged nations may have no minimum wage (0,0) and they would operate on the low end of the line. As nations improve their standard of living they would probably adopt a minimum wage and move their range of operation up the line as their standard of living and national productivity improves.

Initially it should be easy to apply the concept nationally and internationally at the aggregate macroeconomic level and at the corporate level where we have the most data. Over time, improved measurement methodology will provide average productivity data for each 10% income group so that we could ensure that average wages and average productivity have the correct linear relationship (straight line graph). By using the salary correction mechanism of Title 11a the ECA will ensure that the (P,W) point of each 10 percentile income group is a point on the straight $W = M \times P$ line. This axiom would end the bad idea of cheap labor as an economic concept once and for all!

All products and services produced on this straight line would have equal labor cost no matter what country they are manufactured in and no matter how high or how low their country's productivity may be! Consequently all nations will compete equally and fairly over a wide range of living standards and productivities eliminating exploitation of labor rates and exploitation of currencies. See Title 7 below for discussion on currency normalization and topic "The Role of Profits in Humanism" for more discussion and ideas on axiom 2 and fair wages.

The equal pay for equal productivity axiom 2 and the income increase axiom 5 are relative axioms. So they tell us how to balance labor rates to achieve equilibrium. But they can only provide quantitative wages once we choose an initial condition. The easiest and most effective way to choose this initial condition for the USA is to use the minimum wage of Title 8 or axiom 4 since it is an inherent starting wage by its very nature. Other nations could choose minimum wages of their preference provided the points chosen are on the $W = M \times P$ line.

This fair "level playing field" idea of axiom 2 is very important to understand. Let's take a hypothetical example. We will contrast two extreme cases comparing the same exact product. Let's imagine a souvenir type product that can be made two ways. It can be made totally by hand at home requiring no factory, no management, and no other infrastructure or capital which would be ideal for the most underdeveloped economies at the low end of the productivity range.

On the other hand it can be made by robots in a robot factory which would be ideal for the most developed economy. Any real world economy would be somewhere between these two extreme cases. The two product sources are tested to the same standard and are identical and indistinguishable from one another. Based on axiom 2, the two sources will produce products at exactly the same cost and value excluding trade/transportation costs that provide no product value!

This means the two product sources will be highly competitive; they are the same cost and quality! We would expect each source to be equally competitive and achieve an equal proportion of market share. Suppose that in the robot factory the capital depreciation for the robot is $10/ hour and that the robot requires a full-time technician at $30/hour. So the total direct labor cost is $40/hour and further assume that the robot can produce 400 units per hour. Thus the direct labor unit cost for the robot is 10 cents per unit produced ($40/400 units). While the competing handmade producers make $1 per hour because they can produce 10 units per hour. Therefore the unit cost of the handmade product is also 10 cents ($1/10 units) as axiom 2 requires.

Notice that the productivity (P) of the two sources varies 40 to 1 (400 units per hour/10 units per hour) and their pay (W) also varies 40 to 1 ($40 per hour/$1 per hour). Therefore we have equal pay for equal productivity. So axiom 2 is satisfied and both of these (P,W) points are on the same $W = M \times P$ line. **This straight line represents the fair level playing field for international trade**. The slope and especially the straightness of the line are what provide this level playing field fairness. You might think that $1 per hour is low pay but that is 60% more than the minimum wage our neighbors make in Mexico and Mexico is not even considered "competitive" in the cheap labor war!

Now we see that because of axiom 2 the same exact product can be produced throughout the world at exactly the same price and quality even though labor productivity is drastically different (40:1 in the example above). Therefore every product could be produced at the same cost anywhere in the world. So it follows that similar products that are competitive would be equally competitive no matter where in the world they are produced. Thus the competitive nature of a product becomes solely a characteristic of the product or company itself, **not** a characteristic of **where** it is produced. Notice how different this idea is compared with our current ideas. Indirect labor and profits are treated in a more detail model in topic "The Role of Profits in Humanism".

As you can see in Humanism economic competition is maintained and even enhanced while economic exploitation and distortion are eliminated because **all humans** are treated equally based on their productivity. Competition will increase because now competition will focus on attributes of a product or its company that make it more or less competitive not on more or less distorted and exploited labor rates. Product quality will improve as well because now product quality will distinguish a product or its company as more competitive not just as more expensive. **No country will ever again lose jobs to another country** because of cheap labor rates only because of true competition where the product with the largest benefit-to-cost ratio wins!

No employer in the world will ever again be able to extort its employees with threats of moving its production to a cheaper labor source because there **cannot** be a cheaper labor source according to axiom 2. Furthermore the motivation and justification for protectionism will be drastically reduced if not eliminated entirely and our markets will be fair and open to all. Finally production local to consumption will have better efficiency because trade/transportation costs are separated making local production naturally advantageous. See topic: "It Is Time for a New World Order" for more trade ideas.

Notice that there is no need for exploitation of currencies or exploitation of wage rates in the low productivity economy in order to compete with the high productivity economy. Massive amounts of very low productivity employment can be generated with minimal capital investment and infrastructure without wage or currency exploitation! Furthermore there is no reason any other product could not be produced at the equally competitive cost in the high productivity economy as well. Productivity will be protected for all.

So there is no reason that the highly paid, high productivity workers cannot make any product that their market demands without sending any jobs abroad provided there is no shortage of labor or shortage of natural resources. This means that all the loss of jobs and loss of productivity caused by exploitation of the global economy were mandated by greed and corruption not by good market economics!

In this corruption whoever is willing to work for the lowest wage gets the rationed job! So in Capitalism's profit paradigm workers compete to see who can work for the lowest wage (achievement?). While in Humanism's prosperity paradigm, workers compete for the highest productivity (achievement!) and this corresponds to highest pay. This change in paradigm is so profound that it represents a true renaissance!

Notice that there is a "night and day" difference between the two paradigms. It's the difference between competing for the lowest pay instead of competing for the highest pay! It is amazing how much difference there is between wealth economics based on profits and prosperity economics even though they are both based on Capitalism! So our economic axioms and rights make this profound difference.

Axiom 2 creates a level playing field for national and international competition where all workers compete to improve their standard of living by improving their productivity and every worker has equal access to the international market no matter how high or how low their productivity may be! So trade protectionism will no longer have a motivation because fair and open trade will be encouraged in a systematic scientific way where fair is **fair** and foul is **foul**. There is no need for protection against fair economics only protection against foul economics! See topics: "It Is Time for a New World Order!" and "Beware! Economists, Greed & Productivity" for more discussion.

One way to implement this fair and open, level playing field idea is to expand the use of international technical standards similar to the ISO 9000 series of standards already used for international quality standards. Two different methods could be used to achieve an auditable international certification of compliance. For developed nations the entire nation could be certified as compliant and recertified periodically. Then each company of that nation would just have a minimal certification process for international trade compliance.

For emerging nations that might not be able yet to achieve certification as a nation, their leading individual companies could still achieve certification using the more extensive certification process that is auditable periodically and based on the companies' detailed financial reports. This alternative approach makes trade arrangements even easier than the current WTO system and all companies have equal access to the fair trade system as their economies emerge and develop.

National compliance could be achieved gradually company by company. In general the certification process consists of measuring and documenting compliance with the wage value formula $W = M \times P$, the annual pay increase formula: $W\% = Ip\% - Iw\% + P\%$ (see Title 11a), and the currency value formula discussed next in Title 7 below.

We intend to avoid most tariffs by seeking an international agreement that recognizes the inalienable right of all humans to equal value pay for equal valued work. International equal currency pay will be determined by Title 7 below. It will be very interesting to see which nations will argue that their workers deserve less! Indeed, which nations will argue that their workers deserve more? Both arguments are preposterous because **all humanity must be treated equally**!

So this leaves us with only one conclusion: establishing a fair and open level playing field for economic competition would be a long term boom for international business and the prosperity of all nations. If such an agreement were to reduce trade, the only explanation would be that the trade, so reduced, was only justifiable because of human exploitation since the absence of exploitation made the trade less attractive. This powerful concept can replace an Export Led Economy!

In conclusion notice how the axioms provide economics with an inalienable national and international economic discipline based on **economic first principles** that has been so lacking. It is this discipline that other forms of science like Chemistry or Biology have that sets them apart from the undisciplined (no meta-principles) field of Economics. Moreover this lack of discipline also "opens the door" to corruption and privilege afloat in a sea of financial funds to fuel them.

It is interesting to note how recently there has been so much discussion about reversion to a "Gold Standard" or digital currencies to provide some of this needed discipline and standardization. The viability of this gold reversion is not what is interesting but rather its element of economic desperation! In many ways the axioms, particularly axiom 2, create a new national and international discipline and standardization for economics that provide a new "Labor Standard" idea instead of the old "Gold Standard" idea. This truly represents a renaissance in economic thought that will transform economics into a brave new era!

The $W = M \times P$ formula represents this new Labor Standard. This standardization of the labor-hour rate/productivity relationship provides economics with a "unit of productivity" as the economic standard for value. This will achieve a broad and powerful internal discipline and standardization that provide much more than the wildest promises of a "Gold Standard" reversion. It is time for a new economic science to replace the barbaric relics of the medieval past. See topic "The Role of Profits in Humanism" for further discussion.

Title 7: Equal Currencies Buy Equal Goods and Services

In Humanism all international currency equivalence will be based on equal value of purchased goods not solely on a traded market based on supply/demand and massive manipulation. This concept is mandated by axiom 3 and item 3 of the Economic Bill of Rights. It is impossible to have a market based on supply and demand if unlimited supply can be printed at will. This axiom would end the idea of cheap currency as an economic concept once and for all. Gleeful riddance to a bad idea!

Thus currency equivalence is a calculation based on a measurement, not just a broken market. A fiat currency has no intrinsic value. Its value is determined by its economic performance which can be measured easily and accurately. It is worth whatever the fiat currency can buy. If two currencies have the same purchasing performance so that equal denominations of each can buy the same exact goods and services in their local markets, they must be equal valued currencies!

This idea like almost all ideas in this book is not new. It is usually called Purchasing Power Parity. What is new is putting these ideas together into an integrated axiomatic system of thought to produce a systematic prosperous economy for all mankind! No doubt this idea of prosperity based on meta-principles is new, novel, and can improve the religion of market economics radically. So it is clear that a currency's long term relative value compared to other currencies can be measured with stability rather accurately without depending totally on a manipulated currency market. We will continue the existing currency market as well using a hybrid market solution. See topic "The Role of "free" Markets in Humanism" for more market implementation details.

The ECA will define and maintain a minimum cost of goods and services "basket" representing the annual cost of goods and services for a married couple and 2.2 children. To be most effective this basket of goods and services should be basic and closely related to basic labor costs that are used to produce all products and services worldwide.

This basket is used as a metric in many other calculations such as the cost of living. The local currency cost of this basket must be calculated by all nations with which we trade. In addition each nation will provide forward guidance as a linear daily rate. Equivalent product substitutions will be specified to handle local preferences and availability such as rice caloric equivalent to potatoes or beans.

Equal valued currencies will have an equal annual cost for the basket or be proportional. This proportionality will determine the currency's exchange rate for use in analysis and computation of tariffs as well as a nominal trading target price. In this way the measured currency value is decoupled somewhat from the volatile traded market valuation price.

It is interesting that this system allows for direct conversion between any two currencies using the measured data supplied above without the use of a reserved currency or a market mechanism. Technically this valuation mechanism could be implemented as an international standard similar to the ISO 9000 series that are already used for our international quality standards as first discussed above in Title 6.

This axiom is so fundamental and so inalienable that it is hard to argue against. Consequently we can expect those opposed to attack this "basket" as wrong, inappropriate, unfair, or inaccurate. For example some would attempt to argue that this "basket" does not include tractors or airplanes and is therefore not broad enough for economics?

However extraordinary tractors, airplanes, and all other goods and services are made by ordinary workers whose ordinary wages are directly related to the minimum cost of ordinary living. So the cost of these items is directly related to the cost of the "basket" and the "basket" is a very economically basic measure well suited for this use.

Others will argue that the basket is not "perfect" enough for their economy and that they need their own basket. Thus they can manipulate their basket and achieve the same goal as manipulating their currency. Isn't economics ugly? If greed can't spin it corruption will! Needless to say, it is important that the basket is internationally designed to have local equivalences such as rice caloric equivalent to potatoes and beans. It should be universal and multinational in every respect. Our global economy would accept nothing less. But there is a much more fundamental counter argument that is important to present. Unfortunately it takes a paragraph of background explanation first.

There is a fundamentally important measurement theory idea. If two variables A and B have the same error (inaccuracy, uncertainty, anomaly, fault …), then their difference A-B will not contain that error, even though the error was unknown or unmeasurable it will disappear! Thus it is possible to measure A-B more accurately than either A or B. The proof is simple high school algebra. Designating the error as "e", then $A+e - (B+e) = A-B$ because the error cancels out.

Applying the measurement principle to our problem is easy. We wish to know the difference between two currencies A and B. We only need to know their difference because we wish to make them equal (A-B=0), or proportional with an exchange rate. We do not need to measure the absolute value of either one of the currencies just their difference. If our basket has any errors, inaccuracies, uncertainties, anomalies, or faults they will all cancel out if we use exactly the same basket in all countries evaluations. Science is so fair yet trade is so not!

So the most important characteristic of the basket is that it always be the same so the errors will cancel. For example, we suggested that the basket be based on a family with 2.2 children because we believe that 2.2 is the long term international average for sustainability and zero population growth. Some country could argue that their birth rate is actually 1.8 and so our basket is "wrong" and they should use 1.8 in their evaluation. This is nonsense. It is not important whether we use 1.8 or 2.2; it is important that we use the same exact number in both evaluations. So if the number has an error, the error will cancel out!

All trade with other nations must be based on this equivalence or tariffs applied to approximate the equivalence. Unfortunately tariffs must be a legitimate option on the table if the majority of tariffs are to be avoided by applying the fair and open trade concept of Title 6 above. We expect to use tariffs only for temporary correction. We expect to avoid tariffs long term by agreement between most nations to keep their currencies within a narrow range of the calculated nominal value by joint action of all central banks according to a predetermined supply/demand elasticity formula including linear forward guidance.

No agreement – no trade! In effect we will keep the manipulated international currency market as it is now except that the manipulation will have a calculated common target rather than a protectionist goal of isolated self-interest. This is an example of a hybrid market concept where the nominal trading price is determined by a guiding principle yet the day to day trading has the same effect as a regular free market.

Of course if all nations agree, some disadvantaged emerging nations can be given special dispensation on a short time-frame and on an agreed compliance schedule for trade equity. See "The Role of Profits in Humanism" for a standardized suggestion. Every nation worldwide desperately wants fair and stable currency values. We expect that any international agreement that provides fair and stable currency values will naturally increase the volume of international business drastically.

Title 8: Minimum Wage Equals Minimum Cost of Living

As discussed in Title 6 in Humanism each nation can choose any minimum wage they deem appropriate including none at all (0,0) providing the point chosen is on the $W = M \times P$ line. In the USA the minimum full-time wage of any worker must be greater than or equal to the cost of a dignified living needed to accomplish a human's right to "life, liberty, and the pursuit of happiness". The minimum goods and services "basket" of Title 7 above will be used for this metric. In addition the minimum wage for any worker with more years of full-time economic service will be increased by formula for each year of economic service up to a maximum of 30 years of full-time service.

So our new minimum wage will establish a minimum value wage for experience as well and protect the older worker as well as the entry level worker. This new experience feature will improve the minimum wage idea significantly. Furthermore part-time workers will be paid at the same rate as full-time workers. Exceptions will be allowed for disadvantaged workers such as students or disabled workers. The ECA will manage the minimum wage using its Economic Labor department.

We have a minimum wage currently but it is set to a fixed hourly rate, does not adjust automatically as a formula, does not compensate for the true cost of living, and does not compensate for experience. Unfortunately wealth economics has drastically corrupted the current ideas on measuring the cost of living. In order to justify a low minimum wage, many costs have been removed or distorted. This is one of many reasons why Economic Labor needs to be part of the ECA rather than a political department led by a political appointee to satisfy the political goals of the current Presidential party. Instead Economic Labor will be driven by first principles of metaeconomics!

To establish the "basket" of goods and services, the ECA should start over by actually measuring every penny spent by thousands of target families and carefully determine which expenses should be included. The appropriate value will be determined later, but current estimates using the proposed method (Wagstaff, 2013) were around $16/hour or more for an entry level wage in 2013 or about $18/hour in 2018!

The current discrepancy between the minimum wage paid now ($7.25) and the proper minimum wage ($18.00+) is a national embarrassment. Each year the gap widens. The gap is so wide that the size of the gap is now used as a justification for not closing the gap because it is too large. Seemingly mismanagement justifies even more mismanagement. Yet this misleading justification only makes the ugly gap even wider!

This humiliating intellectual embarrassment affords us an opportunity to better appreciate formulaic governance. The minimum wage law should have been a formula as proposed herein not a fixed number. Then Congress would not have to haggle over the number every year over and over again. Instead the number would track the cost of living mathematically and automatically for hundreds of years or more without any haggling, bribery, or political deals at all. So in a quest for our economic "moon" achieved with economic engineering based on metaeconomic principles, we find this path also leads to better politics!

Although this idea is usually referred to as the "minimum wage", it would be far more accurate to refer to it as the "minimum productivity". Consistent with the W = M x P relationship, the "minimum wage" is a (P,W) point on this line. So rather than refer to this point by its minimum wage value (W) we should refer to this point by its minimum productivity value (P) emphasizing its productivity.

The idea here is not to pay more for a job than it is worth which would decrease productivity and therefore prosperity. Rather the intention is to establish a minimum standard for productive job creation. So we want to use the minimum wage to motivate businesses to increase productivity and thus increase prosperity throughout the pay scale.

We want businesses to avoid creating "junk jobs" below the minimum productivity so we expect that they will upgrade the minimum jobs with automation and other productivity improvements to meet the new productivity standard. Notice that including a minimum wage for experience will help further to increase productivity at the higher pay scales. Notice also that axiom 2 mandates productivity pay at the higher pay levels by ensuring that the (P,W) point of each 10 percentile income category is on the straight W = M x P line. See Title 11a for implementation details. See more discussion in "The Role of Labor Efficiency" and "Beware Economists, Greed & Productivity".

Title 9: The National Fund and Public Capital Formation

Economic Humanism will use a public capital concept where workers provide a significant part of our economy's capital deployment needs directly. Retirement payroll deductions will be held in a National Fund passively managed by the NF department of the new ECA. This idea will help achieve the mandate of Axiom 1 to make all humanity principals of our economy. The world's leading nation deserves the best retirement system in the world. Moreover the National Fund can achieve that goal as part of the prosperity mandate. So a robust retirement system can keep our economy confident. What a celebration of good Capitalism! Why should our nation strive for anything less?

The Benefit

The goal of "twice the benefit for half the cost" is really an **easy** goal to achieve once an individual's payroll deductions are multiplied by the growth of compound return on investment for many future years. Compound return on investment is what made the perpetually wealthy in the first place and it will work just as well for the rest of us. This approach will make everyone who works into a capitalist (literally) in our democratic economy! Each and every person of each and every generation will pay for their own retirement and medical care with gains from their own savings without any taxation at all! They can tailor their savings plan up to as much as double the minimum 6.2% (12.4% max) to suit their own ideas of a wholesome retirement plan.

Unfortunately in the current retirement system some welfare costs were paid out of our retirement funds as a sly political trick to avoid charging them to the welfare budget and the general fund. Of course disability and other such benefits are social welfare programs that have nothing to do with the economy or retirement. All welfare programs should be managed under one general welfare budget line item category so they can compete efficiently for available welfare funding.

The funding and management of these programs should be associated with other social welfare programs not the NF or the ECA. The 14% of GDP national budget mandate was intended to be sufficient to cover continuation of disability and other welfare program funding. The administration will stay with Congress and the current welfare administration that Congress has already established. See "Capitalism vs Humanism" for more economic welfare discussion and evaluation.

Baby booms or demographic changes will no longer be a problem. Self-employed persons will be treated the same as everyone else and they will not have to pay double! The new system does not depend on never-ending growth to achieve benefits so it is consistent with the success of our future economy and our planet. It will work well even in a situation of reduced or flat economic growth even negative growth. Furthermore the new system would be sustainable without **any** taxes for **all** generations in the future! What an epic achievement! This breakthrough would help ensure the economic success of our nation indefinitely. See Title 18 for more discussion about growth concepts.

There is only a one-time (45 year) non-recurring cost required to pay off the liabilities of the old defunct system. The funding for this payoff will come from the one-time windfall of the inheritance tax of Title 5 and the wealth tax of Title 23. Once those old liabilities are paid off in about 45 years the new system is self-sustaining indefinitely with only the 6.2% minimum individual savings deduction and the Medicare savings deduction with no further taxation **ever** needed in the future!

Let us look forward one working lifetime 45 years from now. Let us assume we realize that the existing system is fundamentally flawed, cannot be fixed, and must be replaced. Our descendants will look back at our historic decision to make this transition by absorbing the one-time liability costs in exchange for never-ending retirement prosperity for our children and for all future generations. Twice the benefit for half the cost without taxes would be a historic human accomplishment of epic proportions. This is an easy trade-off decision between a one-time liability that ends gradually over 45 years and a perpetual, recurring benefit that continues indefinitely for **all** future generations!

Making visionary sacrifices like this is what made our nation great in the first place. Our forefathers accepted sacrifices so that all future generations could prosper. Are we going to allow wealth power to write our history for us? How could we not have the courage to make this trade-off decision for our children? What will they think of us if we do not? Will we just stand back and watch as the old system erodes benefits and crumbles into insolvency? I feel shame to even admit the remote possibility that we will not stand and demand this benefit now!

The importance to our economy and our prosperity of having a robust, affordable, and sustainable retirement system is so large it is hard to put into words. Better yet our NF fund stabilizes our nation's capital formation system. Our economy is inherently a democratic human thing. Axiom 1 reinforces this idea as fundamental for our economy. A robust retirement system creates and sustains collective faith, hope, security, and confidence in our economic future. These prevailing feelings and attitudes permeate and energize our economic lives. When humanity lives and works in such a positive environment we become more creative, more inventive, more enthusiastic, more confident in taking on risks, and better able to navigate those risks successfully. Clearly this is the starting point of our path to our economic "moon"!

Moreover this is just the beginning because our economy is also a generative system. Your confidence increases my confidence and my confident response further reinforces your original confidence! So to a great extent our economy is a "confidence system". If we encourage and maintain our collective confidence our economy booms with prosperity but if we collectively lose confidence our economy crashes into depression. A robust retirement system creates and sustains collective confidence more than any other single idea in economics. With a robust retirement system our economy can withstand periods of **great crisis with ease** because we are confident that our futures are secure and full of exciting possibilities. There's no gloom and doom!

Unfortunately our human characteristics magnify the same way in the negative direction. If I lose confidence you lose confidence as well. For example it seems like our entire nation is constantly embroiled in a never-ending controversy about how and when to cut retirement benefits in an effort to reduce the unfunded liabilities of the old retirement system. Every time we cut we immediately begin the controversy again for the next stage of never-ending cuts. Therefore our children have completely lost faith and collective confidence that the current system will ever help them with their retirement. They know the current retirement system is defunct and will eventually fail.

It seems to them that all they can hope to do is minimize their burden by paying less and less for our retirement. Thus their negative fear becomes amplified as a self-fulfilling prophecy! We do not want to haggle over **less and less** especially with our children. We want to positively achieve much **more** for all! This controversy is morbid, putrid, and it has demoralized our economy and our nation; we have all had enough! It is time now for the "twice the benefit for half the cost" sustainable system that we should have had in the first place! It is time for metaeconomics that will begin our new age of prosperity.

Here is how the new NF fund will be managed to achieve our goals. The current cash surplus, if any, of the old Social Security fund will be included but accounted separately to offset against future benefit payouts. This increase in economic capital for direct deployment is intended to more than offset any 'trickle down" shortfall that might be caused by the inheritance tax of Title 5 or the wealth tax of Title 23 that will be used to pay off the liabilities of the old defunct system.

As first discussed in Title 2, each worker will save a minimum 6.2% of their income as currently and will receive shares in the NF which will be paid out as a tax free annuity at retirement. Each worker can increase their individual savings to as much as double the 6.2% deduction minimum. The annuity benefit for the minimum 6.2% deduction is estimated at 70% of your average lifetime income.

Medicare premiums will be covered in a similar manner using the existing Medicare retirement deduction. This deduction will support approximately a 400% larger medical benefit or medical cost if needed and any excess could be paid out as a general cash premium added to the annuity or used to aid the transition funding. The 6.2% is a nominal value but the ECA will increase or decrease this amount from time to time as a powerful economic management control tool as well.

Here is how the economic control tool will work. If the amount is increased by the ECA above the nominal 6.2% then the contribution to the NF will increase which will increase available capital directly for deployment, increasing consumer supply to deal with excessive consumer demand, and simultaneously decrease consumer demand in an inflationary environment. Moreover if the amount is decreased below the nominal by the ECA then the differential will be monetized to keep the nominal contribution to the NF at the 6.2% minimum.

This control method will maintain capital deployment and simultaneously increase consumer demand in a recessionary economy. So this becomes a powerful direct tool that can be combined with monetary policy, investment policy, and tax policy to provide an integrated approach to economic policy. This integrated economic management approach is one of the key hallmarks of the Reform Act. See a detailed example of such an economic control system in Title 23.

It should be noted that capital liquidity is always provided to worthy capital demand independent of the payroll deduction since the ECA will monetize any payroll deduction shortfall. This contrasts with trickle-down capital where the risk appetite of the capitalists can grow or shrink drastically in direct opposition to the capital market's needs. When we need it most they "hide under the bed" or "leave town". This flawed idea of capital liquidity creates economic instability. Instead we will directly inject any emergency liquidity into consumer hands.

This is exactly what happened during the recent 2008-2018 crisis. The Fed injected QE into the hands of our trickle-down capitalists who "hid under the bed" or "left town" during that period and our recovery suffered. Direct demand driven capital formation into consumer hands is fundamentally superior to any conventional trickle-down economic capital formation system and we deserve the absolute best system!

The NF will invest funds according to a formulaic model. The fund's managers will be passive and will not make any investment decisions. They will simply execute the transparent formulas and methodologies specified by this reform legislation for all to see and scrutinize. We could call this method a "piggyback" investment system. The fixed investment model will be driven by four parameters which will be approved by the ECA board prior to the beginning of each fiscal year.

The parameters are: 1) the total amount of funds to be invested this year, 2) the percent of funds for each venture capital investment, 3) the percent of funds for each public offering investment, and 4) the percent of funds for each primary bond issue. Investments will be made in three of the most important economic investment categories: 1) Venture capital financing, 2) Public equity offerings, and 3) Primary bond offerings by bond rating. In addition the ECA should launch a task force to determine a powerful new capital support system for small businesses. Once the new plan is formulated the ECA will seek legislation from Congress to enact the new capital support system and integrate it with this plan by adding a fourth investment category.

    a) Venture capital is the most economically important type of capital formation. Each year venture capital investment firms will each decide whether or not to participate in the NF program for the upcoming year. Those who participate will guarantee that a fixed percentage of each and all deals financed will come from the NF fund as a silent partner. In this way the venture firm must accept the NF in all deals or no deals. There is no deal discretion allowed.

In this way the NF makes no investment decisions but rather they ride "piggyback" on the venture capitalist's decisions. The share percentage is fixed for the year and is one of the parameters approved by the ECA board. The absolute maximum is limited to 30%. The benefit to the firm and our economy is more venture capital deployment. The NF funds so invested will be held for 10 years and then liquidated as soon as possible with the proceeds returned to the NF to be rolled over and reinvested as new funds.

b) Equity public offerings, NYSE and NASDAQ, are the second most important form of capital formation. The NF will take a fixed percent of each and all such public offerings including IPOs. Thus they will "piggyback" on other public offering investor's decisions. No deal by deal discretion is allowed. The share percentage parameter is approved by the board for each year. The absolute maximum is 30%. The NF funds so invested will be held for 10 years for IPOs and 7 years for PO's and then liquidated with the proceeds returned to the NF to be rolled over and reinvested.

c) Any funds not committed to a) or b) above will be invested in the primary issued, 10 year corporate bond market. A fixed percentage of each AAA rated corporate bond issue will be taken by the NF. If funds are still available then the fixed percentage will be taken of each bond offering of the next highest rating and so on until all funds specified by the board are committed for the year. No deal by deal discretion is allowed. Thus they will "piggyback" on other bond investor's decisions. The share percentage parameter is approved by the board for each year. The absolute maximum is 30%. The NF funds so invested will be held until maturity and then redeemed with the proceeds returned to the NF to be rolled over and reinvested in an ongoing fashion for all future generations.

It will take 60 years or so for the NF to reach its mature size. In later years the fund's size may require different parameter controls and different strategies that can be added by subsequent legislation. New markets can be included when the fund's size dictates. For example the NF could take a fixed percent of every stock in the S&P or a fixed percent of each stock in the NYSE, NASDAQ, or both. The secondary bond market could be used as well. The possibilities for "piggyback" investing are almost endless. It is intended that parts a) and b) should be the majority of the fund's commitments and that c) should be the smaller commitment. Notice how this Humanistic application of capitalistic ideas is so like Capitalism yet so different and humane. This contrast could only be explained as an economic renaissance.

The Risk

This public capital concept will provide our economy with a reliable and stable source of base capital deployment and simultaneously provide us with the best retirement system in the world. It will also recycle perpetual wealth in an economically viable way and make all those who work capitalists in our democratic economy! What a powerful combination of ideas! Multiple "unsolvable" problems are solved with one comprehensive solution. It's a common theme of HERA. For more ideas see "Understanding the Power of Design".

Some would be concerned about the seemingly risky nature of these investments. It is not the risk of the investment types that is most important but rather the risk on the fund's size, time horizon, and investment methodology that are important. The fund's mature size is huge by mutual fund standards. Moreover the time horizon is even more secure and stable. There would be a roughly 65 year time horizon (45 working + 20 retired) over which risk could be absorbed.

The methodology is mathematical in nature involving no judgments required for execution. The absence of judgment means that the "law of large numbers" applies because bad or accidental judgment is not possible nor is corruption. So the return on investment for the fund will be the weighted average return of the markets chosen over 65 years with a high degree of accuracy, stability, security, and certainty.

The NF's ability to predict future returns on investment are probably more accurate than the actuarial prediction regarding life expectancy! The only real risks to these investments are risks to the future of our economy. There is no way for any citizen to ever avoid the risk of his national economy. Any suggestion to the contrary is based on Capitalism's idea of the exclusion of humanity from the economy. Capitalism suggests that our economy belongs to the rich and powerful capitalists and that we are delegated to be helpless victims! No wonder we were so fearful and suspicious of investing in our future economy!

On the other hand in Humanism our economy is not separate from us; we are our economy and our economy is ours. We depend on it. We contribute to it. And we benefit from it. Furthermore this legislation and the NF will make very beneficial contributions to our economy and will keep our economy strong and secure for many future generations indefinitely. Humanism will initiate a renaissance that will rocket us into a new age of economic stability, security, and success never before imagined! So our renaissance comes with much less risk.

Nevertheless, to ensure the safety net characteristic of the old Social Security system, the new benefit will be guaranteed at a minimum of the old benefit level! So the safety net will be maintained exactly as it is currently even though the payroll deduction is only half as much. Yet the reserve over minimum is a hefty 2:1 instead of the nearly zero reserve of the current cash system. This new system is so superior!

The Promise

Let's look in detail at the idea of "political promises" intended to achieve social security. Political promises are just "words on paper" that can be erased as easily as they were written. So the real security of these promises depends on the structural soundness of the mechanism that delivers the security. Otherwise these are just empty promises intended to trick humanity into believing in the **illusion of security** that cannot be delivered. No delivery mechanism – no security! As soon as these empty promises are threatened they crumble because there is no strength of delivery behind them. Worse yet our entire economy worldwide will crumble in a breach of confidence as well!

The detail nature of our current social security promise is that the previous administration promised through laws that it enacted that the current generation would pay the retirement and medical costs of the previous generation now retiring. But the generation that made this agreement was **not** the generation that is burdened with the obligation to pay. So it is like **he** and **you** agree that **she** and **I** will pay for you!

In other words the old administration passed laws that force the young to promise to pay for the old! Indeed the beneficiary of the agreement was the same generation that made the promise not the generation that has to pay the cost of the promise. The current generation made no agreement. Instead they seem to be the victim of the agreement! So it is like "Obamacare". One day we have it. The next day it's gone. Erased and repealed with ease after years of effort to gain security! It's an ugly "time trick" where one generation tries to exploit its successor.

Consequently this social security promise will stand only to the extent that the current generation does not change the law again and again because it is too burdensome. Yet of course it is too burdensome. So we continue to reduce the benefit endlessly! Is this security? Worse yet there was no mechanism whatsoever that could help deliver the promise. No funds were accrued. No savings were set aside that would shoulder the burden. This is truly an empty promise because there is no money in the promise fund! In fact there is no promise fund at all!

On the contrary the proposed new system does not have these catastrophic faults. The generation that makes the promise is the same generation that fulfills the promise and the same generation that in turn benefits from the fulfilled promise. Furthermore the funds to secure the promise are accrued by continuous savings deductions into a safe separate account as an asset owned by each citizen and protected by property laws and rights that prohibit confiscation or attachment.

Moreover each citizen has visibility for 45 years or more over the projected valuation of their NF account based on current economic conditions and continuous future projections of the NF. So if the economic outlook underperforms expectations, the fund's managers and/or the individual citizens themselves can increase their deduction many decades in advance to offset any unusual retirement shortfall.

Finally let's look at the idea of "reserve" regarding a security promise. In the new system the unsecured promise made by the system is that each citizen will receive a guaranteed minimum benefit that equals the old benefit minimum even under catastrophic circumstances. Notice the target benefit is twice as large as the guaranteed minimum benefit. So the investment system could fall short of its goal by a reserve of 2:1 and still meet the entire promised minimum benefit from the NF fund itself without any additional funds or burden on the general budget.

The old system could have a small cash reserve but the old system had no accrual reserve at all because all the funds including any shortfall came directly from the general budget. There was no accrual. It should be obvious that the new system delivers much more social security than the old system could even hope to promise much less deliver! Don't we deserve the absolute best possible retirement system? Hell yes we do and it is time we engineer it as part of our own destiny!

Title 10: The Responsibility for Worker/Consumer Rights

The government is fundamentally responsible for protecting workers, consumers, and all of humanity from manipulation, distortion, extortion, and exploitation nationally or through international trade. Every nation is responsible for protecting its citizens from abuses of wealth power locally or globally. Indeed the responsibility for this economic governance is more fundamental than the constitutional responsibility for national military defense. As a negative issue this responsibility is clarified in item 3 of the Economic Bill of Rights.

As a proactive issue this responsibility is clarified in Axiom 1 with the terminology "to serve humanity in facilitating the worker/consumer duality by achieving maximum prosperity". All the necessary functions of a labor union will be provided by labor laws. The basic benefits of unions must be available to all workers. Disputes will be settled through due process with the Labor Department acting as public prosecutor representing the workers. This is why the Labor Department must be independent from the political process, chartered by the rights and axioms, and protected as part of the ECA instead.

This is also why we must maintain the legal standing of labor unions. The voice of labor must be organized in order to balance with the extreme voice of wealth power. Strikes will not be allowed until due process has been exhausted. Labor unions will still be allowed and the laws protecting the workers will give unions an added advantage and a much better balance of power. Titles 7, 8, 11, and 12 are examples of protections that make this possible. In the future the unions are likely to become more like economic "watchdog groups". They will monitor the situation and ensure that the ECA and its Labor Department fulfill their primary responsibilities. If not then unions have legal standing and they are free to take direct action and represent human labor.

Consequently much of what unions do now will be included in basic labor laws enforced by the ECA through its Labor Department. So this will free unions to focus on **proactive economic ideas** improving productivity and **offensive prosperity** for Labor. This can be done at the local level working directly with the employer, at the industry wide level, and at the national level by proposing new national economic goals to improve prosperity of the workers they represent. This will achieve a drastic improvement in our human economic representation.

Title 11: Management of National Income and Wealth

In our reformed economy national income and national wealth will be managed by axiomatic formulas not dependent on power, exploitation, manipulation, extortion or happenstance. The minimum wage schedule and the direct wage controls together with various taxations such as income tax, wealth tax, inheritance tax, luxury taxes, and management pay controls will be used by the ECA to achieve these requirements.

a) **National Income Increase**

Beginning immediately, the national income must increase each year by the amount of labor hour growth (population), plus product price inflation, plus the amount of the annual productivity improvement. The formula for axiom 5 simply says that all workers are entitled to wage increases to compensate for product price inflation, not caused by wage inflation, plus any increase in labor productivity. Let's put this into a proactive wage change compensation formula where:

W% is the percent change in wages, salaries, and other human labor that should be applied as correctional compensation to achieve full labor valuation for the current period using the monthly wage control.

Ip% is the percent of product price inflation actually measured for the current period and I% is total inflation (Ip% = I% - Iw%).

Iw% is the percent of wage inflation actually measured for the current period and I% is total inflation (Iw% = I% - Ip%).

P% is the percent change in labor productivity actually measured for the current period. Labor productivity is actually M x P and M is estimated to be about .95 so labor productivity is about 95% of GDP.

Then the inequality compensation formula for the current period required for axiom 5 is:

W% ≥ Ip% - Iw% + P%

For example suppose for a given year that wage inflation Iw% is 3%, price inflation Ip% is 1%, and the labor productivity increase P% is 2%. According to the compensation formula W% would be 1 – 3 + 2 = 0% of additional compensation is required. So the wage inflation that occurred naturally during the period exactly matched the growth required and no additional compensation was needed. This example is typical of what we would expect for a minimal growth situation.

Looking at other examples suppose the wage inflation is 5%, price inflation is 2%, and the productivity increase is 2%. Then W% would be 2 - 5 + 2 = -1%. So in this case wages would need to be compensated by reducing them by 1%. Likewise if wage inflation was 2%, price inflation at 1%, and the productivity increase is 3%. Then W% would be 1 – 2 + 3 = +2%. So in this case wages would need to be compensated by increasing them by 2%. The measurements and corrections would be cumulative so if the corrections are not exact the error would just carry forward to the next period for further correction.

The pay increase mandate of axiom 5 is just another way of stating the equal pay for equal productivity mandate of axiom 2 over time. For example suppose productivity increased by 2% year-over-year consistent with the sub mandate. Wages would need to increase by 2% as well in order to keep equal value pay for equal productivity in both years. Likewise if the value of currency dropped 1% year-over-year because of product price inflation then wages would need to increase by 1% as well in order to keep equal value pay for equal productivity in both years. The ECA will use two separate yet coordinated mechanisms to achieve this goal at the macroeconomic level.

First the ECA will issue salary directives to modify wages and salaries of each ten percentile income category each month to ensure the formula is met. If the only data available is annual it will be divided by 12 to get the monthly correction. If data is not available for each 10% category the correction will be applied equally to all categories until data is available. Employees will declare their income category by W4

(IRS employment) form declarations based on current earnings of all jobs including gender, race, and other economic control information.

Employers would use the W4 information to determine the percentile group of each employee. In the early years the correction will be applied equally to each ten percent category. Once productivity data is available each ten percent category will be compensated separately to straighten the $W = M \times P$ line. Currently this line "sags" down in the middle depressing the middle class and increasing the wealthy class.

This measurement/correction system will be able to directly track pay by gender as well so any gender bias can be measured and then continuously corrected each month using the same system! Most other kinds of bias could be addressed as well such as racial or ethnic bias. In general if we can measure it; we can correct it. And with economic engineering if we cannot measure it today we will soon be able to tomorrow. See further discussion in topic "Justice in Economics".

Furthermore there can be no wage inflation nor any wage erosion for the economy as a whole! Notice that wage inflation ($Iw\%$) is directly subtracted out of the formula for $W\%$ above. So there **cannot** be any wage inflation because it is mathematically eliminated. In other words the correction system is always more accurate and precise than the underlying measurement system. So wage inflation is always exactly zero within the accuracy of the measurement system to compensate.

The second mechanism needed to achieve axiom 5 is that each employer is responsible under penalty of law "to pay prevailing wage rates". The Labor Department will take legal action against any employer that allows a statistical tendency to under or over pay by job category. Labor Unions can also participate in this scrutiny as well. New hire salaries will be audited especially because wage inflation and wage erosion will show up in this category first and be compensated.

Moreover new hire salaries will be controlled as a separate vector to make it easier to combat wage inflation/erosion. This mechanism will ensure that the statistical deviation allowed above or below the average is very small. So combined together the first mechanism controls the statistical average and the second mechanism controls the statistical deviation. Together they control our labor rate valuations statistically.

Combined together these two mechanisms implement the differential formula of axiom 5 that does not specify any particular pay scale. Rather the formula will only specify how pay will change with changing economic conditions. The minimum wage in Title 8 above and the income and wealth management in Title 11b below will establish long term pay levels. Furthermore once productivity data is available for each 10 percentile group, axiom 2 will control the linear distribution of wages and salaries by 10 percentile income groups according to the W = M x P equation. Notice how proactive this is. Review Title 6 for details about the importance of wage linearity.

It is interesting to contrast this axiomatic approach of Humanism with Capitalism. Capitalism tries to achieve the **lowest** possible wages and salaries to maximize return on capital and wealth of the capitalists. So this year's min is next year's max in a never ending downward spiral stair step. On the contrary Humanism using axioms 1, 2, and 5 will achieve and maintain the **highest** wages and salaries possible without causing wage inflation! This is like a 180 degree difference in prosperity goal from a goal to achieve the lowest prosperity to a goal to achieve the highest prosperity! Furthermore the correction is proactive and automatic so there can be no more **accidental** wage loss.

What a profound difference this will make in our economic lives and the lives of all future generations! A crude analysis suggests our average salary over one working lifetime would more than double at about 131% to as much as 172% without wage inflation. This is just one of many improvements and it is proactive for all generations. For an analysis of the income difference see topic "What Would Adam Smith Have Thought" and "Conclusions" in the last discussion topic.

This methodology represents a powerful "hybrid" approach between pure calculation and pure market. The microscale market still determines the relative (one job to another) value of each job's labor rate but a macroscale calculation scales that labor rate up or down slightly to achieve the total national income by percentile category. Furthermore the "pay prevailing labor rate rule" makes sure that each job shares in the statistical scaling proportionally. Yet the employer is still responsible for salary administration in the normal manner including "cost of living increases". These ideas represent a new renaissance in economic thought to begin a "New Deal" for humanity.

In addition the national aggregate is managed by the ECA to balance each percentile group by issuing monthly directives to slightly increase or slightly decrease wage rates in each of the ten, 10 percentile groups. Thus the ECA ensures that the metaeconomic axioms are achieved in the aggregate even though a market mechanism determines each job's relative labor rate and balance of one job compared to another. Furthermore the employer still determines the pay and promotion of each of its employees. Two vectors of 11 items each will be used one for new hires and one for regular employees. An 11th category will be added for top management pay inflation. For details see Title 21.

Continuing to use the labor market unchanged as a relative market has another important advantage as well. We want to manage all human labor costs to match our axioms. But the measurement and correction system suggested only controls wages and salaries because they are easy to measure and correct and they are in the majority already.

The market system creates and maintains relative equilibrium within the total labor market so it is not necessary to measure or correct every data point. As long as the majority of the data points are measured and corrected, the market will automatically track the rest of the data points as well without measuring or correcting all data points. Furthermore wages and salaries do represent a significant majority of GDP labor (Ryle, 2015). This system is simple and easy to understand.

Eliminating wage inflation and erosion proactively is a very significant economic accomplishment on our road to prosperity and our economic "moon". Workers will be included as principals of our economy rather than being treated like zinc or soybeans! As economic principals, labor will be protected from wage erosion and they will be guaranteed to receive productivity gains and be protected from product price inflation. Likewise product price inflation is much easier to manage when wage inflation is absent. See discussion "The Role of Profits in Humanism" for more discussion on product price inflation and control.

Low and well managed inflation is the objective of every economic system. Furthermore businesses will be protected from excessive and erratic labor rate demands ensuring that they compete with all other businesses on a level playing field where **every** business pays the same rate for the same productivity worldwide. So this is a perfect win-win accomplishment for both business and labor. For further discussion see: "The Role of "free" Markets in Humanism", "The Unification of Business and Labor" and "What Would Adam Smith Have Thought?".

b) National Income and Wealth

Over time, as the ECA determines, the national income and wealth of the B90 (bottom 90%) group should be greater than or equal to 70% of the total national income and greater than or equal to 50% of the total national wealth. So the T10 (top 10%) group would be limited to 30% of income (Excel file Tab Fig 2006, 2006) and 50% of wealth (Domhoff, 2010). In fact these targets are based on actual distributions in the early 1970's, one of our most prosperous periods. We should be able to do better than these goals with a concerted effort of the ECA.

Contrast this with the USA now where 77% of the wealth is held by the top 10% and the B90 has only 50% of the income. For reference, in a mathematically perfect economic democracy the B90 group would have 90% of the income and 90% of the wealth. As our goals are achieved, income of the B90 group will increase at least by 20% while the B90 wealth will increase by about 27%. Prosperity, here we come!

The national income of 11a is a differential equation that can be applied immediately and continued indefinitely. The formula of axiom 5 is based on very fundamental principles that are basically timeless and indisputable. It will be very interesting when we re-analyze historical economic data and re-compute the estimated current income and wealth figures if the formula had been used for the last 45 years!

You will be amazed at how much larger your income should have been! For a preview see discussion "What Would Adam Smith Have Thought". The tools to apply this formula were readily available hundreds of years ago when our political democracy was formed! Can you imagine how much higher your income would be today if it had been applied all these years? The difference in your prosperity would be mind-boggling! This difference is the benefit your children and grandchildren will enjoy if you have the courage to act on their behalf. For the first time in economic history we would have wage increases and "**wages as if people mattered**". Metaeconomic democracy really does matter for all of humanity and it is time to make it a reality now.

The formulas of 11b are absolute value formulas that set minimum national goals for the distribution of income and wealth. These formulas are estimates of likely or reasonable goals that are not based on any indisputable or timeless rules. However they are based on actual historical achievement in the early 1970's. Furthermore these formulas will require about one life span before they will apply fully.

The distribution of income and wealth are strongly affected by "old money" that has been perpetuated forward from generation to generation compounded into a massive concentration of wealth and political power that is choking our democracy and our economy with wealth stagnation and corruption. The inheritance tax of Title 5 will slowly and gradually correct this maldistribution so that the change will not shock our economy. This will take about one lifespan of between 80 and 90 years. Notice that "new money" is not affected by the inheritance tax yet, not until it is passed on as the "golden spoon".

New money represents exactly the kind of economic investment that we need to perpetuate prosperity too. New money will eventually become the only kind of wealth concentration that we will have. We will end perpetual wealth. In addition new wealth opportunity and new wealth achievement will increase substantially over this same period. Our new entrepreneurs will lead and certainly benefit from the national prosperity achievement. They will benefit from the new capital available from Title 9, 15, 16, 17, 18, 19, 20, 21, 22, 23, 24, and other improvements below. See topic "Capitalism vs Humanism" for more discussion on wealth reform and wealth opportunity improvements.

So the formulas of 11b are future goals that will be refined as we make progress towards our overall economic goals. They were included here to give the reader a specific idea of where we are and approximately where we should be in the future. They were also included because it is important to understand that the differential equation of 11a is not sufficient alone to track national income and wealth goals over the long term. The ECA should monitor and report the distributions of income and wealth yearly and see to it that they continue to move in the right direction and magnitude to achieve our national economic goals for many millennia into our future. For the first time in history **perpetual prosperity** is our **national economic goal** not perpetual wealth for the privileged, self-declared elite. And we are long overdue!

Notice how strange the term "national economic goals" sounds? Do you know what our current national economic goals are? What were they in 1950, or 1980, or 2000? In our history did we ever have even one such formal economic goal? I am well read and well educated yet I have difficulty grasping any sense that our nation has or ever had any national economic goals except some vague sense that we all want growth, wealth, and economic security. These vague desires sound more like wishful thinking in the midst of economic oppression rather than any formal proactive national economic goals. How could we have ever gone to the real moon without having a clear formal national goal to get there? Could we have just "showed up" on the moon one day as a national accident? No goals – No plan – No achievement!

Yet without Humanism we have no national economic goal to get to the economic "moon"! No economic goal now of any kind and we never did. To make a perfect match we don't have a "NASA" type organization to proactively achieve getting us there either! What a coincidence. I guess our economists are waiting to achieve prosperity as a "national economic accident"? Could it be that they never wanted nor intended to achieve national economic prosperity at all mankind?

On the other hand our Humanistic axiomatic approach to economics provides such a striking contrast: five simple, clear, concise, and quantitative guiding principles that are indisputable and inalienable. Applying these axioms to our economic system will provide us with national and international economic goals for the next millennia and beyond combined with an ECA organization to achieve them. What a clear, distinct, and proactive difference in economic governance!

Title 12: Equal Access to Available Employment

In Humanism equal access is guaranteed to **all** available employment by **all** qualified workers. This is a powerful democratic idea that no single person or subgroup should be singled out to suffer the draconian punishment and burden of unemployment. Rather all workers and all management should share equally in the burden of underemployment and thus share equally in the available employment. This idea achieves the democratic rights of item 4 of our Economic Bill of Rights.

The Flexible Workweek

In order to adapt to the business cycle, employment needs elasticity. Our current employment system uses a fixed 40 hour workweek combined with elastic hiring and firing to provide the elasticity required. The proposed new system uses an elastic workweek and almost no hiring and firing to provide the same elasticity in a humane way! This new system together with the wage inflation control of Title 11a and Title 23 also provides an ideal basis for achieving the full employment sub mandate of Title 2. Notice that in HERA many problems are solved with the same comprehensive improvements.

For example conventional layoffs will not normally be allowed. Each business will be a little different, but the average recession results in less than a 5% swing in unemployment from the boom max to the recession min. This would put the boom max at 41 hours per week and the recession min at 39 hours per week. If a business needs to reduce employment by 5% from the max to min, then everyone including management will go home 1 hour earlier than the nominal 40 on Friday for a 39 hour week instead of the 41 hours they had been working at the max. So a flexible workweek substitutes for layoffs.

The difference is 2 hours or a 5% swing of the nominal 40 hour week. The human impact of the flexible workweek approach is trivial when compared with the singling out of 5% of workers for a catastrophic layoff termination at a time when replacement jobs will not be available. How draconian and inhumane! In addition the ECA has policy options as well to offset some or all of the pay loss to stimulate the economy using the NF deduction discussed in Title 9 and an example of a full employment control system discussed in Title 23.

This new approach will also make 100% full employment (0% unemployment) easy to achieve and manage! With the current fixed 40 hour week, as full employment is approached, labor elasticity approaches a "brick wall" where elasticity approaches zero because labor growth becomes impossible and wage inflation especially for new hires explodes. However in the new flexible workweek system at full employment labor growth is still possible by expanding the workweek by 5% or more. Furthermore wage inflation will be manageable because of the special compensation vector of 11 items for new hires.

This idea is intended to be applied to all employment across businesses and industries as well. If a company's average underemployment rate exceeds the national or regional average by 5 percentage points they will be allowed to lay off workers on a buy-out basis, volunteer first, and then reverse seniority. Any unemployed worker has a right to be hired by the nearest employer with the lowest underemployment rate that currently has employment that fits the workers qualifications.

Workers could work at more than one company to ease the work balancing effort without putting undue burden on any one employer. As mentioned above part-time rates must be the same as full-time rates. The local labor authority is responsible for facilitating the placement and balancing coordination between employers and the employee since unemployment benefits will no longer require their attention. These transitions must be prearranged and seamless with no temporary interruption of income providing humane employment.

Underemployment

Unemployment has always been a "curse" for humanity. The old paradigm dealt with the issue in a draconian way. It then added costly and inefficient unemployment benefits to attempt to soften the ugly draconian effects. Substituting proportional underemployment tames the curse of unemployment and eliminates the need for unemployment benefits, yielding a substantial economic savings. This includes federal unemployment benefits, state, and employer contributions. The old unemployment benefit system should be maintained as a safety net system to be used in rare cases where benefits would still be needed, such as when a major company files for bankruptcy in a small town.

Furthermore taming unemployment reduces the "job security fear factor" that magnifies the onset of recessions making economic management of recessions easier with less recession depth and less duration. See Title 23 for an example of the improved recession swing range. During the onset of recessions a **few** layoffs scare **all** workers that their job may be next. These scared workers cut back consumption in preparation for what could happen to them. This consumer cutback causes more layoffs as a self-fulfilling prophecy. Clearly fear has no productive place in good economics. Yet fear is used extensively in promoting and motivating the bad ugly ideas of wealth economics.

This is a downward spiral caused by a positive feedback loop with a feedback gain approaching unity (see Engineering 101). Proportional underemployment has no fear factor and thus results in a measured and more proportional consumer response. Indeed most workers will look forward to recessions since they get to start their weekend early on Friday! No more debilitating fear and insecurity! Instead they will be replaced with powerful economic emotions of optimism, confidence, security, and a sense of wellbeing. It feels exactly like a renaissance!

Also business management is easier and less likely to under-react or over-react to recession conditions. Businesses want to avoid layoffs because rehiring and retraining are expensive. So when inventories increase they tend to lag in response. But lag causes the unstable positive feedback mentioned above. With a proportional employment system, layoffs are not needed so businesses can provide proportional and immediate response and keep inventories under control. Likewise the flexible workweek allows expanding labor hours without adding new employees so there is no longer any risk to increasing output.

Furthermore, avoiding layoffs keeps the workforce on the payroll and ready for a proportional recovery. No risky hiring is required and no expensive retraining will be needed. Businesses can respond to the recovery in a measured, riskless, and proportional manner. There is no chance that the employer will miss anticipating the recovery or miss participating in an early recovery. Our current economic situation (2015) is being affected by exactly this problem. Employers are afraid to risk adding new workers and that is holding back our recovery.

Management of Full Employment

Some would think that this proposed approach could place undue burden on employers. But the situation is quite the opposite. Scaling the workforce for a business is a difficult task. You must supply the work hours needed using an integral number of standard definition, 40 hour jobs. For example, with the receptionist, one is not enough but two is too many. So you must balance work to utilize the unused fraction of a receptionist. It is like juggling a large number of balls. Once you get it right, the demand for your business increases or decreases and you have to start balancing over again. Two important structural improvements make the new system much easier to manage.

The streamlining of Title 15 below and axiom 2 will make part-time employment just as attractive as full-time employment with one employer. Part-time pay rates are the same as full-time and remaining benefits are proportional to hours worked. Thus two or more part-time jobs totaling 40 hours have exactly the same benefits and pay scale as any full 40 hour job. Employees do not have to be in full 40 hour jobs.

Employees now have the flexible option to make their full-time employment out of two (or more) part-time jobs that could be less, equal, or more than 40 hours. In addition they can utilize flexible employment to adapt their work schedule to make their own quality of life vs work week choices. Likewise this makes it much easier for an employer or the labor authority to utilize part-time employment. More importantly employers can schedule proportional workloads to match their variable demand exactly by using a proportional workweek and flexible hours. No more juggling is required and scaling is trivial!

Some might also wonder "will employers be required to hire even though they do not have open requisitions"? The answer is "yes" if their weekly utilization statistics qualifies them and there is a qualified employment match. Furthermore in a full employment situation most all employers will have "perpetual" open requisitions anyway because boom or bust there will **always** be a shortage of labor! With 100% full employment most employers will jump at the opportunity to hire new employees that otherwise would not have been available. With 100% full employment this hiring opportunity is a solution not a problem!

Is it any surprise that employers are responsible to ensure equal access to employment? Employers benefit substantially in reduced unemployment taxes, reduced training costs, reduced recruiting costs, better job scaling, and better inventory management; is it too much to ask their support with intercompany employment balancing?

Employers benefit from our economy and "yes" they are expected to contribute to our economy as well. It is a "win-win" solution and usually winners do not complain! Full employment is a new mindset. Once we adapt to this mindset these new ideas on employment will seem natural and much easier to manage than our current system. Most importantly this flexible system is more humane and less draconian. Let's eliminate fear as motivation in our new prosperity paradigm.

Overtime pay will have to be modified slightly as well. No overtime pay for the first hour per week would cover most cases (+/- 2.5% range). No overtime pay for the first 2 hours per week (+/- 5%) would make the system more effective for a wide range of crises situations. Employees could be protected by the Labor Department from abuses such as operating with a higher than normal average workweek. The best way to implement this would be as a differential to the national average workweek. Overtime would be paid if an employer's workweek exceeds one hour more than the national or regional average.

If the average is 41 hours at the boom max then above 42 hours would trigger overtime pay and if the average is 39 hours at the recession min then above 40 hours would trigger overtime pay. The benefits of full employment (0% unemployment) and no layoffs are certainly worth the loss of one or two hours of overtime pay occasionally. Moreover just the stimulus pay benefits discussed immediately below will more than make up for any overtime loss and there are many other benefits.

To complete the recession management aspect of this discussion, as stated in Title 9 above, the ECA will have payroll controls available. So the ECA could reduce the nominal 6.2% NF payroll deduction to 1.2%, monetizing (printing money for) the 5% difference. This would increase take-home pay by 5% to offset the 5% reduction in pay for reduced flexible hours and induce a painless (full pay) recovery! The Medicare deduction could also be used if needed in the same way.

It is quite likely that the improvements in integrated economic policy (9 above), with improvements in managing inflation (11a above), combined with improvements in managing underemployment we could eliminate recessions entirely. There would be periods of higher growth and periods of lower growth but no more recessions (negative growth) and no more draconian unemployment lines and layoffs.

Just imagine that after all these years of draconian unemployment we could have **"employment as if people mattered"** instead! If we had had this system the Great Depression would not have happened. What a breakthrough! This is truly a renaissance in economic thought and action. It is made possible by axiomatic metaeconomics and economic engineering. For examples of economic controls see Title 23 and "The Role of Labor Efficiency" for more discussion on full employment.

Title 13: Business Competition on a Level Playing Field

In Humanism the economic cost of a product or service is measured in labor hours needed to produce the product or service. It is not measured in currency. If businesses wish to reduce cost they must do so by reducing the total labor hours and thereby improve productivity. Reducing the currency cost without improving the labor hours would reduce labor rates. Each business is required to pay prevailing labor rates and they can be fined and forced to reimburse for any statistical tendency to underpay. In this way all businesses compete on a level playing field regarding equal labor productivity rate costs nationally and internationally. Review Title 6 to refresh new wage linearity ideas.

This level playing field idea establishes a new concept for competition between businesses. Businesses will no longer compete by driving down labor rates. Instead they compete by improving performance of their product, improving customer support, improving the reliability of their products, improving product function, and reduce product cost by reducing labor content which will directly improve labor productivity.

In this way competition will change from an excuse for wage and currency exploitation into an opportunity to improve prosperity and our economy. What a significant change! And it is made possible by our axioms. This paradigm shift *from profits to prosperity* makes this improvement in the quality of our lives and improves the international competitive posture of our streamlined businesses substantially!

Title 14: The Prosperity Mandate Guides Business Optimization

A business is a legal entity that organizes workers and capital to produce a product or service usually for a profit. In a humanistic economy the responsibilities and privileges of business are somewhat different than with Capitalism. Capitalism relishes the slogan "what is good for business is good for the economy". The idea of this slogan is that no one, not even economists, need to worry about what is good for the economy because businesses guided by greed, corruption, and privilege inherently do what is best for the economy automatically!

Of course Humanism realizes that this outrageous slogan is false. We also realize that metaeconomics provides a much better optimization. Many examples of exceptions to the slogan will suffice to prove its falsehood, some of which are addressed in specific topics below. See discussion in topic "The Renaissance of Economics as a Science".

Once we abandon this idiotic slogan how do we find out what is good for our economy? So Humanism, primarily using taxation incentive controls, will strongly encourage (not regulate) businesses to achieve those activities that maximize the prosperity of the M80 majority consistent with the prosperity mandate of axiom 1. Prosperity will be measured by a prosperity index = average income of M80 divided by the minimum cost of goods and services basket of Title 7 above.

Thus this prosperity index is a currency-less number that measures the number of "baskets" in the average M80 earner's income. For example a prosperity index of 2.8 would indicate that the average M80 earner makes 2.8 times the minimum cost of living. Since the prosperity index is independent of currency it can be used internationally as well as a comparative index of prosperity between international economies.

The prosperity mandate will become fundamentally important in achieving a much higher quality of life for the vast majority. This represents an important contrast between Capitalism and Humanism. In the profit paradigm of Capitalism general prosperity is diminished to the lowest level possible in order to benefit the privileged capitalists by minimizing wages and salaries and maximizing shareholder profit. While the prosperity paradigm of Humanism mandates, through the axioms, the achievement of prosperity for the vast majority of all mankind by maximizing wages and salaries to the highest levels that can be achieved without causing wage inflation. What a difference!

Thus increasing prosperity becomes the economic goal of each business not necessarily just what businesses perceive as in their self-interest. This idea that the optimum economy cannot be achieved by selfish optimization of the profits or revenues of each business is a fundamental idea that contradicts conventional economic thinking!

Conventional wealth economics says that capital and capitalists are in chronic short supply and that they are the only key to the success of our economy. Therefore we must constantly and mindlessly pamper and mollycoddle the capitalists, their enterprises, and their management in order to achieve "prosperity" (profits for the wealthy) which will "trickle down" to humanity (maybe a little sometimes).

This wealth economics concept is the single most farcical and silly idea in all of Capitalism. This economic alchemy has produced fat, bloated, and perpetually overindulged capitalists, businesses, and management that are inefficient and consequently unprosperous for humanity! Yes they are even less prosperous for the capitalists as well! Because bloat, fat, and inefficiency benefit no one; they just harm some more than others in a lose-lose more fiasco of wealth economics!

Eliminating this conceptual flaw will require an economic renaissance that will shift from a profit paradigm to a prosperity paradigm. This swing from profit maximization to prosperity maximization will result directly in an estimated 88% to 129% or larger improvement in your lifetime income without increasing wage inflation! Moreover your children and grandchildren will receive similar improvements. See topic "What Would Adam Smith Have Thought" for more analysis.

Under the prosperity paradigm, the optimization of each business will be directed towards the metric of maximum prosperity **not** maximum profits. It is easy to apply the prosperity mandate at the macro-economic level but it is more difficult to understand how to apply the idea to the microeconomic level of businesses. To achieve this goal, we must analyze each attribute of a business as a function of the prosperity index and then maximize that function as in axiom 1.

Maximizing the function is a standard engineering technique that involves setting the first derivative to zero and solving the equation for the maximum. You could think of these attributes as being the line items in the Income Statement or Balance Sheet of the company's financial reports. This makes humanity a principal of our economy not its subject because humanity's prosperity becomes the primary measurement and goal of the economy consistent with axiom 1. This general process embodies the concept of systematic economic engineering made possible with axioms that systemize economics.

We can understand this issue theoretically by considering our new economy to be the summation of all of its possible businesses, selected "most efficient" first until 100% labor utilization is reached. Then we could repeat the process by selecting "most profit" or "most revenue". Now we could ask which selection method has the highest GDP. The answer is highest GDP will be obtained by maximizing the prosperity efficiency of each and every business not maximizing their profits or their revenues because there is no shortage of efficient business ideas! A general idea of "prosperity efficiency" would be to maximize the ratio of maximum product value divided by minimum product cost while maintaining full wage rates consistent with the axioms. In other words maximize the product's "bang for the buck at full pay". Other metrics of efficiency are: business efficiency (Direct labor/Total labor hours) or labor productivity (Total revenue/Total labor hours).

One interesting insight of this engineering approach is that "more is not always better". As we look at these attributes we will find that many are functions that have maximums. In other words as we begin to increase the attribute, prosperity will increase until it reaches a maximum but then prosperity will start to decrease as the attribute continues to further increase. So the process of prosperity optimization involves finding the optimum value of the attribute not mindlessly increasing it to the point of inefficiency. Notice that **profits** are of this attribute type. The axioms and their prosperity mandate fundamentally change our conception of good business practices! See specific examples of how to apply this efficiency optimization approach to some specific attributes below in Titles 15, 16, 17, 18, 19, 20, and 21.

This good business practices idea is at the heart of the economic issue especially for profits. So let's look at this contrast between Capitalism and Humanism in detail. Capitalism insists that businesses should maximize shareholder profit which is usually achieved by maximum revenue and income. Yet Humanism says there is an optimum profit.

Capitalism's microeconomic idea is simply not effective at the macroeconomic level or much less the new metaeconomic level. It is an economic idea that has simply outlived its usefulness at best! It is an economic idea that only makes sense in a world that suffers from a chronic never ending shortage of capital and a chronic never ending surplus of labor. See Title 18 below for further discussion and ideas.

On the other hand Humanism insists that each business should always maximize their products and services for the maximum efficiency at full labor valuation. We refer to this as maximizing "bang for the buck at full pay". Notice that these two ideas are not completely different at all. Many of the attributes that increase shareholder profits will also increase efficiency and likewise many of the attributes that increase efficiency will also increase shareholder profits. However only focusing on efficiency will achieve the optimal prosperity goal while only focusing on shareholder profits and other preferences will not!

The similarity of the two paradigms makes the shift easy to implement. Clearly the maximum efficiency idea will always prevail in the long term under competition at the national or global macroeconomic level. Businesses that insist on maximizing short term shareholder profit will be taxed so they actually find their longer term profits are dwindling away because their products and services are less and less competitive until they are finally absorbed by high efficiency competitors. More importantly, reducing corporate profits directly increases efficiency while it directly reduces product cost without reducing product value.

Thus the maximum prosperity paradigm based on maximum efficiency could be so successful that it will soon drive down aggregate corporate profits. High competition in a mature minimal growth, global economy could achieve dangerously low corporate profit levels. Thus we are proposing that average aggregate corporate profits be managed by the ECA at about 5% of GDP as optimal. Review the profit model in Title 6 and see "The Role of Profits in Humanism" for more discussion.

Now that we are starting to solidify the basic intellectual concepts of Humanism, let's look at the human changes involved in the transition from wealth economics to prosperity economics. In other words what emotional, moral, social, and political changes are required to support and achieve these conceptual, intellectual ideas in a practical way?

Will the morality of mankind have to improve substantially to eliminate exploitation, corruption, extortion, and greed? Will we need better religion to accomplish our goals? No! Economic Humanism will work just fine with the human nature, ethics, and religion we already have. There is no reason to wait for evolution to improve the morality of humanity. Axiomatic metaeconomics is all we need to guide us!

For example it is likely that big business, big banking, big wealth, and Wall Street will still feel just as greedy in the future as they feel now. There is no need to reduce their greedy feelings. Instead what we will change is that their opportunity to cause harm with their greedy feelings will be drastically reduced by the better prosperity paradigm.

We will force adherence to axiomatic economic principles enforced by the ECA and mathematically monitored, measured, and confirmed by us and our watchdogs as "the economic law of the land". All we are asking from the greedy is to choose efficient, prosperous greed over inefficient, draconian greed. We and the ECA can measure and analyze the difference so we will **tax them heavily** until they comply! We don't need their agreement, permission, or their cooperation!

All we are asking from our political system is "law and order", the key responsibility of any government. However make no mistake we are demanding an economic, academic, and journalistic change that stops the perpetual glorification of greed as a great human accomplishment.

Instead economics will become its own science free for the first time in history to seek and tell the truth, to paint greed as the selfish, stupid, dangerous, and harmful human fault that it is, always was, and always will be! Then we can begin to treat greed like we do all the other ugly faults of mankind. So the prosperity of good economics can coexist successfully in a greedy world. We don't need to wait for better humans or better religion; we just need better economic governance based on axiomatic principles that represent all of mankind ethically!

Title 15: Streamline Businesses for Efficiency

Our prosperity paradigm for Humanism will flourish based on maximum efficiency guided by axiomatic **first principles** that are mathematical in nature so that good economics can be achieved by proactive economic engineering. The responsibilities of businesses in this new economic system will be streamlined to maximize efficiency not maximize profits or revenues. Health care, pensions, retirement plans, and other such fringe benefits are no longer appropriate responsibilities for a streamlined maximum efficiency business.

The Model

In Humanism holiday pay and vacation pay will be paid by all our businesses according to the same national plan. No business variation is allowed. All of humanity is entitled to equal holiday and vacation pay according to axiom 2. Any inferior "junk" business that cannot afford to pay prevailing labor rates or the standard benefits needs to be revamped or replaced by new businesses that meet this requirement.

It is the ECA's responsibility to ensure that investment funds and tax incentives will be instituted and managed to produce as many new businesses as our economic labor capacity and labor productivity will support according to the full employment sub mandate. Once the last worker is fully employed there is no reason other than ECA failure to have an ongoing shortage of businesses, capital deployment, or jobs.

In the worst-case crisis scenario if capital deployment was too low the ECA would simply print money and inject the emergency capital deployment required directly as discussed in Title 23 until the crises shortage is corrected. In Humanism our only legitimate shortages are of human labor and natural resources! You could think of this basic economic optimization process as a continuous never ending process of identifying the least efficient businesses and revamping or replacing them with more efficient businesses in a continuous unending business revitalization that fully utilizes available labor under all circumstances.

In the Humanistic economic model each consumer has a wide range of desirable products and services that they would be willing to spend their earnings to acquire. Their desires and imagination will always vastly exceed their income except in the case of a very few very wealthy. Likewise the imagination of entrepreneurs will always provide us with many more business ideas, product ideas, and capital than we have labor to support. The average consumer will always adjust their consumption mix to achieve the maximum acquisition of humanly valuable products and services within their fixed income.

Thus they will always opt to acquire the most efficient products and services they desire because this is how they will achieve the most "economic bang for their limited buck". Under this economic model the ECA only needs to provide sufficient revitalization capital for enough new businesses to replace or absorb the inefficient ones and provide capital for depreciation and productivity improvements.

In our mature economy virtually all of this incremental capital requirement could be satisfied from the NF and the retained earnings of those existing companies. In a minimal (productivity only) growth economy no other capital is needed. The consumers will choose the most efficient businesses and products especially if taxes encourage efficiency as discussed in Title 16 below. Any excess wealth or capital must be "mopped up" or "throttled out" of our economy or it will create capital inflation, wealth perpetuation, and wealth stagnation.

Streamlining

Now let us return to the objective of streamlining our businesses under this Humanistic model. Holiday schedule will be determined by Congress in the normal manner. Vacation pay will be earned by equivalent years of full-time economic service of the worker. Vacation pay will **not** be dependent on any particular service at any particular business as it is currently. It will depend on years of economic service.

Part-time work is proportional to full-time. Congress will determine the schedule as part of this legislation. This makes holiday pay and vacation pay a portable standardized benefit protecting the employee. The following schedule would be a likely candidate for vacation pay:

1-5 years	2 Weeks
6-10 years	3 Weeks
11-15 years	4 Weeks
16-20 years	5 Weeks
>20 years	6 Weeks

Theoretically many employees currently receive vacation benefit promises similar to that suggested. But the vast majority of employees never actually receive those promises! Under the new system every employee will receive the same benefit based on years of equivalent full-time economic service that cannot be lost or taken away! These benefits are not dependent on the good faith or the performance of the employer. They are a matter of labor law and economic governance!

For example many employees work for companies that theoretically offer the vacation benefits described above but by the time they qualify a cost reduction, layoff, demotion, restructuring, bankruptcy, merger, acquisition, or other reason forces the employee to change jobs or she loses her benefit. Indeed most businesses do not last long enough to fulfill their future promises. Consequently we have lots of promises but very little vacation! So nationwide only a few employees with 20 years of experience actually get the 20 year benefit. Under the new proactive system **everyone** with 20 years of experience will get the 20 year benefit! What a change; your vacation is an earned benefit. It belongs to you and it goes with you wherever you go. It's yours!

In addition there will be standardized rules for leave of absence, maternity, and other employee benefits and services as determined by our new Labor Department. This approach will minimize the burdens placed on businesses and standardize the responsibilities and benefits. It will also provide security to the employees that their benefits are not dependent on the employer's performance or good faith and are easily portable from employer to employer, even multiple employers for part-time workers. The NF will manage the accrual funds for vacation pay.

Part-time work will be much more attractive since benefits will be proportional to hours worked as a percentage of the standard 40 hour week. One of the most useful benefits that must be supported by all employers is automatic payroll deductions and transfers to other accounts such as their vacation accrual account or their health care account so that the employer can no longer be involved in the account.

Pension and retirement plans will be covered by the NF as discussed in Title 9 or in 401K below. Health care is somewhat more difficult to streamline because of the unknown flux of the currently enacted health care mandate. Before we can propose a specific solution we must wait for the new legislation to "shake down" and stabilize. Nevertheless, we believe the best exit strategy for business involvement in health care is for businesses that now offer healthcare benefits to "buy out" their employees with a one-time salary increase that will compensate.

We believe that the buyout should be priced at about 120% of the employer's current average cost of coverage. Over time we believe the employer's gain will substantially exceed 100% and we want the employer to share some of the future benefit to make the initial transition more attractive. No more underfunded pension plans! No more changes in health coverage when you change employers! Retirement and health care you control and you own; it is yours and it's paid for with your wage increases and your payroll deductions!

The employee's current health care contribution combined with the salary increase would then be available to purchase private insurance under control of the employee and as required by the existing health care mandate. The one-time salary increase is by nature an ongoing increase because it would automatically carry forward in later years. However over time incomes would re-establish a new equilibrium that would be attractive for streamlining businesses and their efficiency.

Using taxation and competition we would ensure that the windfall profits would be passed back in terms of higher efficiency and reduced product costs. Also Title 11a above will be adjusted to carry forward the salary increases in the aggregate. We are concerned that the buying power of an individual may be eroded compared with the buying power of the corporation. So if the health care mandate does not deliver competitive coverage, then additional changes will be needed to accomplish every citizen's right to affordable health care insurance.

401 K contributions will be treated in a similar manner. Companies will buy out their company contribution portion of the plan using the same 120% rule discussed above for health care. The employees will take the salary increase and their employee contribution and they will have a choice to contribute those amounts to an IRA, Roth ... or increase their NF deduction or a combination. Cash payments would not be allowed to ensure that buyout funds are fully reinvested.

Defined benefit pension plans will require a unique resolution. First, those already retired will continue to receive benefits as defined by the plan. The employer will be responsible for making contributions to the plan's fund to ensure these obligations are satisfied. For all other employees their defined benefit will be prorated down based on the number of years they have been on the plan and the number of years left until retirement. So as time passes the employer's defined benefit obligation will be gradually reduced until it is eliminated totally.

The difference between the employer's annual contribution under the old plan and their contribution under the new prorated plan will be paid out as a salary increase to the existing employees using the 120% rule above. The employee will have a choice to contribute those amounts to an IRA, Roth … or increase their NF deductions or a combination. In this way their defined benefit will decrease but the defined contribution will increase more to compensate. Cash payments would not be allowed to ensure that buyout funds are fully reinvested.

Some will ask: why are we reducing the responsibilities and burdens placed on businesses? The answer is that businesses are the engines of our prosperity and burdening them will only burden our prosperity. Only with healthy optimized businesses will we be able to achieve the prosperity we all want. We want businesses that are "lean, clean, productive machines" that are not fat, bloated, and inefficient. Instead of mollycoddling businesses we intend to streamline them efficiently.

We will go out of our way to produce a level, fair playing field for competition as discussed in Title 6 above for both national and international trade. But without competitive and productive businesses we will not realize the benefits nor achieve the prosperity we want and deserve. This is a perfect example of "win-win" prosperity economics!

There is another reason as well. Efficiency and effectiveness are always best when those with the self-interest have the self-control. Why should my employer choose my health plan for me? Give me prosperous wages and I will choose my own! Why should an employer increase the price of his product so that he can contribute a portion to my retirement? Give me prosperous wages and I will do it myself! If the purchasing power and ease of group purchasing is an issue then the government should provide the group organization not businesses.

For example for health care plans, government could architect standardized plan options (A, B, C, …) similar to existing Medicare Supplemental Insurance. Then each employee could just choose from one of 5 or 10 different standardized plans or their own custom plan. This would give each employee easy choices and provide far more purchasing power than even the largest company could hope to offer. Better yet there would be efficiency and no cost to taxpayers at all!

Businesses should concentrate on "taking care of business" not on healthcare, retirement, and other fringe distractions that reduce their competitiveness and increase the price of their products or services. Efficiency dictates that businesses must specialize and concentrate on their own line of business not health care and other fringe benefits.

Many falsely believe that businesses are "paying" for these benefits out of their "pockets" so to speak. But this is, and always was false! Businesses do not have "pockets" for such purposes. There is no way for a business to charge back costs to its owners or shareholders. All a business can do is add the cost of these benefits to the cost of their products or services making them less competitive. They simply add the cost on to the product or service for the consumer to pay for these benefits out of their "pocket". So they just pass the cost on as a useless and inefficient "middle man" and they do not actually "pay" for any of these costs! Worse yet all workers do not receive the same benefits.

Instead you, the worker/consumer, end up paying 100% of the cost of these benefits anyway! You pay part of the cost as the employee and the rest of the cost as the consumer! So businesses might as well add the cost of prosperous wages to their products and let the employees decide what the benefit should be for themselves. In this way the cost becomes a labor hour cost and is protected by the equal pay for equal work rule. The next Title has a discussion and an analysis of how the economic benefits are passed back to the employees over time.

Title 16: Streamline Business Taxation for Maximum Prosperity

Business taxation will be streamlined as well. Two general concepts will be employed to guide the ECA in managing taxes on businesses.

- 50% of all businesses should pay no federal tax whatsoever. Tax thresholds will be adjusted to achieve this goal. The intention of this restriction is to protect against excessive business taxation. This goal might not be achieved initially because it will take time for businesses to adjust. But this goal will be achieved within the first 5 years. Notice that the 50% of businesses that pay no taxes will likely be very efficient and very internationally competitive!

- Taxes should be constructed and applied in a manner that supports and encourages our central maximum prosperity mandate, our four sub mandates, and our ongoing national economic goals.

The current Social Security 6.2% employer matching tax will be eliminated provided the windfall inheritance tax revenue and the wealth tax revenue are sufficient to finance the old Social Security benefit liability, the Medicare retirement liability, and the sovereign debt reductions. If not then the matching amount will be reduced until it is totally eliminated as soon as possible. In the worst-case scenario this tax would automatically end gradually over a 45 year schedule and we should be able to eliminate it much sooner than the worst-case!

So beginning immediately the NF retirement fund will be financed using **only** the 6.2% employee deduction currently in force. Thus the 6.2% matching tax on business and about 75% of the Medicare deduction will be available to offset the costs for paying down the old Social Security liability, the Medicare retirement liability, and the sovereign debt liability. It will be used only if the inheritance tax of Title 5 and the wealth tax of Title 23 are insufficient in the early years.

This change is consistent with the "twice the benefit for half the cost" goal of Title 2 and Title 9 above. In addition the current 15% to 35% corporate income tax will be eliminated in favor of the prosperity tax suggestions listed below. This will eliminate the current need for businesses to keep profits offshore returning them to be reinvested here in the USA. Also the unemployment tax will be substantially reduced as discussed in Title 12 because of 100% full employment.

In general it is intended that the total business tax revenue will be the same as current revenues less the 6.2% matching Social Security tax reduction, 75% of the Medicare deduction, and the unemployment tax reduction. The nature of each prosperity tax below is the same. Each tax has a variable threshold and below the threshold there is no tax.

Above the threshold the tax rate will be substantial and it will increase substantially more as it increases above the threshold. This will strongly encourage management to comply with our prosperity efficiency goals. So the best managed companies will strive to stay below those thresholds so they pay little or no tax. Each year the ECA will adjust the thresholds to achieve the "50% pay no tax rule" and they will adjust the rate structure above the threshold to achieve tax revenue goals. The taxes below are likely candidates for prosperity tax controls and all will be used if appropriate and others added as needed:

- Tax on excessive profits above a specified threshold (say 5%)
- Tax on excessive cash or securities above a specified threshold
- Tax on Debt/Equity ratio below a specified threshold
- Tax on excessive advertising, marketing, and sales costs
- Tax on excessive legal costs above a specified threshold
- Tax on poor labor productivity below a specified threshold: Productivity = Total cost/total labor hours.
- Tax on poor business efficiency below a specified threshold: Efficiency = % Direct labor / Total labor or Direct labor cost/total
- Tax on any reduction of product value/cost at full pay valuation
- Tax on poor economic quality of the product or service below a specified threshold

The ECA will develop a "Delphi ranking system" using a broad internet based consumer panel under Congressional committee review to determine the economic quality of a product or service using a 1:10 scale. Health care and education would be examples of high economic quality products or services that benefit mankind (rank 10). Payday lenders, gambling, and junk food are examples of products or services that are of dubious value to mankind (rank 1). Economic quality taxes will be applied as a percentage of revenue on products ranked below 6.

Now let us turn our attention to how these streamlined changes will benefit the vast majority. Many will not realize that eliminating the 6.2% matching cost and the elimination of unemployment benefit costs (.8%) will directly benefit the worker/consumer far more than the business itself. In fact all of the streamlining improvements discussed in Title 15 and 16 will result in the same kind of benefit returns for worker/consumers. Let us just analyze the benefits of the matching tax and unemployment benefits as examples to understand the full benefit.

When these costs are eliminated from the business very quickly competition will force all companies to reduce the price of their products and services. After a short period competition would return profit levels back to their pre-change equilibrium levels. There is no economic reason that the equilibrium will reach a new equilibrium; it will just return to its previous equilibrium level. Moreover aggregate corporate profits will be managed by the ECA at 5% of GDP as discussed in "The Role of Profits in Humanism". So any aggregate macroeconomic increase in corporate profits will be compensated at the national level further ensuring profit normalization and reduction.

Initially the business profits would increase but within a year or two everything will be about 7% less expensive across the board. Workers' salaries would be the same but all products and services would be less expensive so everyone would have 7% (6.2% + .8%) more they could buy! It would be similar to everyone getting a 7% raise. But that is not all. Since salaries are the same there is no reason for consumers to save more or spend less so the 7% increase in buying power would increase business volume by about 7% and thus business employment would increase by about 7% to produce the added product volume needed.

In addition each business would have a 7% improvement in international competitive pricing that would further increase our international competition and further employment. The added employees would be available from improvements in achieving full employment, improvements in employee participation rate of Title 2, and improvements in general productivity. This is an example of win-win prosperity economics in action. Our shift from profit optimization of Capitalism to the prosperity optimization of Humanism is a profound change in economic thinking. Our renaissance has begun!

Title 17: Eliminate Dividends and Stock Buybacks

The prosperity mandate fundamentally changes our conception of good business practices. Dividends, the practice of paying cash to shareholders when profits are excessive, will not be allowed as it would conflict with an excessive profits tax of Title 16 above and the maximum prosperity mandate. Stock buybacks will not be allowed for the same reasons. Prosperity economics does not pamper shareholders.

Both of these business practices represent profit "leaks" that divert retained earnings away from efficient reinvestment in the business! If businesses cannot reinvest their profits in product or service increases, expansions, mergers, acquisitions, or corporate venture capital then they need to reduce the cost of their existing products and services. This will improve their business efficiency, competitiveness, and benefit the greater prosperity of our economy the goal of axiom 1.

This is a good example of the conflict between the greater good of humanity referred to in item 6 of the Economic Bill of Rights and the self-interest of the business as seen by greedy management and their shareholders. Humanism dictates that the majority of society provided the labor, the natural resources, the capital, the infrastructure, and the product demand that made the business possible and the majority deserve their "prosperity dividend" too as principals of our economy.

For dividends there is already a business model for this idea and it is called the "growth model". Many businesses already use this growth model successfully. So requiring all businesses to use this growth model will not create a major burden but it will result in significant growth! Shareholders can still realize their profits by capital gains, selling their stock to realize the profit at a lower capital gains tax rate. See topic "The Role of Profits in Humanism" for more discussion.

Title 18: Tax Excessive Sales, Marketing, and Advertising

The prosperity mandate fundamentally changes our conception of good business practices. Advertising, marketing, and sales costs are areas of particular concern. These are examples of costs that the business community is convinced are necessary or desirable to improve their businesses or more likely to satisfy their shareholders and make their bonuses. Much of these costs are defensive in that they are motivated by a desire to match their competitors. So these costs become a self-fulfilling prophecy. To make matters worse, these costs add **no** value whatsoever to the product or service reducing prosperity.

So the efficiency of the business and the cost of the products or services suffer. Seldom do the incremental sales increases produce some offsetting efficiency to compensate for this loss. Even in rare cases where there are offsetting "economies of scale", these same economies could have been achieved more efficiently by product expansions, mergers, or acquisitions without these recurring costs. So these costs help us contrast corporate efficiency vs corporate profits.

To make matters worse pesky sales personnel and intrusive advertising are not welcome advancements to the quality of life or the common good of the vast majority of humanity. In short, we consumers are forced to pay for what offends us and then does not benefit us. What a draconian combination, harm and no benefit! Consequently, sales costs in excess of mere customer support and advertising and marketing outside the storefront or business website will be taxed. Each business has an economic mandate to find its most efficient size and then scale itself to fit that size most efficiently consistent with our axioms.

Consequently revenues or profits of some businesses may actually **drop** in order to improve economic efficiency! Remember that increasing profit **directly** increases product cost without **any** increase in product value. Furthermore efficiency will produce a larger number of new businesses using the same labor shortage providing a greater variety of valuable products and services to achieve the same GDP goal. So we will achieve the same GDP goal with a more efficient mix of goods and services that better maximizes our prosperity. Thus our prosperity paradigm vastly exceeds the old profit paradigm. For details review the Title 15 discussion about the Humanistic economic model.

These new ideas represent a new renaissance in economic thinking. Mindlessly increasing revenues or profits at all cost only produces economic inefficiency and reduced prosperity. It should be obvious that our economy benefits more from two business of size "X" that are efficient than one business which expands to size "2X" inefficiently. In all cases just reducing these undesirable costs will directly reduce the cost of the product or service and directly improve our prosperity.

Consumers will be able to buy more products and services of greater variety with the same income. In addition the savings from elimination of these undesirable costs could be reinvested in further reducing product or service cost so that the consumers could buy even more with the same income further compounding their prosperity gains!

The ECA has a full employment sub mandate that guarantees that there will be sufficient economic investment to produce all the businesses, products, services, capital, or jobs needed for 100% full employment. There is no economic benefit for expanding revenues or profits of any business beyond the point of maximum economic efficiency. In this steady-state Humanistic model for prosperity economics, there will be **no** shortage of businesses, products, services, capital, or jobs **only** a shortage of human labor and natural resources.

So maximum prosperity will be achieved by focusing the limited labor resources and the limited natural resources on the most economically efficient products and services! Obviously this will produce the greatest "economic bang" for our "GDP buck". In contrast notice how the wealth economics of Capitalism makes very different assumptions about our future economy and its natural shortages.

Namely that labor and natural resources are abundant and that profits, revenues, businesses, products, services, capital, and jobs are in short supply. The contrast between the profit paradigm and the prosperity paradigm is clear and concise. For more discussion see Title 23 and the discussions in Titles 2b, 12, and "The Role of Labor Efficiency".

Let us change our perspective for this same discussion from our current economic situation to our future situation. Let us look forward just one working generation of about 45 years (age 20 to 65). The profit paradigm of Capitalism is based on assumptions that might have been true in 1850 but these assumptions are glaringly incorrect and harmful for the next working generation and beyond indefinitely.

Our planet is quickly reaching its limits and we are already well beyond sustainable limits in many cases most importantly population (labor), resource consumption, and pollution. Furthermore there is no worldwide or national plan to manage population, resource consumption, or pollution even on the distant horizon leaving our planet in **grave danger**! What is wrong? Our concept of economic governance is fundamentally and intellectually flawed. Economics is usually considered to be: a social (non) science concerned with production and consumption of goods and services using **scarce resources**. Yet wealth economics is so flawed that it does not even know which economic resources are scarce and which are not!

Population represents the single largest load on our ecosystem and our economic system. For example population growth directly increases resource consumption and pollution. We must make a transition from a paradigm of unlimited labor, unlimited natural resources, and high growth into a paradigm of limited labor, limited natural resources, and "minimal growth". "Minimal growth" will be defined as productivity growth only with zero population growth. Clearly minimal growth is sustainable indefinitely once we achieve a sustainable population.

We are in the midst of an economic sea change from high growth to low growth and eventually minimal growth. Although growth will be limited prosperity through productivity will not be limited! So AI, robotics, and automation will become a godsend. Furthermore the full employment sub mandate insures that labor will **always** be in short supply boom or bust. Indeed labor in the developed nations has already been in short supply ever since the economic recovery from WWII.

Since this time employment in the developed nations has been asymptotic to full employment already even without any consideration of planetary limitations. Full employment was deliberately avoided by artificial rationing employment using interest rates at about 5% unemployment as the Central Bank's definition of "full employment". This deliberate rationing of employment was the only reason we avoided achieving full employment by about 1970 or sooner! With the direct wage inflation control of Title 11a we could have achieved full employment and lower interest rates long ago! It's time to understand for the first time in history that a successful economic system must inherently produce, manage, and sustain a never ending shortage of labor and natural resources as its normal scarcity equilibrium state!

Furthermore if our economic ideas depend on high growth to be successful we will certainly **not** be successful! Our old Social Security Retirement System is a stark example of this reality because it depends on high growth to maintain its benefits. New workers pay for old workers. So if there are fewer new workers; it is doomed to fail! Likewise in the profit paradigm our sovereign debt is only feasible if we increase growth beyond sustainable limits otherwise it will fail.

On the other hand we propose a new prosperity paradigm with ideas to drastically improve minimal growth retirement benefits, reduce sovereign debt, and increase prosperity through productivity and efficiency. When this paradigm is combined with sustainable natural resources including antipolution we would be quite successful and prosperous in a minimal growth, labor, and resource limited situation.

So our prosperity paradigm and its axiomatic Humanism are our **only** hope for the future anyway! Our steady-state future equilibrium is clear and obvious. Humanism matches ideas with our unavoidable future while Capitalism matches ideas with our distant and dark past. Let's consider the likelihood of two different risk scenarios: 1) the risk we will make this transition too quickly, and 2) the risk we will make this transition too late. Which do you think is the most likely risk we face? Too much prosperity economics too soon or too little too late!

Why not get a head start on achieving our economic "moon" right now rather than being forced into it anyway in the near future in a desperate catch-up effort to survive. We want prosperity for the vast majority of mankind not just desperate survival. Do **not** underestimate the threat!

Wealth economics through big business, big banking, Wall Street and perpetual wealth depend heavily on excessive growth to produce high profits that **cannot** be sustained. Yes they are blind to their blindness because of their greed. So they will force this excessive growth on us using wealth power even though it is unsustainable and catastrophic. Only the axiomatic prosperity of metaeconomics can guide us away from this greedy insanity and its inevitable catastrophic conclusion!

The economic fate of the world that we leave our children and grandchildren is under grave threat right **now** and nothing less than an economic renaissance will be needed to **save their lives**. Greed and corruption can be tamed before they result in the inevitable catastrophic conclusion. But we must realize the intellectual truth that the true idea of Capitalism is **prosperity** not profits or wealth!

Title 19: Eliminate the Burden of Consumer Credit

The prosperity mandate fundamentally changes our conception of good business practices. Consumer credit is another concern. To help us understand this issue let us review some basic fundamental economic ideas. At the macroeconomic level, the main issues facing any economy are supply and demand. Our macro-demand is relatively easy especially in a managed economy such as that we are proposing.

In many ways demand is as easy as printing money, not too little and not too much. Supply on the other hand is much more difficult. Trying to provide the right capital to the right companies to provide the right products and services at the right price is difficult. But it is only the beginning of the difficulties. Motivating businesses to make and keep such commitments is the proverbial "wet noodle". So it can be said that macroeconomics is all about increasing supply-supply-supply.

Interestingly the issues facing the microeconomic business level of the economy are opposite to the macro level. Namely that supply is relatively easy but demand is much more difficult. For example, most manufacturing companies could manufacture almost any product of a general class or type. But what product will consumers buy and at what price? So business is all about finding demand-demand-demand.

Consumer credit is an idea to temporarily boost demand. Regrettably consumer credit is a "one-shot" idea that can only work once when it is first enacted and only for a short term benefit that is long past. But the costs of consumer credit are recurring because of interest costs. What a bad economic combination: a one-time benefit with a never ending cost! That's an idea we can live without. So in the long run consumer credit reduces demand by the amount of consumer interest costs. To make matters worse, human management of consumer credit is problematic for most consumers and this accelerates its excessive depressing effects on the demand that it was intended to increase!

Since demand is the easiest side of macroeconomics and since the ECA has many direct and highly effective tools (Title 23) for increasing or decreasing demand, we should avoid such a highly ineffective tool as consumer credit. Needless to say, the advantages and convenience of "plastic" or electronic transactions can still be maintained without any consumer credit using debit cards, non-credit cards, or newer transfer pay systems. Furthermore the so called "big ticket" items such as cars and homes will continue with bank loans. Only our high interest, unsecured revolving credit will be affected.

The consumer's savings in interest costs will then buy more products and services with the same income providing more prosperity for both consumer and worker! It's just like the 7% example in Title 16 above. Revolving consumer credit is a "cash cow" for banks but it is an anchor dragging on our economy. It is time to get this problem fixed and to stop pampering and mollycoddling the banks as if they were the "little darlings" of our economy instead of as our economic servants!

Unfortunately the confusion about the "benefits' of consumer credit is partially supported by an economic measurement anomaly exploited by economists at the pleasure of the banks. In this anomaly interest paid to the banks is measured as a "product or service" supplied by the banks to benefit the consumer who paid the interest! In other words the model for this economic transaction is: that the consumer demanded recurring interest costs, and that the consumer satisfies his need for these costs by paying the bank for the "service of collecting interest" and therefore increase GDP. What a distorted idea to benefit banks!

However in fact this interest cost is an economic **loss** that could have been used to purchase more real goods and services over our lifetimes instead, thus increasing prosperity! Interest paid is just an economic loss cost added to the product with **no** corresponding tangible increase in the economic value of the product. To see this more clearly, imagine trying to recover this "value" by reselling the product; it's impossible because the imaginary value is not there! There is no difference in resale value between a product originally purchased with credit and a product originally purchased with cash. Their resale value is the same!

Consumer credit also makes managing the stability of our economy more difficult for the ECA. For example, when the economy heats up the ECA would like to reduce consumer demand by reducing disposable income. But consumer credit allows demand to continue to grow instead. Likewise when the economy cools down the ECA would like to increase demand by increasing disposable income. But consumer credit allows increased disposable income to be diverted to debt repayment instead of buying goods and services. This reduces the control and delays the effect (lag) both of which create instability in the control system as discussed in more detail in Title 23 below.

The exact method to deal with the consumer credit problem most effectively will require much debate because the "little darlings" are so spoiled. To get the debate started we will propose a two dimensional approach phased in gradually over a ten year period to end this issue.

First the ECA will reduce the interest rate cap on revolving credit gradually over ten years. They will monitor new credit and continue reducing the cap until we accomplish reducing newly issued credit by 95% over the ten year period. Reducing the cap will make the revolving consumer credit business less and less attractive for creditors in preparation for eliminating it entirely as a national economic goal. Reducing the cap will also reduce the negative impact of consumer credit since the recurring interest cost will fall. The falling interest cost will help reduce the principal as well directly increasing prosperity.

Secondly, the ECA will increase the minimum monthly payment gradually over the ten year period. They will monitor the revolving credit principal to make sure it also reduces by at least 95% over the ten year period. The interest rate cap and the minimum monthly payment are already regulated so this legislation is just an updated improvement. After the ten year period the ECA can recommend to Congress how to finally conclude this national economic goal.

Title 20: Tax Excessive Legal Costs

The prosperity mandate fundamentally changes our conception of good business practices. Excessive legal costs are an issue as well because they reduce efficiency. Legal costs provide no value or benefit to the business's product or service; yet they add cost. Every effort should be made by the ECA to simplify the legal complexity of operating a business. Our prosperity mandate dictates that this inefficiency be reduced. The ECA should institute, through its

Economic Management department, a task force specifically to reduce legal costs and propose legislation to Congress to achieve that goal. However, many businesses find it more profitable to operate on the fringes of illegality or operate with offensive, exploitive, or abrasive policies that generate the need for excessive legal costs that add no value. Consequently their excessive legal costs will be taxed heavily.

Title 21: Restrict Management Pay at a 40:1 Ratio

The prosperity mandate fundamentally changes our conception of good business practices. Let's look at the labor market which has some relevant peculiarities. In the labor market equilibrium is achieved by general forces affecting the broad market and local forces. Since the CEO pay divided by worker pay is a ratio within the general market, the general forces do not affect the ratio because they affect both items of the ratio equally. On the other hand with the local forces in this hierarchy of jobs, each job class is affected by jobs above it and jobs below it. Jobs above it push down on the current class while jobs below push up on current class creating a local equilibrium condition.

However there are two exceptions at the extreme ends of the scale. Jobs at the extreme bottom have no jobs below to push up. So equilibrium cannot be achieved and we have the proverbial "downward spiral". Likewise jobs at the extreme top have no jobs pushing down from above so we have no equilibrium and an "upward spiral" instead. The downward spiral of the floor of the market is corrected by the minimum wage. But we need a corresponding correction for the upward spiral by correcting the ceiling with a CEO ratio pay cap that will eliminate management wage inflation the same way we eliminated worker wage inflation as discussed in Title 11a.

Pay restrictions on top management are required to accomplish axiom 2 the equal pay for equal productivity rule and the maximum prosperity mandate of axiom 1. Clearly the economic productivity of management is directly related to the productivity of the business and its workers **not profits**. This has always grown out of control because there is no "balance of power" at the extreme high end of the pay scale to create equilibrium. So overpaying management reduces business efficiency and that is unfair for its workers and bad for our economy.

As top management wage inflation is decreased the efficiency of the business will clearly increase as will our macro economy. However if top management pay is reduced too much corporate performance will suffer. Therefore in between these two extremes there is an optimum choice for top management pay that will achieve maximum prosperity.

The ECA will achieve this optimum pay using improved measurement and monitoring techniques. Herein we are estimating this optimal aggregate average was historically at a 40:1 ratio or less. Remember this is a ratio between CEO pay and worker pay. There is no reason this ratio should increase as our economy grows in time because as worker pay increases so does CEO pay keeping the ratio the same.

There is no reason the 40 to 1 ratio would not be appropriate for the next 1,000 years or more! So if CEOs want a pay increase all they need to do is manage the company so productivity and efficiency increase worker pay! Then worker pay and CEO pay will increase **together**. Using the CEO to worker pay ratio as an indicator (Huff-Post Live, 2013), we have the following unequal and unfair history:

1950, 20:1

1980, 42:1

2000, 120:1

2013, 204:1

2016, 347:1*

Does this obscenity look like equilibrium to you? Do you think management's productivity justifies a 1735% gain **over** labor? Do you think this will magically fix itself if we just wait leaving it alone as we have been doing? Remember the discussion about how mollycoddling businesses just produces bloat, fat, and over indulgent excesses that diminish economic efficiency and general prosperity? Here is a good example. This historical data paints the same ugly picture reinforcing the same ugly idea. We have let wealth power ravish our economy. Clearly this is out of control and our economists are too corrupted by wealth power to fix it! So we must intervene and fix this "ugly" in a systematic way without permission or cooperation from wealth power!

Management pay is a classic system consisting of a single force opposed only by resistance that has no equilibrium. All we have to do is stop pampering CEOs and their management entourages as if they were the "spoiled brats" of our economy. We know that our economy operated just fine in 1950 (20:1) and 1980 (42:1). There was no management shortage then or at any other time in history much as there was never a shortage of kings or queens during the feudal era!

Axiom 2 dictates management pay based on productivity the same as worker pay. Consequently a gradual goal of 40:1 would work well for starters and we could optimize from there. This goal would correspond approximately to that of 1975 one of our most prosperous periods. It will be easy to manage as wage inflation compensation just like other employees as discussed in the macro wage correction system of Title 11a. These inflation controls have two aspects: salaries and bonuses.

> a) Wage inflation of top management will be included in the general national monthly inflation management discussed under 11a by providing an 11th pay category. Salaries of the top tiers of management will simply be reduced by a fixed percentage of 2.7% each month until the national average CEO pay ratio reaches the goal of 40:1 and other management pay is reduced proportionally (same %). After the CEO cap is reached the ECA will continue measurements each month combined with pay deviations up or down that will continue to track the cap goal of 40:1 indefinitely.

> Notice that the relative market mechanism is still effective and only the aggregate ratio is managed so any individual CEO or company can achieve any ratio that they are capable of achieving and all relative pay is determined by the market mechanism the same as now; there is no market change! This macro inflation correction process will take approximately 60 months or 5 years to reach equilibrium because this market is so corrupted. Imagine that: an axiomatic fair pay system **"as if people mattered"**. For

more explanation review market hybridization ideas and details in Title 11a and "The Role of "free" Markets in Humanism".

b) Bonuses will be limited by regulation so that the maximum payout possible does not exceed the salary that is appropriate in a) above. In this way maximum bonuses will track with market salaries. Bonuses will be restricted as to what can be incentivized. Here are some likely bonus incentives for business applications.

- Bonuses can be incentivized based on profitability improvements not to exceed the tax threshold maximum, provided business efficiency and labor productivity do not decrease in the current year or the next year after the profitability improvement.
- Bonuses can be incentivized based on revenue, ROA, ROE, and other similar metrics provided profitability is less than the tax threshold and business efficiency and labor productivity do not decrease in the current year or next year after improvement.
- Bonuses can be incentivized based on improving business efficiency (Direct labor/Total labor) or labor productivity (Total revenue/Total labor). These two economic metrics, business efficiency and labor productivity, are the most beneficial for the prosperity mandate. Notice that once the profit tax threshold (5%) has been reached, these two attributes are the only attributes that can be incentivized.

Another control approach would be an excessive pay tax on the businesses themselves that progressively discourages excessive pay in excess of the 40:1 ratio and bonuses other than those specified above. Both methods could be combined as well. Also special provisions will be needed to ensure that corporations and top management do not thwart the intentions of the management inflation, pay ratio cap.

For bonus purposes it is best to measure these attributes as year to year differentials using the same measure basis for both years. In this way the differentials can be quite accurate even though the measure basis could have some anomalies. Year to year product price increases should be compensated as should be year to year labor rate changes.

As Title 14 explains, the prosperity mandate fundamentally changes our conception of good business practices. In Titles 15-21 we considered specific business practices and how they could be evaluated as good business practices under Humanism's prosperity mandate. Notice how the axiomatic prosperity mandate combined with a proactive ECA can continuously identify new national economic goals and then achieve them as an ongoing, never ending prosperity engineering process to attain our quest for our economic "moon".

For the first time in economic history the economics profession has an economic engineering role to play in setting and achieving our national economic goals in a systematic, scientific, and ongoing fashion. For the first time in history we will have a department of government that can proactively propose new national economic goals to Congress and then execute those goals while we, humanity, democratically control this metaeconomic process with our axioms and Constitutional rights!

Let us try to evaluate the impact of these changes on our prosperity. I will estimate the following distribution of prosperity improvements:

Tax	%
Matching Social Security Tax	6.2%
Unemployment Tax	0.8%
Holiday & Vacation pay	1.2%
Consumer Credit cost	3.0%
Sales, Marketing & Advertising	6.0%
Excessive Legal costs	0.8%
Dividends & Stock Buybacks	2.0%
Excessive Management Pay	3.0%
Total	23. %

The accuracy of my estimate is not so important because I only want you to get a general idea of the quantitative measure of the benefit to you is about 20% or more. We already analyzed how these improvements affect your prosperity in the discussion about the 7% tax reduction. The analysis of the total 23% follows a similar general rationale. The point here is clear; the optimization of prosperity instead of profits matters tremendously to humanity. Having an ECA that is guided by axiomatic metaeconomic principles allows us to focus on the prosperity mandate using proactive economic engineering that will make a profound difference in our prosperity initially and for many generations to come. We deserve the best and we are long overdue!

Title 22: Scientific Tax Methodologies

In order for the ECA to achieve our national economic goals, the ECA will have to have some delegated management control of taxation. Taxes are one of the key controls of our economic control system. As mentioned above Congress will be provided from the ECA bank a national budget of 14% of GDP to meet the national budget mandate.

The ECA, an independent, apolitical, non-partisan department of government, will manage taxation with Congressional oversight based on guiding principles such as the prosperity mandate and other goals and restrictions discussed above. Regarding tax responsibilities there are four separate key questions to consider. The first question, "How we spend our national budget" is very much a political question. Congress and the President are capable and until recently they had a long and successful track record for resolving this political issue.

However, they also have a very poor track record of not being capable of deciding the second question, "how much total they should spend". The only decision they can agree to is MORE! That is because the two questions, "how much to spend" and "how to spend it" are not compatible for the same authority to decide because one is a conflict of interest to the other. This conflict is the cause for our big deficits.

This is an intellectual systemic flaw in our system and it is now time that we must fix the flaw! The budget process only works effectively if those deciding the amount of each budget line item have the enforced discipline of a fixed total to spend. If the total budget is also a variable in their control then the inherent budget discipline is lost completely!

This loss of discipline is the primary cause of our deficits, sovereign debt, unfunded liabilities, and other budget related problems. Since Congress and the President must decide "how to spend the budget", then they must delegate authority to decide "how much to spend". They tried to solve this problem and hold on to the authority to do both with the "debt limit" idea but it failed completely! So it is time to answer the question of "how much to spend" by a voluntary political restraint herein delegating control to an agreed to budget formula mandate of 14% of GDP, directly enforced by our new ECA bank.

Likewise decisions on the third and fourth questions "how much to tax" and "what to tax" are separate questions and both are **economic** questions – NOT just political questions! If you politically wish to tax less, simply reduce expenditures using the political authority discussed above! So the issue about deficit financing becomes a delegated ECA economic management issue not just a political issue to haggle about!

The question of "how much to tax" is a long term strategic economic question and we know the answer is very close to "how much we spend" from the above discussion to minimize deficits. In actual practice it would be economically beneficial from time to time to tax a little more or tax a little less depending on the state of the economy. So you can see that the question of "how much to tax" is indeed an ECA economic management question **not** just a political haggling question!

Similarly the question "what to tax" is a short term tactical economic management question. Our second biggest tax flaw has been treating the question of "what to tax" as just a political question. As a political question the "answer" is pointless. You want to tax him and he wants to tax you. So your political parties haggle about it over and over incessantly, generation after generation and whatever the "answer" they haggle up this time, it is always wrong for our prosperity. Imagine that! Good haggling is not the path to economic prosperity. To achieve maximum prosperity for all, both questions must be decided by our scientific, independent, economic authority that has **no** political motive and **no** vested interest in the outcome except maximum prosperity, sub mandates, and national economic goals approved by Congress.

As with any problem, good results depend on having a sound and solid guiding principle. Our principle will be called "smart taxes". The idea is that politically anything could be taxed to raise the required tax revenue but all taxes are **not** equal economically. Some are economically "smarter" and much better for prosperity than others. Furthermore prosperity matters as axiom 1 reminds us. Prosperity is the single most important aspect affecting the success of our lives. Shouldn't our taxes be as smart as our phones? Here are some ideas.

1. The efficiency of the tax is important so the cost of collection should be minimal.

2. Avoid taxing features that are economically desirable or should not be reduced because they provide prosperity.

3. Instead tax features that are economically undesirable or should be reduced to increase prosperity in proportion to the tax.

4. Measure and monitor the results of a tax to see if it is economically performing as intended. Do not just increase taxes to increase revenue. Increase the tax to accomplish a measurable economic goal that benefits prosperity in proportion to the tax.

5. Once a tax has achieved its economic prosperity goal stop increasing and design a new tax to achieve more tax revenue until your revenue goal is achieved separately.

Notice that our current broad scale income tax is a good example of an economically "dumb" tax. To maximize prosperity we certainly do not want to reduce the incomes of the B90 group! How we tax has a great impact on our economy and our prosperity. So the ECA will be responsible for designing and managing taxation for maximum prosperity and Congress will provide oversight. However they will not be involved in tax collection. All tax collection will be conducted by the Treasury as it is now and this will include any new tax ideas.

It is not intended or necessary to transfer general tax authority to the ECA. Rather this reform legislation will authorize specific tax authorities and tax ranges within which the ECA can operate initially. In later years new authorities can be added and old authorities modified by recommendation of the ECA and approval by Congress and the President. In this way the economic control of taxes can be delegated to the ECA as a management authority without loss or interference of overall legislative authority or executive authority.

Trade tariffs deserve special consideration. Although the power to levy tariffs is necessary to achieve fair trade and fair currency valuations, their use should be restricted to extreme cases where negotiations fail. The Economic Trade Department will monitor the Executive's negotiations as Congresses' agent in preparation for ratification.

Import taxes can be used especially if only a few products are at issue. Import tariffs should only be used to enforce the trade rules discussed above. Trade balances are different and would be best dealt with by using voluntary export taxes instituted by recommendation of the ECA. See further discussion under international trade discussions.

Title 23: Wealth Tax to Encourage Economic Investment

Before we discuss the tax structure details it is important to distinguish between capital availability and economic capital deployment. Our developed economy is characterized by huge capital availability surpluses and reserves combined with limited and very erratic capital deployment in economic investments. When we need it most, it "hides under the bed" or "leaves town". This unreliable, frivolous, and often fickle capital deployment is usually referred to as the "trickle down". It's not a shortage problem but rather a management control problem.

Capital Availability and Deployment

This is why we have stated repeatedly that there is no shortage of capital availability. During the business cycle there can be a shortage of capital deployed or an excess of capital deployed corresponding to an excess of labor availability or a shortage of labor availability respectively. This "mismatch" is caused by inadequate Central Bank controls **not a shortage**. So clearly labor is the shortage **not** capital. Thus we could manage our economy with far less capital availability excesses and still attain the same exact economic performance using a better control system that separates **labor utilization** from **inflation control**. This would be possible because we will have the same exact amount of capital deployed and the same exact full utilization of labor.

Once labor is fully utilized more capital deployment is in excess causing a shortage of labor. The unemployment we have been plagued by is not caused by a shortage of capital availability. Rather it is caused by deliberate rationing of capital deployment under the guise of "fighting inflation". This throttling of job creation with interest rates is intended to drive down and hold labor rates to achieve price stability.

Instead we propose direct mathematical control of wage inflation (W% = Ip% - Iw% + P%) with a separate control mechanism (Title 11a). So there is no longer a need to throttle back capital deployment to force an excess of labor unemployment as a convoluted, surreptitious way to discourage the "boogeyman" of wage inflation. Capital deployment can then be controlled more directly and succinctly to obtain full employment and maximum prosperity instead! With these new ideas in mind let's construct a wealth tax designed for the labor utilization control structure. See discussion "The Role of Labor Efficiency" for more discussion about labor efficiency and wage manipulation tactics.

Wealth Taxes

The inheritance tax of Title 5 was carefully chosen because it is very gradual and it only affects deceased taxpayers. So it is a very benign way to accomplish our national goal of eliminating excess perpetual wealth in one generation. Wouldn't it be nice if the rest of us had the same special privilege and did not have to pay taxes until after we die!

In effect the inheritance tax allows perpetual wealth to simply expire over one lifetime as a national economic goal. So the personal and economic impact of this wealth transition will be minimized. That makes it a perfect match to finance the one-time old Social Security liability cost (45 years), the one-time Medicare liability cost (45 years), and the one-time sovereign debt pay down cost (60+ years).

Unfortunately it is unlikely that the inheritance tax alone will be sufficient to meet all the goals of Social Security reform, Medicare liability funding, and sovereign debt elimination. In the early years these costs are all frontloaded, larger in the beginning smaller in the end. So we will need additional taxes in the early years. A wealth tax is the most likely candidate for a new tax to accomplish our goals.

This would be implemented as an annual "flat" tax on Net Worth = Assets − Liabilities in excess of some tax threshold. Furthermore this tax would have little or no economic impact because we are primarily removing excess capital availability that was **not** yet economically deployed. Furthermore Title 9 will add substantial sources of new base capital directly deployed reliably and stably that will more than offset any unreliable "trickle down" loss caused by the wealth tax or the inheritance tax. So it is reliable and easily controllable boom or bust.

A good choice of a tax threshold would be ten times the average net worth of the middle 80% of wealth earners. This threshold would ensure that only the wealthiest would pay the new tax. A two tier and a two dimensional system should be used. Special lower tax rates should be applied to net worth that is committed to economic investment as defined in Title 24 below and produce 70% of their employment in the USA. Notice how strong this control is compared to the trickle control.

Furthermore taxes on perpetual wealth should be higher than taxes on new wealth. New wealth will be defined as wealth above the threshold without the prior generation being above the threshold. The table below gives likely tax rates. The differentials could be the same as shown or different from time to time as the ECA decides within the operating ranges approved by Congress to control labor utilization.

Investment Tier	Investment Dimension	Tax %	Differential %
Economic Investment	New Wealth	0.5%	Economic/non
Economic Investment	Old Wealth	2.0%	1.5%
Non-economic	New Wealth	2.0%	New/Old
Non-economic	Old Wealth	3.5%	1.5%

Tax rates shown are annual rates but tax rates will be applied on a monthly effective basis to make the tax more responsive monthly so it can be used as a powerful economic control tool. The economic/non-economic tax differential can be increased or decreased to encourage or discourage economic capital deployment on a revenue neutral basis that does not necessarily increase tax revenue. The ECA will monitor available economic capital and adjust the tax differential to ensure that adequate economic capital is deployed to meet mandates such as the full employment sub mandate while maintaining sufficient capital availability to ensure stability. Tax rates could be spread as in Title 24.

These wealth taxes would help ensure the immediate or early elimination of the 6.2% employer matching tax discussed in Title 2 and Title 9. Furthermore if the inheritance tax on perpetual wealth is not totally effective in reducing perpetual wealth at the rate desired, the New/Old differential tax rate should be increased on perpetual wealth. This will ensure that the national economic goal of eliminating perpetual wealth in one lifetime is achieved as intended and scheduled.

In later years instead of reducing this wealth tax the ECA and Congress should seriously consider the gradual elimination of the personal income tax on the B90 tax group. We could begin gradual phase-out after $1/3^{rd}$ of the sovereign debt principal is retired. This will help the gradual achievement of the distribution of wealth described in Title 11b above. The wealth tax is an excellent prosperity type of tax consistent with the standards outlined in Title 22 above. Obviously B90 income is highly desirable for prosperity and should not be taxed. Wealth, especially perpetual wealth and wealth not committed to economic investing are undesirable and should be taxed substantially!

Notice also that this two tier tax benefits new wealth creation which is almost always derived from successful economic investments, still deployed. Furthermore, the newly wealthy have a greater proportion of their wealth committed to economic assets while old wealth tends to have much more wealth in undeployed wealth assets like mansions, yachts, limousines, airplanes, art, jewelry, excess cash, gifts, and such.

Labor Utilization Control System

In conclusion, let us now look at a simple economic control system for labor utilization that the ECA can implement using the tax controls we just suggested. We will focus on a simple yet powerful system using the NF payroll deduction for short term control and the two tier wealth tax for longer term control. This "two punch" system provides a fast and effective economic control system that is much better than the current Central Bank/interest rate system. The NF 6.2% payroll deduction is fast and the economic wealth tax differential is effective.

We will assume that 100% full employment (no unemployed) has been achieved at the outset and that the national full-time proportional workweek starts at its quiescent 40.0 hours per week. We will also assume overtime would be paid by each business whenever their workweek exceeds one hour more than their Fed regional average and that the NF deduction starts at 6.2% its nominal quiescent value.

Case 1: The Economy Heats Up.

In this case demand for products and services increases above nominal (40.0) supply driving the flexible workweek above 40.5 hours per week to increase supply and match demand. This would be a likely initial threshold for the ECA to act. The ECA will begin by increasing the NF deduction above 6.2% which will decrease disposable income directly and immediately, thus decreasing demand for products and services. Simultaneously the ECA will decrease the monthly economic /non-economic wealth tax differential to reduce economic investment deployed and thus reduce new job creation (reduce labor demand).

This differential change could be revenue neutral if desired. The ECA has other controls as well. They could increase the wealth tax on economic investing in addition to the differential, they could decrease corporate taxes (Title 16) on cash and undeployed working capital to decrease deployment and offset other revenue gains, and they could increase interest rates. In more extreme cases they have direct monthly control over wages, salaries, and the Medicare deduction as well, as already discussed in the wage compensation controls of Title 11a.

Employers may respond by opening more requisitions for new employees because they do not want to operate above 40 hours per week. Since there is already full employment they will not be very successful. At any time if an employee became available for employment they could be easily absorbed by any open requisitions or the nearest employers with qualified work. The laws that require paying prevailing labor rates will avoid wage inflation and the ECA can compensate any wage inflation tendency measured at the national macro level using the compensation formula discussed in Title 11a. Notice that the inflation control loop is separate from labor utilization.

The NF deduction control should correct the flexible workweek back below 40.5 hours/week quickly. The ECA will continue with the wealth tax differential reducing job creation until the NF deduction can be gradually returned to the nominal 6.2%. Part or all of the wealth differential tax change could be maintained indefinitely as part of a new labor utilization equilibrium but the NF deduction will always return to the nominal 6.2% ready for the next correction situation.

Case 2: The Economy Cools Down

In this case demand for products and services decreases below the nominal (40.0) supply driving the flexible workweek below 39.5 hours per week to decrease supply and match demand. This would be a likely initial threshold for the ECA to act. The ECA will begin by decreasing the NF deduction below 6.2% and also monetize the difference to keep the NF at 6.2%. This will increase disposable income directly and immediately, increasing demand for products and services. Simultaneously the ECA will increase the monthly wealth tax differential to increase economic investment deployed and thus increase new job creation (increase labor demand).

This differential change could be revenue neutral if desired. The ECA has other controls as well. They could decrease the wealth tax on economic investing in addition to the differential, they could increase corporate taxes on cash and undeployed working capital to increase deployment and offset other revenue losses, and they could decrease interest rates. In more extreme crises they have direct monthly control over wages and salaries that provides for a direct consumer liquidity injection instead of crude QE or Ben Bernanke's famous "helicopter".

Employers may respond by closing requisitions for new employees because they do not want to operate below 40 hours per week but many will just leave their requisitions open permanently. Since there is already full employment they would not be very successful anyway. At any time if an employee became available for employment they could be easily absorbed by any open requisitions or the nearest employers with qualified work. The laws that require paying prevailing labor rates will avoid wage erosion and the ECA can compensate any wage erosion tendency at the national macro level using the separate compensation formula discussed in Title 11a.

The NF deduction control should correct the flexible workweek back above 39.5 hours/week quickly. The ECA will continue with the wealth tax differential increasing job creation until the NF deduction can be gradually returned to the nominal 6.2%. Part or all of the differential tax change could be maintained indefinitely as part of a new labor utilization equilibrium but the NF deduction will always return to the nominal 6.2% ready for the next correction situation.

What a powerful, direct, fast, multifaceted, and responsive control system! Many of you may recognize this control structure as a standard engineering Feedback Control System. These types of systems have been used for nearly a hundred years to solve a wide array of engineering control problems and they are extremely well understood. Similar control systems could be used for inflation control discussed in Title 11a and profit control in topic "The Role of Profits in Humanism". Each region could have its own control loop. Now the ECA would have so much better control of our economy with many direct controls instead of relying solely on loosely coupled interest rates that have collateral consequences and take time to be effective.

We could reserve interest rates for longer term controls like currency control and trade balance control. We could also achieve lower and more stable interest rates. Furthermore full employment was solid and never wavered! Under both cases of the business cycle there were no layoffs, no unemployment, and no wage inflation or wage deflation. Furthermore the flexible full-time workweek stayed in a very narrow range of 40.5 to 39.5 hours per week during the business cycle. Once this feedback control system is perfected and optimized by standard engineering techniques and modeling, the regulation range could be reduced to ½ that achieved initially (40.25 to 39.75 hrs./week).

The system proposed above is just the beginning. Even more advanced engineering ideas should be considered. A proportional, continuous correction system would respond quicker with tighter regulation than the threshold system discussed above. Also the NF has direct and instantaneous control over substantial economic investment. So the NF could shift economic investment deployed directly as needed rather than depending only on slower, indirect taxation controls.

We already know from classical engineering that fast, small lag feedback controls are inherently stable, quick to respond, and tightly regulated. While slow feedback systems with large amounts of lag are inherently unstable, slow to respond, and poorly regulated. Our economic "moon" is clearly visible and achievable using the same engineering techniques and technology that we used to get to the real moon! Economic Engineering and stable prosperity, here we come!

Title 24: Economic Investment and Capital Gains Tax

Economic investment is very important for the prosperity of our economy. Unfortunately it is poorly understood and poorly managed primarily because economists, Wall Street, and the financial news media have destroyed the word "investment". The word investment is almost always used as a euphemism for speculation leaving us with no word to differentiate true economic investment! Worse yet we are left with the deliberate misconception that frivolous speculation is actually good for our economy. So herein we will use the term "economic investment" to mean real investment not speculation. We will define "economic investment" deployed as any risk of funds for one year or more as capital formation for a business that is intended to produce a product or service by employing people as the main business activity.

Speculation is risking funds usually short term solely for the purpose of making a profit. There is usually no business or capital formation involved. Usually speculation sounds like "buy low and sell high". There is no significant economic value to speculation. Worse yet, economic investment and speculation compete for the same source of funds from capital available that is not yet deployed. So the more funds are committed to speculation, the fewer funds are available for economic investment. The common term used for this kind of speculation is "making money" and it is glorified as a monumental achievement worshiped as "high religion and magic" on Wall Street!

This idea is that money can be used in some financially skillful or tricky way to "make more money" by "financial magnification" without economic investment. In Title 25 below this is referred to as "gaming the system". Buy it for $2 and sell it for $3 and "make" a buck out of thin air! Who needs alchemy? This is easier without all the "double double toil and trouble". Yet it is just "capital inflation".

Notice if this "financial magnification" was actually economically beneficial that the Central Bank could just print the money to provide the amplification without this risky unstable inflation. If you think this is just a harmless "game for the rich" that does not matter, then try adding up all of our finest minds and their salaries that are working on schemes for "making money" as we speak. Speculation wastes our most precious economic resource – our minds. We could easily cure cancer for the same cost and mental effort, but we get to indulge our greed fantasies and achieve zero economic benefit instead! How sad!

For this reason HERA will revamp the capital gains tax to make it more of an incentive for real economic development and less of an incentive for "making money" or speculation. A likely variable tax structure for capital gains is shown in the table below:

Capital Gains Type vs % Ordinary Income Tax

Reinvested Business Profits	0%
Seed Venture Capital	10%
Small Business Development	15%
1st Round Venture Capital	20%
2nd Round Venture Capital	30%
3rd Round Venture Capital	35%
Initial Public Equity Offerings	40%
Public Equity Offerings	50%
Primary Bond Issues	65%
Secondary Equity Market	80%
Secondary Bond Market	90%

Note that secondary market activity does not meet the full definition of economic investment and it is only included because it helps slightly to facilitate the primary markets. The table above is a good candidate for the revamped, variable capital gains tax. The percentages given are the percentages of tax on ordinary income. All capital gains are not the same. Investments of one year or more in the secondary bond market would be taxed at 90% of ordinary income. In contrast investments in seed venture capital would be only taxed at 10% of ordinary income.

Capital gains tax improvements alone will not be enough to balance the scales. A broad range of speculation taxes should be considered. We will give some specific examples to illustrate the possibilities. The COMEX commodities futures market is a great example of massive speculation and manipulation that is now out of control. The original idea of this market was sound and wholesome, that producers and consumers would have a market that would ensure the availability and price of commodities in the future. Thus, a farmer could ensure that she will be able to sell in the future all the wheat she intendeds to grow now at a price that is profitable. Or a baker could ensure that he will be able to buy enough flour in the future at a price he can afford now.

Let us look at what actually happens after years of pampering, speculative corruption, and very little oversight. If we study the actual volume of contracts, we will find that the vast majority of all futures contracts close without any purchase or delivery of the commodity by the contract or in any spot market. Instead the contracts are closed by mutual agreement for cash (Butler, 2014). This means that neither party of the contract intended to buy (receive) or intended to sell (provide) the commodity! They only wanted to manipulate or exploit its future price and COMEX was more than willing to facilitate them!

The absurdity of this situation may not be obvious at first blush so let's put this in simple language (Butler, 2014). What this means is that the vast majority of COMEX contracts involve commodity "buyers" who don't want the commodity pretending to buy it from "sellers" who don't have any to sell! But they both want to gamble on, or manipulate the market. So they agree on an imaginary price for this fictitious transaction that has no disciplined relationship to the supply/demand fundamentals of the commodity because there is no real supply or real demand. The market discipline of supply and demand is lost and we are left with just a frivolous yet dangerous betting game. And all we need to do to justify this dangerous activity is to chant "free market"!

If these fictitious cash transactions are in the majority then the market loses its ability to value the commodities correctly so the market becomes useless to fulfill its primary purpose and highly susceptible to manipulation. Furthermore there is risk to the entire financial system because when these fictitious valuations suffer a supply/demand correction the shock wave ripples throughout the larger market. What is truly amazing is that this situation could be rationalized by economists as a "free market" when it is actually the perfect opposite!

So this suggests the following speculation tax. Each year the speculator pays a tax on the difference between his total transactions for a given commodity and the sum of his actual purchases of that commodity plus his actual sales of that commodity. Thus he will only pay tax on his speculations. The farmer who did deliver wheat will pay no tax as will the baker who did purchase flour. Some speculation is beneficial to keep the market robust so there are lots of buyers and sellers available. So the ECA would monitor the activity and increase or decrease the tax rate to obtain a desirable ratio between speculation and non-speculation that allows much less excess capital availability.

There are many opportunities for reducing speculation in other markets as well. The derivatives market is very similar to the commodities market. While in the equities market we have "short selling" which is selling shares you borrowed in the hopes of the price dropping so you can buy them later at a lower price or "naked short selling" which allows you to sell short without borrowing first. These tools have no economic value other than speculation and manipulation and they should be taxed heavily. Likewise, High Frequency Trading has no economic value and should be eliminated or taxed heavily.

In the last twenty years speculation has become rampant. The euphemism for this speculation is called "trading". The ECA will develop metrics to better measure and monitor speculation versus economic investment. Taxes and legislation will be needed to restrict massive speculation and further increase economic investment.

The importance of shifting from speculation to economic investment cannot be overstated. The prosperity we wish to achieve can only be realized if economic investment increases the availability of both old and new products and services in an efficient manner. Then we can increase the income of the M80 group and the prosperity index will increase. Otherwise we will only achieve inflation and prosperity will not improve. It is now time to put our economy first over speculation.

Title 25: Speculation is Threatening Financial Stability

The problems with speculation have morphed into new problems that are threatening the stability of our financial system. Notice that speculation benefits from the dangerous noise of market volatility. Without this volatility speculation would be much less profitable. The ever increasing race to find quick speculative profits has reached a fever pitch. Speculators are impatient waiting for opportunities to "buy low" and then waiting even longer for opportunities to "sell high".

"Greed conquers all obstacles". So they have figured out how to manipulate the markets, lower when they want to buy and higher when they want to sell. High Frequency Trading, insider trading, and price fixing are examples of some of the techniques used but they have become very sophisticated, very quickly and there are many possible methods so new and more dangerous ones are added continuously.

At any other time, in any other case, this would be called "gaming the system" and it would be illegal and it would be prosecuted. But Wall Street makes its own rules! Right now the "gamers" are primarily gaming the institutional and private speculators but soon the "gamers" will start to game each other and then "flash crashes" will increase in scale and frequency. Who will win? Not humanity, the final victim!

It is just a matter of time until one of these tricky monster algorithms accidentally or deliberately decides to "trade" with another tricky monster! This kind of over-the-top desperation behavior is characteristic of a foul, unfair, and failing paradigm in the later stages of self-destruction like medieval "Tulip Investing". We need more advanced ideas for wholesome economic development rather than more tricky schemes and scams from Wall Street. See discussion "The Role of "Free" Markets in Humanism" for more details and ideas.

Our problem is that it is our financial system and our economy that they will destroy in the process! That is exactly what happened leading to the 2008 crisis. AAA Mortgage backed securities were fraudulently created to hide bad debt. So it is time for a new paradigm based on the **first principles** of the Economic Bill of Rights and the mathematical axioms instead of the greed, corruption, and trickery of Wall Street.

It is time we relegate Wall Street to the side lines and take control of our economy putting it under the responsibility and accountability of a special department of government, the ECA, charged and chartered by us to accomplish the prosperity paradigm we so wish for and so deserve. Wall Street can choose to participate with real economic investment or game and speculate themselves into financial oblivion.

Unfortunately this problem is compounded by four important recent trends. First the worldwide central banks have flooded the financial market with excess capital liquidity to stabilize it after the 2008 fiasco. Secondly the developed nations have already been in a capital excess for some time. Until now this excess has capitalized the emerging markets but soon this excess capital will return no longer needed there.

Thirdly our planet's population growth **must be** restricted to levels lower than currently further reducing capital demand. Economic growth requires much more new capital than mere sustenance requires. Fourthly converting our retirement systems to a capital base will substantially and reliably increase stable capital deployed. Furthermore this base capital is committed with 100% efficiency directly to capital deployment not just more unstable capital availability. Thus much less inefficient, indirect capital availability will be needed in the future!

So this "glut" of capital will have to be "mopped up" on a grand scale. Normally this would be an extremely difficult problem risking dangerous instability. However our current problems turn out to be our future solutions! We can use this excess capital to pay off our national debt, refinance our social security in a sustainable fashion, and refinance our medical retirement into a promising and prosperous future! There should even be enough to establish a truly exciting affordable health care plan and affordable education plan for our nation as well! Our economic "moon" is clear and full. Grasp it tightly in your hearts and minds and don't let go of this exciting future!

Discussion Topics:

Now that we have laid out the framework for likely economic reforms, let's look at selected topics that further support and explain the reform ideas, their background, and their future possibilities. Then we can layout a political road map to accomplish these economic reforms.

Is a Humanist a Democrat, Republican, or an Independent?

As discussed in the Introduction, the Economic Humanist Party (EHP like GOP) is very different from a normal political party. It will be thought of by most of us as simply the Prosperity Party. Specifically the EHP is an economic party with no political planks at all and only one economic plank: the Humanistic Economic Reform Act (HERA). Furthermore the EHP is a non-electoral party with **no** candidates.

Many from all political parties will join the EHP as an addendum to their ongoing identity as a Democrat, a Republican, or an Independent without any sense of conflict. Indeed their Congressional candidate may very well endorse HERA so that there is no conflict. In some cases both parties' candidates will endorse the legislation. However, in some cases only the opposition party candidate will endorse HERA. Only in that case will there be an opportunity for any conflict at all. For Independents there should not be any new conflict at all.

Only in those cases where the opposition party candidate endorses HERA but your preferred party candidate does not, will you be presented with a conflict. Should you vote for the opposition party candidate who endorses HERA or should you vote for your preferred party candidate who does not? Your decision may very well depend on how significant the national political issues are compared to the new economic reform issues. However the political issues in the next election will probably be the same ones as in the last election and the one before that. Most of our political issues have been around a long time. Indeed most of these issues are just bait to anger, inflame, and polarize us like "immigration", "abortion", and "gay marriage".

It is hard to believe that any of the old political issues will carry the impact of the economic reform issues addressed in HERA. Considerations of this Reform Act will be a profound legislative event witnessed around the world by all of humanity with great interest and involvement! I believe that the weight of this issue will prompt most conflicted Democrats and Republicans to "take a party vacation", cross party lines and vote for HERA. Of course Independents are used to crossing party lines so this will not be a big issue for them either.

In a very real way HERA is very much a referendum idea that crosses party lines. Yet our political system does not support referendums on the national level the way some states do. So it is clumsy to present a nonpartisan referendum at the national level. We can only elect parties and personalities, not ideas! So to "elect" an idea we must encourage the candidates to endorse the idea first and then we can elect the candidates. This situation unavoidably forces us to cross party lines to be true to an idea. There is simply no other option available to us. So we will have to cross party lines occasionally in order to vote for and achieve a real democratic economy that will represent all of humanity.

What will attract Democrats and Republicans to the Prosperity Party's economic agenda? There is a lot! Consequently let us look at the Republican Party first. Here are some of the original goals of HERA mentioned above that are most attractive to Republicans.

1. Establish an independent department of government primarily responsible for the prosperity and management of our economy
2. Stop further expansion of sovereign debt as taxation without representation
3. Pay off the existing Sovereign debt over the next 60 years or less
4. Eliminate budget deficits by law
5. Restructure Social Security and Medicare to a sustainable system and a substantial increase of benefits
6. Reduce the national budget and regulate the budget at a fixed percentage of GDP
7. Tax businesses so that they are encouraged to maximize national prosperity

8. Replace the 35% income tax on businesses with prosperity taxes
9. Eliminate the need for businesses to keep profits offshore
10. Eliminate the 6.2% matching Social Security tax for business
11. Eliminate business unemployment taxes
12. Streamline businesses so that they are no longer involved in health care, pensions, and other fringe benefits
13. Eliminate the "curse" of unemployment and costly unemployment benefits
14. Implement by international treaty a fair valuation system for all currencies worldwide
15. Manage the national income so that there is no wage inflation and no wage erosion
16. Institute direct, demand driven capital formation using a public capital concept based on a national retirement fund
17. Integrate monetary policy, fiscal policy, investment policy and tax policy into a cohesive unified economic control system
18. Use tax incentives to encourage economic investment and discourage speculation

If we look only at these 18 items, HERA sounds very Republican. Many of these issues have been on and off the Republican agenda for some time. I find it very interesting that some Democrats that review HERA tell me that they believe HERA is a Republican movement with significant Democratic appeal. It is hard to see if there is a bias. Yet there are some aspects of HERA that uniquely affect the GOP Party.

The inheritance tax and wealth tax will be unpopular with the "old money" constituents and "old money" has always had a much stronger voice in the GOP party than mere numbers would justify. How "new money" will react is unclear and will likely be mixed. The bulk of the Republicans are small business owners or business professionals and the majority of both of them will find HERA to be very attractive especially regarding new wealth opportunity and new wealth achievement. Moreover the self-employed will find the elimination of the 6.2% matching tax a big incentive. So judging the response of the Republican Party is going to be more difficult than with Democrats.

What will attract Democrats (DNC) to the Humanist party's agenda? There is more than you might think. Here are some of the goals of HERA mentioned above that are most attractive to Democrats.

1. Facilitate an economic renaissance from a profit paradigm to a prosperity paradigm
2. Establish an independent department of government primarily responsible for the prosperity and management of our economy
3. Institute Humanism: a form of Capitalism with a democratic focus
4. Define economic majority as the middle 80% of earners
5. Define a prosperity metric = average income / minimum cost of living
6. Stop further expansion of sovereign debt as taxation without representation
7. Pay off the existing Sovereign debt over the next 60 years or less
8. Eliminate budget deficits by law
9. Restructure Social Security and Medicare to a sustainable system and a substantial increase of benefits
10. Reduce the national budget and regulate the budget at a fixed percentage of GDP
11. Tax businesses so that they are encouraged to maximize national prosperity
12. End the economic privileged class over the next 80 years with an inheritance tax that heavily taxes inheritances larger than 10 times the average inheritance
13. Eliminate the "curse" of unemployment and costly unemployment benefits
14. Establish a policy of equal pay for equal work that applies nationally and internationally
15. Establish a minimum wage that is at least equal to the minimum cost of living
16. Implement by international treaty a fair valuation system for all currencies worldwide

17. Implement by international treaty an equal value pay for equal work rule worldwide
18. Make sustainable natural resources the right and responsibility of all generations
19. Manage the national income so that there is no wage inflation and no wage erosion
20. Manage national income and national wealth to match a fixed percentage formula
21. Integrate monetary policy, fiscal policy, investment policy, and tax policy into a cohesive unified economic control system
22. Establish the scientific truth that a prosperous economy cannot be achieved by profit optimization of each individual business
23. Use tax incentives to encourage economic investment and discourage speculation
24. Institute a two-tier wealth tax on Net Worth that encourages economic investing
25. Eventual elimination of the personal income tax on the lower 90% of earners
26. Win the "War on Democracy" by achieving a sustainable democratic economy

If we look only at these 26 items, HERA sounds very Democratic. Many of these issues have been on and off the Democratic agenda for some time. It is interesting that many Republicans that review HERA tell me that they believe HERA is a Democratic movement with significant Republican appeal. There are some aspects of HERA that will uniquely affect the Democratic Party. Because HERA seems to have such broad democratic appeal, the institutional side of the Democratic Party may react to HERA as a threatening party competitor. But I doubt this reaction will be strong enough to overcome the broad democratic worldwide appeal of HERA. See further discussion under "The Unification of Business and Labor".

Independents are likely to find all of the goals of HERA to be attractive without any conflict. Maybe the lack of conflict in both parties will bring home the reality that the Prosperity Party is a non-partisan, apolitical, economic movement that represents a win-win situation for business and labor that has worldwide appeal for all of humanity. HERA is all about prosperity! And our prosperity is equally attractive for Democrats, Republicans, and Independents. It is time we focus on prosperity that unifies us instead of personalities, parties, and politics that don't. I know we can do it and I am anxious to get started.

The Wealth Concentration Issue

The wealth concentration and inequity issue is one of the fundamental underlying issues of our current economic crisis (2008 to 2018). There are many measures of this inequality. The top 1% vs the remaining 99% is the most common and it was popularized by the Occupy Wall Street movement recently. A new one arrived more recently. It was reported that the richest 85 people have the same wealth, $1.7 trillion, as the poorest 50% of all humanity on our planet (Shin, 2014). I am an engineer so I like formulas. Let's put this into a wealth formula:

85 "People" = 3,500,000,000 People

According to my high school algebra this equation cannot be true unless the "people" on the 85 side of this equation are exponentially more special and privileged than the people on the 3,500,000,000 side of the equation. Who says there is no privileged class? Even the elite privileged class must have a "privilege" class according to this ugly equation! The inequality presented by this equation is mind numbing.

The news media's presentation and response to this news was telling. It was very matter-of-fact as if they announced this same bad news every year about this same time using a different cute or novel metric to improve the entertainment value of an old morbid subject. Nobody suggested that it was shameful or disgusting. Some elite rich people suggested it was a sign of "progress" implying that 3,500,000,000 were lazy laggards and would eventually catch up with the glorious 85.

However the most notable absence was any thought or suggestion that we should, or even could DO something proactive about this ugly! **No action was appropriate just tolerance**. The implication was that this situation was like a volcanic eruption and that we were helpless to DO anything about it except get out of the way. In fact this is a manmade problem and it has any number of easy manmade solutions that are being disallowed in the name of the voodoo of "volcanic economics".

The numerics of this equation are incomprehensible like the distance to some far star in some far galaxy. This equation represents Gigascale or Terascale inequality, greed, elitism, and exploitation in the late stages of unsustainable, self-destruction caused by bad economics. Let us imagine the likely progression of numbers over the near future:

85 = 3,500,000,000

65 = 3,600,000,000

45 = 3,700,000,000

25 = 3,800,000,000* (We are near this level already in 2018)

15 = 3,900,000,000

4 = 4,000,000,000

Do you think this ends well for humanity? Can you imagine the world with the equation 4 = 4,000,000,000? Each of "the four" would rule from inside their privileged "glass bubble". There would be constant never-ending economic war between "the four" to see which ultra-alpha would dominate this dog-eat-dog nightmare of wealth privilege.

To that end humanity, outside the privileged bubbles, would be expected to reduce prosperity lower and lower and lower yet until humanity and our economy were exhausted with "working poverty", extortion, exploitation, and finally "working homeless", or worse yet "working starvation". Obviously humanity would not survive! In its final conclusion the economic **prosperity inefficiency** of this system of privilege is mind-boggling. To support the achievement of just one ultra-elite requires the exploitation, impoverishment, and enslavement of one billion humans! What an ugly future has been forced upon us!

The system that produced this equation is sick, as in "terminally ill"! The obscenity of this equation makes us numb because it is beyond human comprehension. The system that produced this equation could not possibly create prosperity! In fact this system is the antithesis of prosperity. Prosperity is intrinsically a broad scale human concept.

Yet the above equation says only 85 people were really prosperous and 3,500,000,000 or more are not prosperous. What a score! 85 win and 3,500,000,000 lose! How could anyone propose this insane score as an achievement? Why would you vote for them if they did? If you did not vote for them, who did and why? Either the 85 stuffed a hell of a lot of ballot boxes or you and I are responsible for this outrageous outcome! Furthermore there is much we can and will DO about it starting now!

The prosperity axioms of Humanism are exactly what "we can do about it". We should wonder what were the axioms of Capitalism that produced this existing system where 85 = 3,500,000,000. It should be no wonder that they are opaque, hidden, and undeclared because they are so ugly! Greed, corruption, exploitation, manipulation, extortion, and elitism are the axioms of our existing system and they harnessed our economy to working poverty. Instead using Humanistic axioms we will harness our economy to prosperity! What a conceptual difference!

I think the crux of the problem is that the only voting choices we had were personalities and none of those personalities could fix the system that was hopelessly broken. Any attempt to fix the profit paradigm is a dangerous distraction that traps us in impossibility and hopelessness. Capitalism can be rejuvenated but we must replace the old paradigm. Maybe we look too much for saving personalities that we do not really need? We are misled to believe we must wait for an ultra-alpha to save us from the ultra-elite! We seem to be stuck in this kind of ultra-ism.

On the other hand our political democracy has already empowered us to solve this problem ourselves! We do not need a savior and we do not need permission to have a democratic economy! Now for the first time we will have a new systematic solution (HERA) to choose instead of a personality or a political party. If we do not stand and vote for the solution, it is an absolute certainty that none of the 85 will stand and do it for us. Our path forward is clear and concise. We must create an economic science based on simple economic geometry that will guide us out of this economic nightmare creating a system of meta-economic prosperity for all mankind based on **first principles**! It is time for what we deserve: "**economics as if people mattered**" (Schumacher, 1973)!

The Invisible Economic Slavery

I have bad news for you - slavery never ended! Not like the history books say. But to understand this we must differentiate between two related but different ideas. One is "economic slavery" and the other is "racial or ethnic prejudice". Like greed, racial prejudice is a human fault that will be with humanity forever. Hopefully we and our future generations can minimize this fault and transcend it with the new idea of **mutual respect** that is inherent in Humanism. I believe we can. Although greed is very much a topic within the scope of this book, racial and ethnic prejudice, outside economics, is beyond our scope.

Let us make a quick review of the history of slavery. In ancient times the model was simple. Raise a big army, conquer your neighbors, and force the survivors to work for you as slaves at the lowest possible pay and the highest possible profit. This allows a privileged class to perpetuate itself indefinitely by exploiting the slave class endlessly.

The privileged class and the slave class are opposite sides of the same "coin" of privilege. We cannot have one without the other. Of course our social conscience is relieved if there is some racial or ethnic difference that can seem to justify, or at least differentiate, this exploitation. That is the role that prejudices play but the primary motive was economic slavery to allow and enable economic privilege.

At the "end" of slavery the model was not much different. Empty ships leaving Europe to pick up sugar and other products from the new world, were forced by the trade winds to go past Northwest Africa. Why not stop and pick up slaves to do the work in the new world for the lowest possible pay and therefore the highest possible profit?

Again economic slavery was the primary motive. The new world wanted cheap labor and the privileged economic class was more than willing to do whatever atrocity was necessary to obtain the **cheapest labor for the highest profit**. Northwest Africa and racial prejudice were only convenient collateral opportunities to facilitate the primary motive of economic slavery that would perpetuate economic privilege.

Slavery was forced to morph into a more economic form because of a worldwide, grassroots movement to stop the cruelty of slavery. By this time the power of wealth economics was better understood. The old slavery concept was based on forced labor. But this left the privileged class with responsibilities and costs for buying, feeding, clothing, and housing slaves. Not to mention the high cost of incarceration and supervision. Slaves were a valuable asset that needed to be cared for to protect their investment. So why not free the privileged class of all these costs and responsibilities for care and improve profit drastically?

So we did. We "freed" the slaves! It was much easier to control the "free" slaves with the new economic power controls rather than the costly old forced controls. We freed the slaves of incarceration but further entrenched them in economic slavery! Moreover, all workers could now be exploited with no restrictions on gender, race, creed, or ethnicity. This would guarantee an ongoing endless supply of economic slaves. "Greed conquers all obstacles"! The Dark Age for the modern profit paradigm of economics was born. The new era of broad scale human exploitation had begun and it has yet to end!

The economic control principle was simple. The privileged economic class controls the economic work by investment and they can ration it as needed to exploit the labor market. It is just supply and demand. It is easy to make sure you do not invest too much so that unemployment remains high; **not investing** is extremely easy! If workers do not work, they are "free" to starve while watching their children starve as well.

Only those desperate enough to work for less and less will work. The others will not. Our "new era" economists called this a "market", a popular new economic idea of that era. How could starvation possibly be a "market"? Unemployment was not a problem – it was a solution! Without investment risk more unemployment creates more desperation which yields even lower wages and even higher profits. This new profit paradigm was a godsend for the economic privileged class and a new plateau for cheap labor slavery that pretends to be a market.

The best feature of all was that the stigma of the slave owner was gone! Now it was the economy, the economists, and the "free" market that exploited the slaves. The privileged class disappeared from view hidden behind the economy and the "free" market idea while **slavery became invisible**! This new concept of privilege was even more outrageous than the old concept of feudal royalty. Draconian progress!

In the old feudal concept royalty had privileges but they also had responsibilities. In the new concept the privileges were maintained and even expanded while the responsibilities were eliminated! The privileged class used the "Invisible Hand" of economic exploitation to accomplish their hidden privilege without any responsibilities at all. This is the real economic version of how slavery (never) "ended".

There are two things about this history lesson that amaze me. One is how ingenious and effective it was. Early Wall Street at their best! The other is how obviously flawed it was and yet it persists today! The draconian ugliness of this profit paradigm is revolting and depressing. If you were an economic prosperity theorist, this profit paradigm would be the last paradigm you would ever propose for prosperity.

It reeks of a "lose-lose more" paradigm in which the privileged class satisfies their greed urge by exploiting the slave class which loses more than they. It is like the factory owner who exploits his workers with lower and lower wages until they can no longer afford to buy his products. What is amazing is that the factory owner, intoxicated with the stupid side of greed, never figures out what is wrong. He just keeps repeating the same greedy mistake in the name of profitability with encouraging confidence that he lost less! Welcome to the stupid and blind side of greed intoxication that can be perpetuated indefinitely!

Since the beginning of time slavery has been the nemesis for mankind. Our first yoke of oppression was political slavery which was ruled by the rich and powerful bloodline elite. It took at least 6 thousand years before we could throw off this yoke for political democracy. Modern political democracy was based on two ideas: 1) that all men were created politically equal and 2) that this right could be protected by a new constitutional government system of **political thought**.

Unfortunately the rich and powerful simply moved to a new venue, the yoke of economic slavery ruled by the rich and powerful bloodline elite. In order to throw off the second yoke of economic slavery we will need an economic democracy. This economic democracy is based on two ideas: 1) that all men have the right to equal economic treatment and opportunity and 2) that this right could be protected by a new axiomatic, scientific, mathematical system of **economic thought**. The parallelism of these two similar ideas should be obvious.

This is a powerful problem and it will require a powerful solution. Our two most powerful worldwide institutions, government and religion have not been powerful enough to solve this problem! We need ideas and methodologies so powerful that they are undeniable, irrefutable, and unarguable. Only mathematics and its application, science, have achieved this level of power and unification of thought for humanity.

Currently the field of Economics consists of a single idea, the supply/demand market mechanism, and an insane asylum of 10,000 different "expert" opinions of what to do with the market mechanism almost all of which are harmful to humanity! It is like the alchemy of times past, there was no science and 10,000 "expert" opinions on how to convert lead to gold! Only science with its mathematical rigor can achieve intellectual power that is inalienable, undeniable, irrefutable, and unifying for all nations and religions with one system of thought!

In this pseudo-science of wealth economics its practitioners became opinion artisans. Every issue in wealth economics has a wide spectrum of opinions. The truth is always a broad and elusive "economic mystery" that inhibits proactive changes and encourages more opinions, more confusion, and more inaction. There are no concrete goals or guiding axioms not even the "free" market chant because it can be extorted, distorted, manipulated, and exploited to agree with a wide range of opinions and valuation results. So our economists tend to suffer from a form of collective paranoia paralysis about any proactive idea for economic change much less economic improvement.

They seem to have a voodoo consensus: "do not touch the economy because it could explode unpredictably at any moment like an active volcano". Just leave the mystery alone and everything will be ok! Thus economics becomes an advise and debate, but **do nothing** profession much like "economic volcanologists" leaving humanity without any proactive professional representation or scientific guidance. But our prosperity economics has a different idea: that good economics can be achieved by proactively following basic axiomatic principles instead of the inaction, fear, and impotence of endlessly debating opinions.

Yet only perpetually privileged capitalists are allowed to be principals of the old economy and the only goal of their economy is to maximize their concentrated wealth. Oh yes, every year a few newcomers are allowed to join and a few old-timers depart. But the 85=3,500,000,000 formula says it all. If left alone without limits, the 85 group will only get smaller, more concentrated and wealthier. We must end the rule of this privileged economic class and find a path to a win-win prosperity paradigm based on truly democratic ideas and scientific methodology!

So humanity cannot be exploited like a commodity. Only slavery treats humanity like zinc or soybeans bought and sold by the tonnage at the lowest exploitable price. Capitalism is flawed at the most basic meta-level. We do not need to abandon Capitalism; we just need to fix it! Old Capitalism does not allow humanity to participate as a principal of our economy while our new Humanism requires it by direct mandate!

Fair Competition vs Foul Exploitation

The International Olympic Games and the competition they sponsor can be used as a very instructive intellectual tool. These international games have been the single most successful, fair, and long lived international competition that humans on this planet have achieved. We can learn a lot from its success that could apply to a global capitalistic economy under a prosperity paradigm. The Olympic Games can represent a very effective model that has functioned and survived under numerous wars, political strife, and economic, cultural, and linguistic differences to provide a platform idea for competition.

Let us try to understand why the Olympics have been so effective for so long under such difficulties. First let us observe how fundamentally intrinsic playing and competition are for all humans and most other animal species. Our instincts to play and compete are an innate drive almost as fundamental as our drive for self-preservation. Just look at how much of our lives are spent playing and competing? Furthermore if we are not competing actually we still compete with our imagination as spectators of games. We even play in our dreams when we sleep.

Secondly notice how fundamental and intrinsic our sense of "fair play" is in us. We seem to be born with built in rules of engagement and rules of fair play. For example watch puppies play when they are young and their instincts are easy to see. Remember when we were kids? There were always those bully kids who tried to rig the game with their biased unfair rules intended to exploit the vulnerable.

Yet it never worked for them because we instinctively and collectively recognized the unfairness and we stopped playing with them. No matter how powerful they were we never capitulated. We just stopped playing with them and went and played somewhere else or played something else or we played alone. But we would not continue with an unfair game. Because it was not a fair competitive game anymore; it was exploitation, power, and privilege intended for unfair competition!

That is why the Olympics have been so successful. They are based on a powerful human need or benefit that could only be achieved with our inherent sense of fair play, **mutually respected** by all humans that innately prohibits exploitation and privilege. In Humanism, economic competition takes place on a level playing field where all businesses pay prevailing labor rates defined by the equal valued pay for equal productivity of axiom 2 and item 1 of the Economic Bill of Rights.

Then each business competes to achieve the highest quality product, with the highest performance, best functionality, most durability, best reliability, easiest usability, best size, greatest versatility, and the lowest labor content. This is real competition not just exploitation that constantly focuses on exploiting lower and lower labor rates and more and more distorted currency exchange rates. So we see our economy is inherently a collective, generative, human thing. It is an oxymoron to try to exploit humanity as a means to achieve economic prosperity. The two ideas, exploitation and prosperity are mutually exclusive!

Likewise the subtle difference between "winning" and "playing" is important to understand. The best games with the most "fun" are the ones that are well balanced. Once the game becomes unbalanced we quickly lose interest or we sympathize with the underdog as part of a greater game called "the underdog game". If one nation dominated the Olympics it would soon destroy the Olympics! Just like when we were kids, we played every day to "win" but if we won too much we just changed the game or rebalanced the players so we could continue play.

Playing is the meta-goal not winning! Only the bullies try to win every game and dominate. Wars are meant to be "won" but international trade is meant to be always "played" and never "won". Wars destroy prosperity while international trade induces prosperity. So for example if a nation finds itself with unbalanced trade favoring its exports, it is time for a self-imposed export tax to restore balance, realize its national gain as a tax benefit, and continue the economic trade "play".

The benefits of trade are all in the "playing" not in the "winning". Furthermore the "winners" are the ones to institute the compensation to keep playing otherwise we all lose! Wall Street's ideas of greed, unfairness, and exploitation have no wholesome role in this process at all! See more discussion on international trade in topics "It is Time for a New World Order" and "Near Term Global Economic Outlook".

The human race has had enough exploitation! If we are to continue with the idea of a global economy, we must do so on a level playing field based on innate rules of fairness and equality for all. Equal value pay for equal work and fair currency values are the beginning of our equality. Reciprocal trade tariffs or better yet no trade tariffs at all are a necessary requirement. Prosperity for all is the final end goal. If we continue with a foul exploitive approach to a global economy based on greed, extortion, and unfairness, we will suffer a catastrophic world-wide collapse! "Fair is not foul and foul is not fair in economics"; they never were! The five key axioms of economics are a perfect basis for "trade science" that will unify the economics of international trade.

Capitalism vs Humanism

In the USA the economic style we understand the best is Capitalism. So it might be helpful if we were to contrast Capitalism and its new axiomatic offshoot, Humanism. In short, Capitalism focuses on profit benefits for the top 10%. Socialism attempts to tame Capitalism by focusing on taxation of wealth from the top 10% to provide welfare benefits for the bottom 10%. Communism focuses on eliminating any benefits at all, except for the Party, as the best way to achieve "equality through equal poverty". On the other hand, Humanism focuses on proactive prosperity for the middle 80%. So Humanism offers an entirely new concept with new economic thinking. This table summarizes this contrast on various issues that we discussed in HERA.

Humanism	Capitalism
Maximize human benefit	Maximize elite benefit 85=3,500,000,000
Equal value pay for equal work	Exploitation of labor into downward spiral
Competition on a level playing field	Exploitive, distorted, and manipulated playing field
Income change: W% = Ip% - Iw% + P%	Unprotected Income drops lower and lower …
W = M x P for trade equality	Export Led Economy for trade
Scientific currency valuations	Exploitive/manipulated currency values
Minimum wage for productive employment	Lower wages justify even lower wages …
Prosperity is the primary goal of the economy	Profit is the primary goal of the economy
Productivity & efficiency lead to higher prosperity	Greed & exploitation lead to higher profits
Equal access to available employment	Rationed employment to drive down wages
Optimize wealth to max prosperity	Maximize wealth concentration
Optimize businesses for maximum prosperity	Optimize businesses for maximum profits
Capitalism:	Inequality Through Profits
Socialism:	Equality Through Taxation
Communism:	Equality Through Equal Poverty
Humanism:	Equality Through Prosperity!

The most distinct contrast between Capitalism and Humanism can be seen by comparing their approach to wages and salaries regarding prosperity as in axioms 1, 2, and 5. Capitalism focuses on driving down wages and salaries, using interest rates, to the lowest levels possible believing this will maximize return on capital and thus the high profits of the perpetually wealthy capitalists. So unemployment rates and interest rates are kept artificially high to maintain low wages.

While Humanism focuses on maximizing wages and salaries to the highest levels possible without creating wage inflation. What a distinct difference! It seems clear that the most democratically prosperous of the four "Isms" of economics is Humanism. The middle 80% group (M80) clearly benefits by axiomatic mandate to the greatest extent economically possible with full employment and low interest rates!

The Bottom 10%

Let's also look at the bottom 10% (B10) group. They clearly suffer substantially under Capitalism and Communism. Socialism attempts to satisfy its conscience by instituting various welfare programs to offset some of this depressing situation. This kind of welfare is more like a "drug" to relieve the pain rather than a "cure" to correct the problem.

It is as if we economically torture the poor (with more poverty) and then provide them with a drug to enable them to endure even more economic torture (poverty)! It pretends to be merciful at the expense of human degradation and humiliation. It does relieve one's conscience but it necessitates perpetual, inefficient welfare that drags down our economy and our collective prosperity. What if we stopped relieving pain (we created) and eliminated the pain instead? What if we stopped focusing on relieving our conscience and focused on what is actually economically best for the B10 group and best for us as well? Win-win!

What if there was full employment so that any entry level worker would have ample jobs available continuously and indefinitely, boom or bust? What if the B10 group were guaranteed equal access to that available employment? What if there was a fair minimum wage ($18+/hr. in 2018) to reward workers enough to be willing to abandon welfare and certainly enough to avoid it in the first place? What if there was an ECA sub mandate to achieve employee participation rate greater than 70% (now 63% in 2018). What if part-time employment was a viable option with temporary fractional welfare support?

This would especially help single parents with preschool children and some disabled or disadvantaged who are struggling with the demands of full-time employment. Part-time employment would provide an intermediate step to help the transition and halving welfare costs is quite an achievement for starters! Now add to this affordable healthcare and affordable education. That is exactly what Humanism and HERA provides for **everyone** and of course it will be available for the bottom 10% group as well. Good economics works for everyone!

The funding savings from the improvements above could be temporarily redirected toward transitional employment support incentives such as health care improvements over welfare levels, affordable education, job training, child daycare supports, disability accommodations, and work transportation benefits. I believe that humans innately prefer independence, self-sufficiency, and pride over welfare. They will instinctively move in this direction if the right economic supports are architected, engineered, and implemented.

Unfortunately getting off the addictive welfare "drug" is much more difficult than avoiding it in the first place. So incentives have to be greater and applied longer to correct the problem once it gets started. Keep in mind that there will always be a B10 group mathematically, no matter how prosperous we are. So it is their standard of living and their quality of life that we want to improve with more prosperity.

Also we want to substantially reduce welfare costs to improve prosperity for everyone else as well. Allowing Capitalism to exploit the B10 group into poverty was a harmful and costly mistake! Trying to appease our conscience with welfare only compounded the problem. Good economics works for everyone! But it takes a long time, extra effort, and extra cost to repair the chronic damage of bad economics!

All we need to do is stop Capitalism from punishing the B10 group for being "lazy laggards" and provide economic opportunity for this group the same as everyone else. As 100% full employment is achieved the number of unemployed in the B10 group will shrink drastically and the majority of the B10 group will be employed at or above the minimum wage. This will eliminate the ugly concept of the "working poor" with little or no welfare cost. Moreover if the ECA will recommend special accommodations like custom prosthetics and business incentives for employing the disabled, great progress will be made. The elimination of the bad economics of poverty and welfare are well within our reach.

In my lifetime the "handicapped" have gone from begging on the street to competing in the Olympics! Our economy would be a stunning success if we did as well with prosperity as they have done with disability! Clearly the problem is not with the "handicapped", but rather with a handicapped economic system that must be fixed now!

The Top 10%

Finally to complete the comparison let's look at the top 10% (T10) group's outlook under Humanism as compared to Capitalism. This group is quite varied so let us look at two different subdivisions: first, the lower 8% (80% of the T10 group) and second, the Top 2% (20% of the T10 group). The Top 2% are dominated by perpetual wealth and top levels of corporate management including some newly wealthy.

Perpetual wealth will be reduced gradually over the next 80-90 years until it is eliminated by design and intention as a national economic goal. Management pay inflation will be reduced as well by design, intention, and national economic goal of a 40:1 CEO ratio. While the situation with the lower 8% is mostly beneficial but slightly mixed:

- Income tax will stay approximately the same but will not be eliminated like B90.
- Lower management pay will not be affected by the 40:1 CEO ratio that affects the T2%.
- Most in the group will not be affected by the wealth tax but some in the very top will.
- Most in the group will not be affected by the inheritance tax but some in the very top will.
- Wealth opportunity and moderate wealth achievement will increase by 10 times or more!
- This group will be able to afford extra NF contributions and the corresponding benefits.
- Most self-employed are in this category and they will benefit from the smaller NF deduction (not double taxed).
- Most business owners are in this group and they will benefit from streamlining.
- Most business owners are in this group and they will benefit from eliminating business income taxes.

- Most business owners are in this group and they will benefit from eliminating unemployment taxes, employment training, and recruiting costs.
- Most small business owners are in this group and they will benefit from the new capital supports of Title 9.
- All members will benefit from recycled wealth, new business formation, and new wealth formation.

So over all the lower 8% sub group will benefit on the whole with almost the entire burden placed on the top 2% with the majority on the top 1% and some on the top 2% by design and intention as a national economic goal. Good economics works for everyone even the rich!

In Title 1 we discussed the rationale for restricting our definition and measurement of prosperity to the middle 80%. But it was never our intention to restrict the benefits to this group! Looking at the analysis above clearly the B10 group benefits the most on a percentage basis! While about 70% or more of the T10 (lower 7%) group also benefit as well. So including only the M80 in the measurement method still results in significant prosperity benefits for 97% or more of earners! That certainly qualifies the term "vast majority" as used in axiom 1.

The Common Prosperity

Humanistic economics is all about win-win cooperation between the capitalists and humanity to attain the same mutual goal of common prosperity. Yet the wealth economics of Capitalism frames the problem with exactly the opposite idea: the rugged individualist, motivated by greed, challenging new economic frontiers by exploiting the rest of humanity who are "lazy" and who "just get in the way" anyhow. Clearly this ugly idea paints the picture that the elite are in control and humanity is just an uncooperative and lazy victim.

This is a caveman like idea of economic achievement. If it was a good idea we would still be cavemen. If we do not do better than this we may end up back as cavemen again! Viewing the economy as a venue for personal greed and selfish opportunity to conquer at the expense of humanity is a narrow and unnatural interpretation of the real opportunities inherent in our economy. Much of this confused ugly idea about individualism comes from generations of propaganda and mythical glorification of the "wealthy successful individual". It's time for this narrow concept to expand, including all humanity **inclusively**!

I can remember a TV program of my youth that explored a different rich and successful person each week. The story was always about the same: "a rugged individualist in spite of a hostile world and with little or no help and constant interference, challenges a plodding world with a novel idea and is rewarded for his hard work and perseverance with the financial success he so deserves". This made for an entertaining TV program but it glorified a very narrow, selfish, and unrealistic idea of success in economics. Maybe good TV programming is not necessarily the path that leads us to good economics for all mankind!

I watched the program every week to see if my success hero would come forward and say: "you know I did have a great idea. I worked very hard. And I persevered but I was also very lucky because many others, who did the same or more, were not rewarded with success. Most of the difference between me and the others was just luck, timing, and the rest was the support of my upbringing, education, role models, friends, family, and coworkers who worked as hard as me for less reward"! Unfortunately, I must have missed the week that my humble hero was on the program? Yes it's time for a much better idea!

I am not sure any particular idea is all right or all wrong but some ideas are just more effective in the world we live in or wish to live in. What if we glorified the impact in our lives of our parents and siblings, of our teachers and fellow students, of our friends and role models, and of our coworkers? Not to mention the powerful motivations of our own families? If we changed our individualistic emphasis our success theme would then become: "How to be successful in a wholesome, fair, supportive, and prosperous world" in which **people matter**!

Instead of: "How to be successful in a foul, dog-eat-dog, exploitive world full of lazy people who just get in the way"! You see it really does matter what we wish for and how we frame our success goals. Humanism says our individual success will be much greater if we concentrate on creating and maintaining a **prosperous world in which to be successful**! Rather than concentrating on creating and glorifying greedy "success superstars" who are obsessed with greed to such an extent that they can even be "successful" in a foul, bleak, and failing world. Notice that **Humanism's idea of prosperity includes wealth but Capitalism's idea of wealth does NOT include prosperity**!

In fact our economy is a beautiful market of synergy where the human producers come together to supply the needs of the human consumers. The beauty is in our duality because we are all both producers and consumers! Our economy is of the people, by the people, and for the people. Wealth opportunity and success will become much more democratic as well. We no longer need "success superstars" because it is much easier to become moderately wealthy and successful in a prosperous world, with cooperation, ample capital deployment, and constant demand for efficient business ideas and improvements.

Under Humanism every generation will have equal opportunity for wealth creation and wealth achievement instead of the constant depression of perpetual wealth stagnation and corruption. Suppose we define "moderately wealthy" as achieving a household net worth of $10 million by retirement (65). I believe we could achieve at least 10 to 30 times as many such wealthy households using Humanistic principles compared to what Capitalism produces! If you think this seems exaggerated, look first at the number of households Humanism will produce with a net worth of $1 million or more at retirement.

A steady-state economy complying with Titles 6, 7, 8, 9, 11, and 14 applied for a 45 year working lifetime will ensure that the average household has a NF worth of more than $1 million at retirement not including any inflation. This is a profound change over current conditions and our goals for the "moderately wealthy" are achievable as well. It is possible because of new concepts of economic thinking.

According to axiom 2 if the moderately wealthy are 10 times more productive than the average household they must have 10 times the income. So they could easily achieve this goal and accumulate 10 times the net worth! Indeed since the average household's NF net worth is based on a 6.2% deduction the moderately wealthy would only need an equivalent deduction of 62% (10 times) of the average household. Thus the moderately wealthy would only need a minimum of just 1.62 times (62%) more productivity and more income (not 10 times) to achieve this goal provided they maintained the same standard of living as the average earner and invested all the rest (62%)!

So in Humanism the path to moderate wealth is well within the will and imagination of **any** citizen. Once we turn away from this narrow unnatural idea of elitism and exploitation, the path to prosperity for all based on productivity becomes obvious. It also becomes clear that the scale of success achievable with win-win cooperation is much larger than without! Humanism can become the bridge that brings all the "Isms" of economics together into one cohesive, new axiomatic idea!

Humanistic Economic Axioms and Guiding Principles

As stated in the beginning summary we wish to create a much more scientific based economic system. Our goal is to change economics into the science of democratic prosperity and sustainable life! To do so we must have a metaphysical goal and a scientific methodology to achieve that goal. First let us state our meta-goal more rigorously as: "We strive to achieve an economy that maximizes democratic prosperity". Furthermore we define democratic prosperity rigorously as: M80 Average Income/Standard Cost of Living. This goal is embodied in the first axiom below called our prosperity mandate.

We also need a set of operating axioms supplemented with a list of guiding principles. The robustness of the system would depend on the strength of the axioms and the guiding principles. Axioms are guiding principles that are so strong, inalienable, and indisputable that their truth is intrinsic and it is virtually impossible to argue against them.

On the other hand guiding principles appear to be true but require extensive debate, study, scrutiny, and testing to ensure their truth in all cases. The first 13 items below are proposed axioms and the remaining 15 are proposed as guiding principles. As discussed in the summary of key ideas, the first five key axioms are believed to be sufficient for a minimum mathematical economic system. And sustainable life is expanded through axiom 6 and item 7 of the Economic Bill of Rights.

Notice that with all these axioms especially the first 6 that the exact goal of each axiom is an exact and precise mathematical calculation free of any doubt, opinion, controversy, or uncertainty and dependent only on the measured data involved. Of course these data collections and measurements will continuously improve through technology and innovation with better and better results the same as all other engineering technologies. Yet the goals are timeless, exact, and will last and guide us to good economics for thousands of years and more! If the mathematics fatigues you, just review the language description of the 5 axioms in the "Summary of Key Ideas". The meaning is the same in English. Mathematics is just more exact for engineering use.

Humanistic Axioms

1. **The fundamental reason our economy exists is to serve humanity in facilitating the worker/consumer duality by achieving maximum prosperity for the vast majority of mankind.** This is the overall mission statement axiom that we call the "prosperity mandate". Mathematically this prosperity is defined as Index (w) = Average(M80) / SCL where Index(w) is the prosperity index as a function of wages (w). Average(M80) is the middle 80% of annual wages (w) averaged, and SCL is the annual standard cost of living basket defined in axiom 4 below. Then the maximum of the prosperity of Index(w) is determined with the differential equation dIndex(w)/dw = 0 excluding all lesser inflection points. Together these calculations specify the exact goal of axiom 1.

2. **Equal value wages must be paid for equal productivity of equal quality.** This axiom is called the "equal pay mandate" and it determines all wages, salaries, and other labor costs worldwide once we chose an initial condition (starting point) of axiom 4 below. The formula that represents this axiom is: W = M x P which means that wages are directly (linearly) proportional to productivity with a straight line slope of "M". The optimum value for "M" can be determined easiest by applying axiom 1 to a nation's macroeconomic data as discussed in topic "The Role of Profits in Humanism" where the value of "M" is estimated at .95 for developed nations such

as the USA (5% profits). It is presumed that fair trade dictates that all nations of equal development would have equal values of "M" if they trade. Review the detail discussion in Title 6 and "The Role of Profits in Humanism" to refresh these ideas.

3. **Equal currencies can buy equal cost of living goods and services in their local economies.** This axiom is referred to as the "equal currency mandate". For any two currencies X and Y the exchange rate ratio converting Y to X is: $X / Y = SCL(x) / SCL(y)$ where SCL is the standard cost of living basket of goods and services discussed in axiom 4 below. Review Title 7 to refresh these ideas.

4. **The minimum wage paid must be equal or greater than the minimum cost of living to achieve life, liberty, and the pursuit of happiness.** This axiom is referred to as the "minimum wage mandate". Every nation can choose their own minimum wage even zero and they can change it at will. However the minimum wage chosen must be a point on the $W = M \times P$ line of axiom 2. For the USA our constitution and its Economic Bill of Rights mandate that the minimum wage $MW \geq SCL(usa)$ to enable life, liberty, and the pursuit of happiness. Likewise other nations will establish their own criterion. Review Title 6 and Title 7 to refresh these ideas.

5. **Wages should increase at least to compensate for product price inflation, not caused by wage inflation, plus any increase in labor productivity.** We refer to this axiom as the "wage increase mandate". This concept can be understood as a wage and salary correction formula: $W\% \geq Ip\% - Iw\% + P\%$. This formula was discussed in more detail in topic Title 11a along with an exact wage and salary correction mechanism that can be driven by this correction formula.

6. **We must ensure that the current depletion cost of natural resources worldwide truly represents their future replacement cost and that pollution costs truly represent their future elimination cost**. This axiom will accomplish

sustainable prosperity and life on our planet using a depletion/pollution tax formula suggested later in this topic.
7. In Humanism the only legitimate shortages are labor (population) and natural resources (including "anti-pollution").
8. Prosperity shall be measured by the ratio: M80 average income/Standard Cost of Living.
9. Economic controls should integrate monetary, fiscal, tax, and investment policy.
10. A democratic economy should maximize prosperity not just profits.
11. Maximizing efficiency and productivity is the most effective way to maximize prosperity.
12. Supply/Demand markets are a fundamental tool and can be improved by hybridization.
13. Perpetual debt is taxation without representation.

Humanistic Guiding Principles

1. The Economy must serve humanity, not humanity serving the economy.
2. Long term B90 income should equal or exceed 70% of national income.
3. Long term B90 wealth should equal or exceed 50% of national wealth.
4. Underemployment is much less economically harmful than unemployment.
5. Perpetual wealth is an unearned and an undemocratic privilege that defies equal opportunity.
6. Taxation should be designed to maximize prosperity not just realize revenue.
7. Old age financial security should be achieved by individual gains from economic capital formation.
8. Businesses should reinvest profits if possible, otherwise minimize product costs.
9. Businesses should be optimized for maximum efficiency using prevailing labor rates.

10. Prosperity cannot be achieved by profit or revenue optimization of each individual business.
11. Formula controlled democracy has the highest quality of representation compliance.
12. Greater axiomatic guidance allows more use of engineering based economic solutions.
13. Supply/demand markets should be free of corruption, distortion, extortion, manipulation, and exploitation.
14. Economic Investment should be encouraged above other forms of risk taking like speculation.
15. Prosperity is a generative benefit. Prosperity induces more prosperity as a self-fulling prophecy.

You might ask if these principles are complete or redundant. As mentioned in the "Summary of Key Ideas" all of economics could be covered by the first five axioms. So I have given them special weight. Mathematicians are very concerned with using only the minimum number of axioms to synthesize a system of thought. Yet I am more of an engineer than a mathematician. I want economic reform now.

I want a system of thought that benefits mankind as soon as possible. Mathematicians could work on this puzzle for years or generations. Fortunately there is no risk in having too many axioms and there is no risk in misclassifying an axiom or a guiding principle. I will leave it to the mathematicians and philosophers to clean up the deficiencies and redundancies as part of our ongoing new study of Metaeconomics.

The ideas of metaeconomics began with Carl Menger in the mid 1930's and were furthered by Fritz Schumacher in *Small is beautiful; economics as if people mattered* (Schumacher, 1973). Unfortunately both of these efforts failed to integrate humanity and humanism with mathematical axioms into a cohesive system of thought. They were able to see the flaws in the ideas of wealth economics but they were unable to replace them with the ideas of prosperity economics instead.

They could not see that the purpose (goal) of economics is prosperity but they knew it was not wealth. Furthermore they could not see that prosperity could be achieved through scientific and mathematical discipline even if human greed continues indefinitely. Instead they believed we would have to wait for or encourage a new morality for mankind that would eliminate greed. They were unable to envision engineering methodology for that meta-shift. They did not see that if economists focus on **macro-prosperity** for all humanity then it will be tolerable for greedy businessmen to still focus on **micro-profits**!

My sense of urgency pushes me to move forward with applying the axiomatic ideas mentioned above for the benefit of all humanity as soon as possible before some catastrophic consequences make the matter mute. The above five axioms clearly indicate that the labor market and the currency market must be revamped immediately and methods to do this are proposed herein. See Titles 6, 7, 11a, and "The Role of "Free" Markets in Humanism".

The Pollution & Depletion Market

There is a third market change that is still a work in process which is the depletion/pollution market. I believe that we need the 6th key axiom added above together with embedded market hybridization. The world's natural resources/pollutions are the key to the future prosperity of all generations and all nations. I believe that global warming and pollution can be best managed using ideas like resource depletion.

In other words: depletion is consuming desirable things we can't replace while pollution is producing undesirable things we can't get rid of. This inverse parallelism suggests the idea of an imaginary substance called "anti-pollution" that can be combined with pollution to neutralize it. Our planet has only a limited amount of this pollution neutralizing natural resource. Consequently pollution can be treated as a depletion of the natural resource of anti-pollution.

My best guess at a wording for the 6th key axiom is stated above. This axiom will balance depletion and pollution for all future generations nationally and internationally. The embedded market mechanism needed for hybridization could be a depletion/pollution tax formula agreed to by all nations as part of a new global trade agreement. For example the depletion tax percentage on each natural resource extracted could be equal to the percentage of cumulative depletion to date. Thus if the depletion of silver available on our planet is 80% then the tax on silver extraction would be 80%. So the tax would start at zero and would approach 100% as the resource is fully depleted.

Of course more sophisticated formulas could be used. Taxes are an inevitable and necessary part of economics. So why not use taxes as a useful tool to accomplish our valuation and sustainability goals as discussed in Title 22. If depletion and pollution taxes generate more revenue than needed we can use tax rebates to balance our revenues.

There is no reason that depletion tax revenues could not be tax neutral. So this tax proposal will not require any increase of total taxation. It would only replace other taxes or be offset by tax rebates. I hope you will join me with more ideas and help integrate other ideas that already exist? Luckily we have a little more time to address this issue but we must proceed forward with implementing the other reforms now.

Once we are successful initiating the democratic reforms, depletion and pollution reform will be much easier with an established base of democratic, axiomatic economics. Furthermore without these democratic reforms, depletion and pollution will never be addressed! The 85'ers and their 1%'er friends live in a perpetual privileged "glass bubble" of their own creation where the plight of humanity and the plight of our planet are *An Inconvenient Truth* and they are in no mood for inconvenience that might reduce their privilege or their wealth!

So it is our responsibility! Humanity must "do the wishing" for the world we wish to live in. Otherwise we are stuck outside the perpetual privileged "glass bubble" they wish to live in. We will die of resource starvation, choking on pollution while they watch from the "glass bubble" unconcerned because they know this system is rigged so they will lose last! They are blind to their blindness so we must lead them out of this darkness for our joint benefit without their permission and without their cooperation. A democratic, axiomatic economy is our only hope to maintain successful human life on our precious planet.

Alternative Communism?

It is interesting to note that Communism, the unquestionably worst economic idea of all time, was proposed by Karl Marx as a desperate reaction to the draconian obscenities of Capitalism. Out of the chronic desperation inspired by Capitalism, Communism became an instant worldwide popularity success and captured the majority of the world's desperate imagination for about 75 years from 1917 to 1992.

If the "beauty" of Communism was the solution to Capitalism, can you possibly imagine how "ugly" the problem must have been? Yet, post Communism, Capitalism has now attained the status of "high religion" through its profit paradigm! However the truth is that they are both variations of elitism. Capitalism promises wealth (and power) for the few capitalists at the expense of the exploited many while Communism promises power (and wealth) for "the party" few in exchange for "the equality of equal poverty" for the masses.

So I have often wondered: could we have separated the goal of Communism from the methodology? Perhaps Socialism wondered the same question? Let's start by identifying the key goal of Communism. Marx's main goal was simple: free the lower class from poverty and give the poor a fair chance to participate in the economy. In retrospect this goal was wholesome, democratic, and would be embraced by any democratic economic solution such as Humanism or Socialism.

Now let's look at the key methodologies of Communism intended to accomplish this goal.

1. Communists believed that they could only achieve their goals with harsh state totalitarianism.
2. Communists believed that they could only achieve their goals by eliminating property rights. So all property would be owned by the State.
3. Communists believed that all individual efforts should be communal. All individuals would share in the effort and all would share equally in the reward: equal poverty.

Clearly the communists believed that it would be necessary to fight inhumane and draconian Capitalism with **even more** inhumane and draconian Communism! This draconian flaw was the undoing of Communism. Yet the fact that Communism was quickly embraced on a broad scale and lasted so long was a tribute to the wholesome nature of its goal. Notice how Humanism has even better goals and a much better methodology! So draconians have no role in good economics.

Axiomatic Capitalism?

The Humanistic system discussed above is a very robust system.

Let us try to contrast Humanism and its prosperity paradigm with Capitalism and its profit paradigm. To do so we will have to take license to create a systemic definition of Capitalism because one does not exist. Worse yet in modern day economics, Capitalism has attained the status of the "high religion" of profits. Capitalism is defined as everything that is good and nothing that is bad. From that voodoo status, a systematic definition would seem to be a big step down!

Nevertheless, let us try to reconstruct Capitalism as a systematic idea. Working backwards, I will try to identify the key principles of Capitalism as proposed below:

1. Profit optimization will create the most successful economy.
2. Perpetual wealth concentration is good for the economy.
3. What is good for business is good for the economy.
4. Greed is good for the economy.
5. Undirected supply/demand markets can be exploited to resolve all economic issues.
6. Exploitation is a necessary part of economic development and growth.
7. Wealth "trickles down" to form investment that returns profits for more wealth.
8. Investment must be carefully rationed to ensure that labor is always in sufficient excess to keep labor cheap perpetually.
9. Capital is always a chronic shortage so we must constantly pamper and mollycoddle the capitalists, their enterprises, and their management to the greatest greedy extent possible.
10. The Golden rule: "Those with the gold, rule".
11. Only the elite Capitalists are principals of the economy, thus the term "Capitalism".

Reverse guessing the mission statement or most appropriate metaphysical goal of Capitalism is a little more difficult. First notice what the meta-goal is not. It is not prosperity since all of the key principles are contradictory with that goal to some extent. We also know that profits and wealth accumulation must be key ideas of the goal. So my best guess for a meta-goal statement is: "We strive to achieve an economy that maximizes the accumulation and concentration of wealth by the capitalists acquired and perpetuated through profits". Thus we have Capitalism and the profit paradigm.

Scrutinizing the above goal statement and the key principles of Capitalism, we can see why Communism was so popular worldwide! The goal statement and the key principles are intrinsically narrow, undemocratic, selfish, exploitive, and elitist. No wonder the outcome was that 85 = 3,500,000,000! As stated before, Capitalism is flawed at the most basic meta-level. We do not need to abandon Capitalism; we just need to fix it with the prosperity paradigm and metaeconomics!

Capitalism only allows humanity to participate as a victim of the economy! Capitalism does not allow humanity to participate as a principal of the economy. Only the perpetually privileged capitalists are allowed to be principals of the economy and the only goal of the economy is to maximize their concentrated wealth. Instead Humanism will maximize sustainable prosperity for all mankind worldwide!

This situation is indicative of a "system" whose only real guidance or principles are greed and privilege to benefit a few self-declared elites! There is no other guidance just chants, slogans, pseudo principles, and greedy goals. You would think that at least the "free" market chant would be used as guidance where it could. But that is not even the case. If the "free' market produces what the greedy elite want then it is good. If the "free" market does not produce what the greedy elite want then they are privileged to rig, distort, extort, exploit, and manipulate the market until it does produce exactly what the greedy elite want!

So the outcome is always the same: "what the greedy elite want". Do you think that a system of economic aristocracy based totally on selfish greed to benefit a small minority could possibly be sustainable in the long term? The greed culture of Capitalism is totally preposterous and it is sustained with a mindless, irrational propaganda of "greed is good" and "foul is fair" no matter how insane the results are. Science led us to the success of our modern day civilization not greed or privilege and science must lead us to sustainable prosperity as well! Scientists, Mathematicians, and Engineers from all fields must have the courage to stand and come forward now. They must join and lead this renaissance of Economics to achieve our economic "moon".

The Planetary Risk

I find it amazing that some of our most beloved and respected scientists have suggested that successfully continuing humanity as a species may require abandoning our economically ravished and decimated planet within the next 100 years (O'Callaghan, 2016). Do you think there will be room in the rocket ship "glass bubble" for all of us or just the economic elite? Can greed and privilege lead our future?

Why would some in our scientific and engineering community abandon all hope that an economic renaissance could be engineered to save our species and our planet with a systematic, scientific, economic plan for successfully inhabiting our planet earth indefinitely? Apparently even our scientists and engineers have been hoodwinked and brainwashed into believing that economic science and economic engineering are impossible! They seem to endorse the hopeless notion that we are doomed to be victims of the economic alchemy of greed and that our only hope is changing planets within the next 100 years!

It took humanity many millions of years for our species' evolution to adapt exactly with planet earth. Why would we expect to find another planet well suited for us? What was wrong with our old planet? Were the sunsets too beautiful or the amber fields too golden? For our part which human flaws would we not take with us to the new planet?

Here is a great idea! How about changing economics with a renaissance instead of changing planets with a rocket ship? Our problem is caused by bad economics; we don't need a better planet! We need better economic governance based on the discipline of economic science and economic engineering! I can only hope and pray that we leave our "greed is good in economics" idea and our ugly capitalistic economic theories of foul "wealth economics" behind!

Or better yet, out of desperation, we could pretend to embrace this silly planetary exodus which would not include us anyway. Perhaps our only hope for earth and its humanity is getting rid of our economic elite. Let's send them to some far galaxy in search of the "Holy Grail" planet under the pretense of perpetual reward for their perpetual privilege! Surely they would want to keep greed and privilege and accidentally save us, left behind, from the curse of their corruption!

Avoiding Class Warfare

One might wonder: "How could we have class warfare in a classless democracy?" The answer is that our political system is a conflicted democracy because our economic system is not a democracy yet. The ideas of Humanism and the reforms of HERA are attempts to resolve this conflict and bring democracy to our economic system as well in a harmonious and unifying way. In the beginning summary I referred to this basic conflict as our democratic dichotomy. We must resolve this!

Until we succeed, we are still confronted with the economic rule of the economic privileged class. The economic privileged class have done very little to avoid class warfare over the last several hundred years. That is why we are in such a "lose-lose more" exploited condition. So it is unlikely they will avoid such warfare in the future unless they fear they might be on the "lose more" side of the losing profit paradigm.

Lucky for all of us, Humanism is a win-win paradigm with plenty of benefits for all. Prosperity is a generative benefit. In other words prosperity generates more prosperity; it is a positive feedback loop with a loop gain (Engineering 101). Economics is **not** a "zero sum game" as Capitalism would suggest where the privileged winners must win at the expense of the exploited losers. Instead we can all win-win together in harmony. We do not need the ugly exploitation of wealth economics nor do we need its old 1850 draconian profit paradigm.

The truth is that the greedy, in an effort to win, exploit the losers to such an ugly extent that the losers cannot contribute to the inherently generative common prosperity. So the "winners" lose a little and the losers lose a lot! Yet the "winners" think they are "winning" instead of losing! They seem to be confused by the 85 = 3,500,000,000 formula.

Predatory capitalists are stuck on a bad idea because they intended that their "gains" would come at the expense of our losses. So they are quick to jump on the fallacy **that increasing our losses will further their "gains"**. They are convinced that "foul is fair and fair is foul in economics" (Keynes, 1931). Remember the factory owner that never figures out what is wrong? But blinded by greed the capitalists cannot see the lost prosperity opportunity or the lost generative possibilities. They are sure that exploiting us will benefit and satisfy their greed.

Capitalists cannot see that on the macro scale humanity is both their **only customer** as well as their **only producer** and that harming and exploiting your producers and customers is **not** a prosperous long term idea for successful commerce! This amazing blindside of Capitalism is motivated by greed and achieved with its ugly intoxicating stupidity!

Their greed allows them to be unable to realize that their capitalistic gains would be substantially greater if they had abandoned their exploitation and supported general improvements in the prosperity for their producers and their customers in a win-win fashion. Yet they are blind to their blindness. So instead they think they are winning and that the 85 to 3,500,000,000 score proves it! While actually the 85 to 3,500,000,000 score is glaring proof that Capitalism has failed on a mammoth scale to provide the common, generative prosperity for all humanity that would have increased their capitalistic gains substantially more. They can't see prosperity creates more prosperity!

Can you imagine the possibility that the meager amount of prosperity that we have achieved so far from greedy Capitalism was actually an accidental, unintentional "mistake"? It was achieved primarily because of humanity's amazing resilience and perseverance under foul, unfair, and draconian circumstances perpetuated for centuries by greed!

Can you also imagine that the capitalists are working hard as we speak on "improvements" to Capitalism that will eliminate the possibility of this "mistake" altogether? Clearly wealth economics is out of control and our professional economists are too corrupted by wealth power to fix it! There is no other choice. We must intervene and implement a democratic sustainable economy that maximizes the prosperity for the vast majority of all mankind indefinitely as axiom 1 mandates now!

It is time to abandon the greed insanity of "fair is foul and foul is fair" as a failed economic idea. The heydays of 1850 Capitalism are over. We need a much better paradigm for economics than "greed is good". We need a scientific, mathematical formulation for economics that establishes formulaic goals and objectives that our economy should be designed to achieve using standard engineering technologies and methodologies. We need to stop pampering and mollycoddling wealth power as if they were our infant economic children. It is time for a new age of **"economics as if people mattered"**. I am ready are you?

Crisis Responsibilities and Liabilities

I do not think anyone could deny that we are in the midst of a serious long term economic and financial crisis. Aside from a chronic lack of prosperity, the crisis has three identifiable subcomponents: 1) The sovereign debt problem 2) the unfunded liabilities of Social Security retirement, and 3) the unfunded Medicare retirement liabilities. In fact every nation is facing these same types of issues. In the discussion of HERA above we clearly put the financial burden for the solutions onto the wealthy class in the form of inheritance taxes, wealth taxes, and income taxes. Perhaps it would help to defuse these class warfare fears if we were to analyze the responsibilities and liabilities for this crisis.

First we should ask: who had fiduciary responsibility in these economic matters? Our choices are between "the non-wealthy class" (B90) and "the wealthy class" (T10). It is sort of a "no brainer" isn't it? Clearly the wealthy class especially the perpetually wealthy by their very multigenerational nature had primary long term fiduciary responsibility. After all perpetual wealth will fail if our future is financially flawed. So they had a vested interest and were in the best position to appraise the problems and they were in the best position to institute solutions before the problems reached crisis proportions.

However instead they used their dominant wealth power and political voice to shout down any wealth taxes forcing chronic deficits that caused these problems. The middle class was simply exhausted and could not shoulder any further tax burden without breaking their back and collapsing the economy. Instead the perpetually wealthy allowed and encouraged the idea of perpetual debt that would provide them with perpetual interest income and cause humanity perpetual harm.

This harmful idea says that sovereign debt is a special kind of debt that can be passed on from generation to generation without the permission of representation. Yet our Constitution prohibits perpetual debt at the individual level but our Economists assured us it was ok at the national collective level! Yes. Our Schools of Economics stood idly by and our constitutional Justices could not see the looming constitutional crises. Worse yet our Scientists and Engineers said "it's not our problem"! So they stood by unsure of how to contribute and participate technically.

Consequently our debt principal grew so large that each generation can only afford to pay the interest cost for their entire lifetime and then hand the **full** principal to their children to do the same for their entire lifetime and continue this process of "hand-me-down" debt forever! My generation benefited from the one-time proceeds (deficits) of the initial debt but all future generations will suffer the cost of the debt burden without any debt proceeds to help them. They will suffer not just once but over and over again generation after generation repeating **forever** or until our economy and our nation are inevitably destroyed.

It is important to understand that this unfair injustice cannot just be corrected later on when our children and grandchildren realize what we have done to them. It will be too late! They have no way to "charge back" the cost for this debt to my generation because they don't have an "economic time-machine" to go back and fix the bad economics of my generation. Likewise there is no way for our children to refuse to pay the debt because they will have become the new sovereign bond holders as well as the new sovereign debtors. They will be both the liability benefactors and the liability beneficiaries locked in a trap.

They could only refuse to pay themselves causing total collapse of their worldwide financial confidence system. They are just hopelessly stuck with the bad debt, unfunded liabilities, and empty promises of my generation that cannot be fulfilled! What is even more stunning is that all of our top Schools of Economics either wholeheartedly endorsed this ugly idea as good sound economics or they did little or nothing proactive to stop it! If our Schools of Economics are not responsible for promoting good economics, who is responsible?

My generation could not afford to pay one penny towards the principal even though we had the benefit of all the loan proceeds to help us. We spent the loan proceeds as well but still could not pay on the principal. Our children and their children will have no loan proceeds to help them so they will not be able to pay down the principal either. Instead like my generation they will not even be able to pay all the interest!

Rather they will be forced as we were to increase the principal (more debt) just to survive a little longer, increasing the inevitable economic collapse! This is a truly diabolical trap whose perpetual harm is so ugly that it is beyond human comprehension! It is a harm that just keeps on harming "endlessly" like the punishment of the Greek god Sisyphus! So it is important to understand that the reforms proposed in HERA will not be effective if we do not act aggressively to implement them before this debt insanity spirals totally out of control and fails.

Perpetual debt is a "poison pill" ingested by my selfish generation that is certain to destroy our own children or grandchildren! None of us would have approved of this ugly idea if we had not been constantly assured and reassured by the perpetually wealthy and their economic representatives that this foul scheme was good sound economics! Do you still think this ends well for humanity if we do not intervene? Clearly this is out of control and our economists are too corrupted by wealth power to fix it! We must intervene and fix this systematically.

To make matters worse, it is a matter of fact that during the period over which the crisis developed the perpetually wealthy class benefited enormously while the non-wealthy class suffered substantially. In law, for a fiduciary to benefit from losses of those entrusted to him is considered criminal negligence! This represents a fiduciary failure on a flagrant scale. If our top universities had provided the professional representation we deserved and denounced these practices we could have reversed this perpetual debt fiasco before it got out of control!

A second key question is who had "deep pocket liability" the wealthy or the non-wealthy? That question is also a "no brainer" isn't it? Clearly the perpetually wealthy class has deep pocket liability in these matters. Right or wrong they are the only ones who can afford the solution! Indeed, clawing back the increase in wealth of the wealthy class during the problem period may be sufficient to offset most of the cost of solving these problems. Do you think this perpetual mess will magically fix itself if we do not intervene? We cannot afford to wait when the stakes are so high. Let's have the courage to do what our children and grandchildren would want us to be brave enough to do!

My intention with this analysis was not to find fault so much as to make a sincere and reasoned plea to the perpetually wealthy class directly. Please, acknowledge that you take responsibility in these matters and that you are the only ones who can afford the solution. Step forward with grace and leadership taking responsibility without blame in these matters while that is still an option. Don't wait!

This approach is the best way to defuse the situation. Otherwise this situation will likely provoke outrage and claims of a "catastrophic crime against humanity" motivating in turn a catastrophic backlash! Under these circumstances the benign inheritance taxes and wealth taxes proposed in HERA could be much worse. Thankfully prosperity is a win-win game for all of us once these issues are firmly behind us.

The Role of Profits in Humanism

Because Humanism is based on the prosperity paradigm and not the profit paradigm, the role that profits should play in our economy is possibly confusing or obscure. Furthermore the valuation and balance of profits and labor is the central most important issue in all of economics. So let us explore various ideas and models for the role profits and labor should play in a prosperous Humanistic economy.

The Investment Model

First of all we should understand that all profits are not the same and that this is the key to understanding the profit issue. In the general sense a profit is a currency gain on a currency risk called the principal. The vast majority of all profits come from gaming, short term trading speculation, long term market investment, and economic investment.

All of these financial activities compete among themselves for risk principal from the same sources of available capital not yet deployed. So the risk principal committed to non-economic investment is lost as a source for economic investing. Let's look at each of these financial activities so we can better understand the profit and investment issue.

Gaming could be as simple as gambling but it is usually a much more complex form I called "gaming the system" in Title 25. This involves scrutinizing the system to find flaws or weaknesses that can be exploited using money to make more money by "magnification". And what if we run out of a supply of faults to exploit? There is a law in economics that says if there is a profitable demand then there will eventually be a supply. So be careful what you create a profitable demand for, because a corrupt supply is waiting just around the corner!

Derivatives have become very prone to gaming to the extent that "Tulip Investing" has become generalized on a very broad and massive scale. There are "weather derivatives" where you can bet on the weather. Obviously gaming profits have no economic value and they are a very high corruption risk. They also represent a serious threat to the stability of the financial system with the flood of excess capital.

The important thing to understand is that this kind of activity is just "money chasing money as a way to perpetuate more money" by magnification. Principal is committed to a risk in hopes of a profit yet this activity results in almost no economic value whether the profit is realized or not. No capital is formed, no product is supplied, no human needs are met, and no workers are employed. If money perpetuating more money was good for our economy, the Central Bank could just print the money instead of all this risky dangerous activity! The economic value of this money chasing could actually be negative if we include the cost of lost stability. Speculation is just "capital inflation"!

Short term trading speculation might be based on some skill but it is much easier to base it on some inside information or knowledge that can be exploited. The success of passive investing implies this skill is small. We already discussed the massive speculation and manipulation in the COMEX market in Title 24. After all short term speculation is a "zero sum game" where every winner must match exactly with a loser.

Every time one speculator buys low and sells high another speculator must sell low and buy high to make the other side of the transaction. Since the losers run out of money it becomes harder and harder to find a loser to match up with until natural selection designates you as the new loser. This dog-eat-dog world was the basis for the win-lose idea of economic exploitation that Capitalism adopted and then glorified.

Nevertheless this kind of profit becomes very prone to corruption as the only way to survive. The only slight economic benefit to trading speculation is that a small amount will help the market improve liquidity. Market liquidity is necessary for efficient speculation. Fortunately it is not so important for long term economic investing. More than a small amount of speculation will increase corruption more than it will benefit the market or certainly the economy. So speculation taxes should be implemented to minimize this "capital inflation".

Long term market investing is a mix of some speculation and some investment but it is not economic investment. For the purpose of this discussion we will consider long term to be more than one year. For example in the secondary stock market the values of stocks depend on the earnings of their companies. As earnings increase stocks increase.

So it is possible to hold the stock and realize a gain that is more than just a trading gain. In addition to trading gains there could be capital appreciation. This capital appreciation is not a zero sum game and it is not just speculation inflation. It is based on factors that are related to the health of the economy and the health of the underlying business.

Long term market investing is mostly appropriate to secondary markets. Aside from providing some liquidity as with speculation, long term investing helps establish more selective valuations of companies stock values which can help the efficiency of forming new capital in the primary market. Yet the benefit is very indirect and fractional. So profits from long term market investing are somewhat more beneficial to the economy than just pure speculation profits.

However it is not economic investment because the principal of the investment is not part of any capital formation. The underlying capital of the company was already formed at a prior time. So buying secondary shares is just a change of ownership of old stock not a commitment to future capital formation. In a mature economy such as ours, corporate capital is provided from retained earnings of the corporations with very little from the primary equity markets. In fact these retained earnings are in such a surplus that dividends are paid out to avoid this excess cash hoard from piling up, instead of deploying it.

Economic investment is the pearl of investing for the benefit of our economy. In Title 24 we defined economic investment deployed as any risk of funds for one year or more as capital formation for a business that is intended to produce a product or service by employing people as the main business activity. Some typical examples of corporate economic investment are small business formation, venture capital, equity public offerings, and initial corporate bond offerings.

Profits derived from this form of investment are extremely beneficial to our economy. Furthermore some types of economic investment profits are far more beneficial than others. Refer to the multi-level capital gains tax table proposed in Title 24 above. The lowest taxes are for the most economically beneficial types of investment profits.

Special consideration should be given to reinvested business profits (retained earnings). In the table they are shown as not taxable at all. This is because they are the most important type of profit that any economy can generate. If these profits do not exceed some minimum the business will not even survive. Above that level they become available for the most efficient and effective type of investment namely when a business expands its current products, adds new products, or invests in increasing supply, productivity, or efficiency.

How these profits are motivated and managed is the key to the prosperity of our economy. That is why we restricted companies from paying dividends or stock buybacks in Title 17 above. That is also why we eliminated the 35% tax on profits until they become excessive and tax excess profit accumulation as explained in Title 16. It is extremely important to keep these profits inside the business that produced them and committed to efficient direct reinvestment. This is also the reason we used a two tier wealth tax in Title 23 above, to encourage economic investment and discourage non-economic investing and "re-trickling".

If these profits are returned to the shareholders they will be "re-trickled" back through the fractional "trickle down" process with a minor fraction returned to economic investment and the vast majority used for wealth accumulation, wealth consumption, gaming, profit speculation, or long term market investing. None of which have any economic benefit even comparable to the potential of the profits inside the business. Even if some profits were to "re-trickle back down" to economic investment they would still likely trickle to a lower quality of investment than the original retained earnings we started with!

As stated in Title 17, if these profits are not reinvested then they must be returned through product price reductions that benefit general prosperity. If not they will be taxed away so other entrepreneurs have access to them from Title 9. If shareholders need to realize gains they have liquidity through the public or private markets. So they can sell their shares and realize capital gains that are taxed at a lower tax rate without negatively affecting their business or our economic prosperity.

In Capitalism a significant percentage of profits come from non-economic risk taking and they were mostly used for wealth accumulation and wealth consumption not economic reinvestment. Humanism intends to significantly improve both aspects of this dual inefficiency. Although we will replace the profit paradigm, we should understand that it was the capitalists and the way they made and managed profits that caused the problems not the economic profits themselves. The old paradigm of wealth economics focused on profits because they generated wealth and seemed to satisfy our greed urge.

So greed dictates that all forms of profits were considered of equal benefit since they all created equal wealth. This is the essence of the paradigm of wealth economics and its "trickle down" justification. On the other hand the new paradigm of prosperity economics focuses on profits that generate economic prosperity and discourages profits that do not generate economic prosperity. So there is an optimum profit.

This is a clear and distinct conceptual difference and it is a good way to contrast the two paradigms. Prosperity economics is fundamentally superior to wealth economics. Understanding and managing economic investment and reinvesting the profits are the keys to a prosperous economy that we so want and so deserve once we find that optimum!

The Profit Model

Finally let us consider a general economic model to expand our economic control systems discussed in Title 6, Title 11a, and Title 23 regarding profits and labor. In the simplest model annual Gross Domestic Income (GDI) is composed of the sum of annual corporate profits plus total annual human labor earnings. In our compensation model of Title 11a we will only control, using monthly corrections, the annual wages and salaries portion of total human labor leaving the smaller balance of labor to track using the relative market mechanism.

For a given GDI (or GDP), if labor earnings decrease, profits will increase and if labor earnings increase, profits will decrease. This interrelationship between income from corporate profits and income from human labor is at the heart of the economic democracy issue. It is like the old "New Deal" idea of FDR; Humanism rebalances corporate profits and human earnings in a much more humane and democratic way consistent with the axioms to achieve widespread prosperity.

Within limits we can achieve any given target GDI goal with a choice of balance between how much is profit and how much is labor. In a simplified formula GDP = GDI = Profits + Labor. We do know how to achieve increases in productivity that improve GDP and GDI. However we do not seem to know how to balance profits with human labor to achieve maximum human prosperity, the goal of axiom 1.

Indeed wealth economics insists on driving down wages and salaries in hopes of increasing profits as the only goal. This unbalanced economic idea is usually called cheap labor. The "high religion" of wealth economics insists that profits are a "good" cost while labor is a "bad" cost even though labor contributes about 95% of GDI. Yet wealth economics insists that labor should be exploited lower and lower so profits will go higher and higher. As this continues profits continue to increase while wages and salaries decrease proportionally in this downward spiral without equilibrium which will eventually collapse.

However prosperity economics presents a very different idea: that humanity's labor is the key economic ingredient (scarcity) to achieve prosperity because humanity is the **key principal** of our economy (axiom 1) and humanity produces and consumes virtually all of our GDP. On the other hand profits are **only** important to the extent that they produce sufficient capital deployment to maintain business revitalization, offset capital depreciation, and increase productivity. No other capital is needed in a minimal growth economy. So profits are only important if there is a shortage of capital and an excess of labor. Yet as we have discussed the true situation is the **exact opposite**.

Except for a small margin to ensure stability there is **no economic benefit** for profits in excess of the minimum requirements. Any such excess is just bloat and fat in the economic system intended to pamper and mollycoddle big business, big banking, Wall Street, and perpetual wealth. Worse yet this bloat and fat directly diminish labor's share and thus directly reduce prosperity which is the exact opposite of our goal!

Moreover humanity can and will supply much of its own investment requirements through retirement funds as discussed in Title 9. Beyond the minimum, excess profits must be "mopped up" or "throttled out" of our economy or they will create inflation or excess wealth concentration, perpetuation, and corruption. Remember the humanistic principle that the only legitimate shortages are labor, natural resources, and antipollution. Capital availability and deployment will **never** again be shortages if the economy is controlled properly by the ECA using guiding axioms to eliminate the employment rationing of cheap labor!

Let us look at the underlying philosophy. Wealth economics seems to be based on the notion that capitalists are precious to our economy beyond limits and that humanity is economic trash of no corresponding value. Thus humanity is an exploitable victim of our economy instead of a principal and our only principals are the capitalists as we have already discussed. After all "fair is foul and foul is fair in economics".

Instead of maximizing general prosperity, wealth economics minimizes general prosperity in a misguided effort to maximize profits for the capitalists. This misguided exploitation simultaneously reduces, diminishes, and depresses all of our economy's producers (humanity) and all of our economy's consumers (humanity) in an effort to benefit the elite capitalists. This self-inflicted economic sabotage is the "blind side" of the profit paradigm of Capitalism that Humanism will end.

On the other hand Humanism intends to make all humanity principals of the economy **including** the elite capitalists. We believe that there is **no** economic benefit to pampering and mollycoddling the 85'ers and their 1%'er friends to the extent of creating worldwide nausea and disgust. Instead we believe that increasing the quantity of capitalists by adding new capitalists is far better for our economy than increasing and perpetuating the wealth (fat and bloat) of the few elite capitalists we already have. Review the discussion in "Capitalism vs Humanism" about the vast creation of millionaires and the huge increase of the moderately wealthy ten-millionaires achievable with our Humanism.

Indeed we believe that all humanity should be capitalists in a democratic style. There is no need or benefit to expanding the elitist style of Capitalism anymore. Furthermore Title 9 achieves that goal with 100% trickle-down efficiency and stability! Of course if we treat the elite capitalists as draconian as they have treated us we could upset the balance of profits and labor to the inverse extent causing a similar collapse. Who would suggest that we intend to treat them with the same greedy stupidity as they have treated us? Not Humanism!

Can the ECA find an optimal balance between corporate profits and human labor that will accomplish the prosperity mandate of axiom 1 while maintaining economic stability? Let's answer that question by building a simple model based on the data for the 1970 to 1980 period our most prosperous era. During this 10 year period corporate profits averaged about 6.6% of GDP (Ryle, 2015) and this value is close to the average for the last 45 years prior to 2008 as well. Based on the analysis discussed in "What Would Adam Smith Have Thought?" we know that using the formula of axiom 5, corporate profits were overpaid by 1.45% compounded annually for the 45 years of the last working generation (Greenhouse, 2013) totaling an 88% loss.

Thus axiom 5 could have been satisfied if aggregate corporate profits were set at 5.15% (6.60% - 1.45%) of GDP. Would 5.15% profits cause economic collapse? No there were many times since 1950 that corporate profits have been below 5.15%. In 1986 profits were at 3.5% while they were 11% in 2014 (Ryle, 2015) and they continue to rise.

Furthermore as discussed in topic "Trickle Down "Magic"" there are many ways to increase economic investment and the NF national retirement fund is just one example. Moreover wealth taxes could have a direct control over economic capital availability and deployment as discussed and demonstrated in Title 23. Finally the wage correction mechanism ($W\% = Ip\% - Iw\% + P\%$) of Title 11a ensures that wage inflation will be 0% eliminating any wage inflation/deflation concerns.

We could have throttled back corporate profits even more since axiom 5 is an inequality equation (at least equal). As we further decrease corporate profits, labor and prosperity will further increase. Eventually product price inflation will start to increase and capital funds available for economic investment will shrink below minimum stability levels. Thus somewhere between profits at 5.15% and profits at 3.5% is this optimum profit for economic prosperity mandated by our axiom 1.

Where this point may lie exactly is an engineering judgement call for the ECA and it could change over time. We will just approximate the result at 5% in our simple model. This control parameter is an aggregate macroeconomic measurement and correction. Any microeconomic corporation or business can achieve any profit within their ability. There are no individual corporate restrictions or regulations.

Only the aggregate sum of all corporations will be managed at the 5% macro level. This profit/labor control would have eliminated the profit surge that occurred since 2008 while prosperity was devastated (Ryle, 2015). Notice that this profit control system is also a protection against excessive profit erosion that could be caused by extreme competition in a maturing, minimal growth economy such as that we are proposing. Review Title 14 to refresh these ideas and concerns for profit erosion.

We already discussed a short term (monthly) wage and salary control system in Title 11a based on axiom 5. We also discussed a short term (6 month average) control system for labor utilization in Title 23. Now we can consider a longer term control system for profits and labor balance. Our goal would be to manage prosperity by keeping the 3 year running average of corporate profits at about 5% of GDP while achieving our sub mandates including our productivity goal of 2%.

Then the $W = M \times P$ equation of Title 6 would have the slope "M" at approximately .95 (1.00 - .05). The ECA would monitor the goal measurements and make corrections using Title 11a and the profit tax of Title 16 slowly over a 3 year running average. Besides achieving our prosperity mandate these controls would dramatically stabilize and standardize our economic performance to an extent that our current Central Bank/interest rate system could only dream of achieving. And it would stabilize and standardize our international economics as well.

In summary the profit paradigm treats profits as the only goal to be maximized by greed and it treats labor as a mere cost to be minimized even though nearly all of humanity depends on labor for its prosperity. On the other hand the prosperity paradigm treats profits as a controlled cost at 5% of GDP and it treats labor as fixed by axiom 2 and 5 at 95% of GDP. So our new system will be much more stable and prosperous.

The International Outlook

We could even use this structure to standardize trade subsidies. For example "developed" nations could use the .95 line with 5% profits we just discussed, while the "balanced" trade nations would use the .94 line with 6% profits, and the "emerging" nations could use the .93 line with 7% profits. This would provide higher profit returns and lower labor cost incentives for developing economies in an organized, standardized, and systematic fashion. Thus all nations would conform to the same general linear concept (W = M x P) where only one key parameter "M" (line slope) varies to achieve temporary subsidies.

This will make the transition from subsidized to unsubsidized economies much easier to measure, achieve, and manage. Therefore the straightness of the line (linearity) provides the most important characteristic of national productivity fairness consistent with axiom 2. This national linearity is nationally fair and easy to achieve internally in the early stages of any of our most undeveloped trade economies.

However the slope of the lines is more related to profit/labor balance and international trade fairness associated with axiom 1 and 3. So achieving linearity first and foremost and then gradually achieving line slope M by optimizing profit/labor balance subsequently will provide the most cohesive international solution. This transitional concept is a vast improvement over the "Export Led Economy" concept of predatory Capitalism. See further discussion in "It Is Time for a New World Order" and the discussion about the Gold Standard in Title 6.

Notice that in Humanism product price inflation is mostly caused by average corporate profits increasing because of price increases without an underlying increase in cost or increase in efficiency. We discussed in Title 11a how wage inflation can be directly controlled and even eliminated by the wage and salary control system. However product price inflation has no direct price control system proposed herein.

Yet it does have indirect controls: axiom 5 compensates wages and salaries, profit taxes of Title 16 will indirectly reduce profits above 5%, labor utilization controls of Title 23 will indirectly smooth the business cycle, and the profit control system (above) can indirectly help control product price inflation in the aggregate. So I do not think product price controls will be necessary but they could be provided.

As with our current system the only direct control of price inflation is competition that keeps costs down but the ECA can shift price inflation to wage inflation to the extent that they believe it is appropriate. Our old wealth economics system has no wage or price controls only the rigged market controls discussed in other topics.

Our new system has direct wage controls and indirect product price controls. Clearly our control of inflation, although not perfect, will be much stronger than the current Central Bank/rate system. Furthermore if it needs to be even stronger, any corporate price increases not justified by non-labor cost increases or component cost increases can be directly taxed by adding a tax under Title 16. I did not propose such a tax because I do not think it will be needed. To the contrary I think that as our world economy becomes more and more mature increased competition will begin to drive down profits to unsafe levels unless we have the protection of a built-in profit control system discussed above.

Let's look forward now to our minimal growth sustainable future that we discussed in Title 4 and Title 18. Once our labor participation rate reaches steady-state our sub mandates reduce to the product inflation rate plus the productivity rate. Now we can achieve zero wage inflation if we think that goal is optimal so our inflation adjusted growth would be about 2% because of productivity plus any product price inflation. As growth further reduces we will likely reduce our product inflation target goal slowly from the current goal of 2%.

My guess for the future is that we will find that a 1% inflation goal mostly from product price inflation is the optimal balance resulting in nominal 3% total growth (2% + 1%). Time and the diligence of the ECA will tell. It is time for a new "New Deal" that will accomplish balance between profits and labor that will stabilize our economy, adapt to minimal growth, and maximize prosperity for all mankind as axiom 1 requires. For the first time in economic history fair will be **fair** and foul will be **foul** in economics! This would be a true breakthrough renaissance and it will begin our new era of metaeconomics.

Science vs Regulation

It would be easy to confuse the control systems that we have been discussing with more business regulation that is already excessive as a backlash to wealth economics. As discussed in the summary there is a "bubble" of anger and frustration with wealth economics. Sadly our political institutions do not know what to do to fix the system. Our economic institutions are too corrupted with wealth economics. And our scientific institutions stand idly by confused on how to participate.

Consequently our political system either does nothing, creating more frustration, or they succumb to rages of petty business regulation that further depress prosperity and make the problem worse. Thinking medically, this kind of regulation would be like trying to cure a disease by outlawing its symptoms! Thus we could cure Tuberculosis by outlawing coughing! Our politicians and bureaucrats make up long lists of symptomatic do's and don'ts for businesses to follow and then haggle about them without understanding the underlying problem or the systemic solution. We must focus on what to **do** not what to not do.

To avoid this frustrating trap Humanism will take a top-down active approach. Instead we have identified our goals at the axiomatic level first and foremost so we can carefully scrutinize these axioms as first principles that guide us to sound economics before we get mired in the do's and don'ts of petty regulation. Therefore once we have the correct first principles, the vast majority of regulations are **no longer** needed.

Instead our first principles guide us to good economics axiomatically. Our first principles guide us under all conditions past, present, and future, nationally and internationally, towards what to do and how to do it. Titles 14 -21 are good examples of applying this methodology. It is like the relation of science and engineering. Good science provides general concepts that already contain all the solutions to our problems.

We only need to do the engineering to reveal the specific solution for each situation. For example Maxwell's famous equations contain all the solutions to problems of electricity and magnetism. We only need Electrical Engineering to reveal the specific solution for each situation. It is not easy yet the historical results have been spectacular. So we can expect Economic Engineering to produce the same spectacular yet difficult results! Therefore our axioms are like Maxwell's equations and Economics is like Electrical Engineering. Provided we follow the axioms we are assured that the results will be as correct as the axioms are irrefutable. It's time for economic science to guide economic engineering to maximize sustainable prosperity for the vast majority of all mankind in a stable safe fashion without petty business regulations!

The Role of Professional Economists

The goals and methodologies of Humanism in general and specifically for HERA are simple and direct. The primary goal of HERA is to establish an independent department of government called the ECA to professionally manage our national economy with cohesive technical control of monetary, fiscal, tax, and investment policy. The ECA's primary mandate is to maximize democratic prosperity as mandated by axiom 1 and implemented with axioms 2 through 5 and eventually 6.

This goal includes a mathematical definition specifying exactly what democratic prosperity is and exactly how it will be measured and managed. Four other sub mandates are defined as well. There is nothing vague or uncertain about the goals, the methods, or the intentions. The guiding axioms are clear, concise, and mathematically unambiguous. They also guide the ECA in developing ongoing national economic goals and achieving them for many generations into our exciting future. So our path is clear to axiomatic metaeconomics.

History of Prosperity

With this clear cut future objective in mind, let us go back in time a little and ask a serious question and explore the significance of the likely answer. The question that comes to my mind is "before HERA and its ECA who was responsible and accountable for our prosperity and how well did they perform for us?" In other words before this book who championed our prosperity? Here are some possibilities.

1. Our democratic government
2. The economic privileged class (wealth power)
3. The economics profession and institutions
4. The labor unions
5. Nobody

Of course the likely answer is anticlimactic. "Nobody" it would seem is the likely answer, but why? Why did it take so long to get started with prosperity economics? The "nobody" answer is not very satisfying at all although it may be the most true. So let us look more closely to the other four answers and try to understand what role they played or did not play in this quest for prosperity. For this purpose we will restrict ourselves to the last 100 years or so of economic history.

The labor unions were the closest on the list above to support ideas similar to democratic prosperity. They focused primarily on fair wages achieved by power negotiations and power strikes as a means to achieve **defensive prosperity** by offsetting some of wealth's excess power. The other three institutions, our government, the economic privileged class, and the economics profession all began the period 1917 to 2017 in strong, near 100% opposition to the labor union cause.

Initially the government approved the use of its Pinkertons as goons by the economic privileged class to beat the unions into submission or death. And the economics profession assured us that this was certainly necessary to protect our capitalistic economy from destruction. There were a few economists who defended the movement but they were just marginalized, branded "dirty commies", and ignored as irrelevant. Their "public execution" set the stage for any future help from future generations of economists who could have inspired our renaissance.

In spite of the initial 100% institutional opposition, during the years from 1917 to 1970 the unions developed as a grassroots movement to their peak in the 1970's. Government support of labor increased to about 40-50% during this period. While the economic privileged class still 100% opposed unions, the economics profession gave less than 10% support to unions or democratic prosperity ideas. After the 1970's the government, the privileged class, and the economists jointly discovered that the lawless global economy could be exploited using cheap labor and cheap currency concepts to drive down wages and destroy the effectiveness of the unions in the USA and worldwide.

Slowly the unions were neutralized until the union movement is just a shell in 2018. This eliminated the only balancing force humanity had to achieve equilibrium and stop the downward wage spiral. After the union peak in the 1970's, the concentration of wealth soared and the middle class was economically devastated. We went from "new deal" to no deal. Of all the institutional groups discussed, the behavior of the economics profession represents the most disappointing and disillusioning of all. I must admit personally that this betrayal was a callous bitter defeat for my youthful fantasies of professional integrity.

Professional Integrity

During the latter half of the 1960's I was a college student on a NSF fellowship studying Electrical Engineering and specializing in computer circuits. Our space quest for the moon had emboldened me. At that time I was very enamored with my profession, Engineering, and I felt empowered that we could do anything that was scientifically possible for all humanity as an ongoing professional achievement.

I was also enamored with other professions like mine believing they were equally motivated like scientists, the medical profession, and many others. I felt part of a grand professional community where I knew that my profession "had our back" when it came to engineering and I believed that the other professions "had our back" too regarding their professions, particularly the economics profession. I felt that each profession participated in the grand camaraderie and together we could take humanity to the moon, any "moon" humanity chose to achieve!

My naive idealism was not prepared for the possibility that greed and power could corrupt a profession intellectually and academically to the point that it was **unable to act on mankind's behalf**. The medical profession has a minimum Hippocratic standard called: "do no harm". What would the world be like today if the economics profession had just lived up to the same minimal standard? It is truly mind boggling!

You decide for yourself. Do you think the economics profession has your back? Did they have the union's back? Do you hear economic professionals incessantly discussing prosperity for all and how they will achieve it? How could economists not be held accountable and responsible for prosperity? If they are not responsible for prosperity, which profession is responsible? Whoever was responsible, their professional performance was certainly amazingly poor. Indeed they became architects of economic corruption rather than champions for engineering **offensive prosperity** for our worldwide economy!

Are you aware of any corruption problem in the field of Geometry or Mathematics? How about any corruption in the field of Physics, Chemistry, Biology or any of the other sciences? Are there two different laws for gravity one the wealthy (85) and one for the non-wealthy (3,500,000,000)? Do the wealthy contribute billions of dollars each year to our scientific academic institutions based on their support of one gravity formula or the other or one chemical formula or the other that better pampers and mollycoddles the wealthy and powerful?

Why do the wealthy have a right to donate $ billions each year to ensure wealth economics is promoted academically at the expense of prosperity economics? Why does the quest for truth in economics need the guidance of greed and corruption? It seems that these scientific fields are immune to wealth influence while the field of Economics seems to be drowning in it. It's time we throw them and us a lifeline!

What other professional field openly espouses the manipulation, distortion, extortion, and exploitation of vulnerable humans as "good market economics" where the greater the vulnerability, the greater the exploitation? Yet economists do exactly this by ruthlessly applying the market mechanism that was intended for zinc and soybeans to the vulnerable human labor market under the guise of "good market economics". What other field of study denies science and openly strives to be a self-proclaimed social (non) science for wealthy elites?

Perhaps economists realize that professional economic science would end the greed, exploitation, privilege, and corruption that is so popular with their privileged elite benefactors. To make matters worse economists insist on rewarding the exploiters directly with the profit proceeds of the exploitation. This would be the Hippocratic equivalent of a doctor who surreptitiously and deliberately exposes his patients to diseases so they can be treated by him later at the highest profit! This is the equivalent of "do whatever harm achieves the highest profit" which is the exact opposite of "do no harm". This contrast is stunning!

Intellectual Corruption

This represents a "circle of intellectual corruption" in which our universities brainwash our economics students with the propaganda of wealth economics that exploits "the many" to benefit "the few" as the proper application of market economics! After all we have been told that whatever is good for wealth power is good for our economy so humanity automatically gets good economics without needing representation - right? Armed with the "free market" chant and the "what is good for business…" slogan, the students then proceed with their career practice and confirm the economic "soundness" of this approach at the pleasure of perpetual wealth and the privileged elite.

"The elite few" then contribute $ billions in rewards to the universities to perpetuate the circle for the next generation. As long as "the many" are deprived of economic representation this circle will perpetuate. It is time to end this malicious alchemy with an economic renaissance. It is time for a scientific basis for the field of Economics with a professional and academic culture of ethics that prohibits wealth influence by the power of Wall Street, big banking, big business, and perpetual wealth! It is time for a long overdue economic renaissance.

I have difficulty grasping how economists actually see their role in the overall economy? Others who were perplexed by the same question have pointed out that economists behave as if they think they are supposed to be "cheerleaders" (David Wiedemer, 2011). They are hired cheerleaders for the economic privileged class to promote wealth economics. They act like cheerleaders for big wealth, big business, big banks, and big exploitation. Yet they are unwilling to represent us!

In terms of my favorite equation, 85=3,500,000,000, economists seem to always identify with the 85 side of the equation and not with the 3,500,000,000 side. They are always the first to pander to the 85 side but seldom if ever do they represent the 3,500,000,000 side. It is as if they have decided that the 85 side is more important to the economy than the 3,500,000,000. Yet, lopsided as it is, it is still an equation! Maybe, just maybe, economists find the 85 side of the equation to be better benefactors than the impoverished 3,500,000,000 of humanity?

Out of frustration and outrage, I have a direct challenge to make to the intellectual and academic community of economists. I have claimed that axiom 2, the "equal value pay for equal value work" rule, is axiomatic for economics in the first degree. I claim that it is the "law of gravity" for economics or like the famous "Maxwell's equations". I claim that it is inalienable, indisputable, and intrinsically true. I further claim that it is quantitative in nature and provides great guidance to structuring economic systems and solutions such as the labor market and global trade, the two most important markets of any economy. So axiom 2 should be a guiding light for our economy as with the other axioms. Yet they are not even allowed as concepts in Capitalism.

My challenge is as follows: prove me wrong or show me that your educational teaching and your textbooks already gave this claim the status of a key axiom like the attention you give supply/demand markets. Any key economic axiom would have several chapters or more dedicated to explaining it such as Title 6, "The Role of Profits in Humanism", and "The Role of "free" Markets in Humanism" herein. Show me those chapters in your Economics 101 textbooks. If you cannot meet this challenge, your hands are "dirty" when it comes to issues of prosperity specifically and economics in general. It is time you dealt with this issue by giving us the representation we deserve!

I know you will not be successful in arguing against the axioms. Furthermore I think you will be hard pressed to find any textbook that even mentions this axiom incidentally. After you justify yourselves on this one simple issue, we will be happy to hear your views on reaching democratic prosperity for the vast majority of humanity whom you find so hard to represent! We're ready for a renaissance. Are you?

The Role of "Free" Markets in Humanism

Capitalism relies on the "free" market idea as the single most important economic idea of Capitalism. The "free" word has become divisive and deceptive in recent years but it originally meant that prices would not be set by governmental rule which was the practice in feudal times. Today "free" means free from any controls that would stop distortion, manipulation, exploitation, and extortion. Since Humanism is an offshoot of Capitalism it's no surprise that Humanism embraces the supply/demand market idea as a fundamental tool as stated in axiom 11 in the discussion "Humanistic Economic Axioms and Guiding Principles". Notice that Humanism has a better balance of 12 other axioms and 15 other guiding principles to present as well.

However Humanism integrates the supply/demand market idea in a different way and with a different balance than Capitalism so we should investigate this difference in great detail. To make our investigation more difficult, the wealth economics of Capitalism in recent times has achieved the status of "high religion" and "free" market is the main chant. On the other hand Humanism has a strong emphasis on scientific principles and scientific methodologies.

Unfortunately, this **economic religion** is very intolerant of scientific improvements and new ideas. The high priests insist that the slogans and chants be kept exactly, and they insist that no improvements are allowed. Any attempt at improvement is considered heresy creating a war-like split between competing ideas even though the two ideas are 99% compatible. We will have to accommodate this unfortunate situation because it will probably persist until wealth economics dies.

Before we consider the humanistic application of supply/demand markets and some of our humanistic ideas, let us look in detail at the shortcomings of the capitalistic implementation of supply/demand markets. Because of Capitalism's full embrace of wealth perpetuation and wealth concentration together with its almost religious fanatical endorsement of greed, the "free" market idea has become intellectually corrupted. The most important corruptions are market manipulation and market exploitation. They sound similar but they are very different even though they are usually used in conjunction to achieve maximum economic corruption and privilege for the self-declared economic elite.

Market Manipulation

Market manipulation was discussed somewhat in Title 24 and 25. The sad truth is that our finest and brightest minds have been hired out of our universities for exorbitant salaries and bonuses to come up with ways to manipulate the markets and make money, with money, for money by magnification. This capital inflation is further motivated by a flood of capital availability seeking yield with no economic place to go (deployment). Our children could have easily cured cancer and then some with the same capital and labor resources but they were enticed to work on "fast buck" schemes and scams for the privileged wealthy class instead. There are many schemes and new ones are created every year. So let me discuss just one commonly used scheme so that you get the general idea without spending too much time on a sad ugly story.

This generalized scheme is used mostly in the secondary stock market but it could be used in the commodity or bond market with some modifications. In this scheme the manipulator wishes to drive the market price down so that he can do the "buy low" part of the speculator's favorite "buy low and sell high" transaction. You can probably imagine for yourself a "sell high" version of the same scam.

First he would use "short selling" to sell a large amount of the stock he has chosen to victimize even though he does not own any such stock. He would present the sale to the market in a most unprofitable way. He would deliberately dump the borrowed shares on the market all at once in one big sale that will overwhelm the exchange system which might even have to stop further trading until his sale is digested completely.

This makes it look like a panic sale by an insider who knows something nobody else knows yet and he is in a hurry to get out quick before everyone else finds out the same bad news. This gets a lot of attention and drives the share price down until the market can absorb the big "panic sale". The manipulator has already calculated or has privileged inside information on how many automatic "stop-loss" sell orders are outstanding at what trigger price. That is how he picked the victim stock and the timing in the first place. Sure enough as he calculated the drop in price he engineered is enough to trigger some of the automatic stop-loss sell orders. The price continues to drop which triggers even more stop-loss sales and so on in a cascading fashion.

Another mechanism is exploited during the next phase. That mechanism is called "momentum trading". This is a style of trading that uses computers to look for certain price changes that meet certain well known patterns and automatically trade on them while the momentum is fresh. Thus the momentum traders' computer algorithms are tricked into joining the "bandwagon" with their short selling that further reduces the price and confirms their momentum trend down.

The manipulator now begins to buy the cheaper stock slowly in small parcels that will not be noticed until he buys several times the amount he originally sold to start the scheme. He paces his purchases carefully to make sure he does not reverse the trend he started. Nobody even notices because it just looks like any other day in the stock market. Just think: we could have cured cancer but we got junk like this instead! Even if this scheme is successful it will only produce capital inflation and more capital availability that was already excessive and undeployable. Wall Street wins and humanity loses – a familiar score!

The general point here should be clear. Capitalism relies on markets like this to provide the valuation mechanism for all of economics. However these "markets" are easily manipulated by wealth power and wealth corruption to support a wide range of valuation outcomes. In engineering this idea would be explained by what we call "Signal-to-Noise Ratio" (SNR). Most markets have a very low SNR. In fact they are almost all noise (volatility) and very little signal (fundamentals)! Look at the stock market for example. Unfortunately the noise is easily manipulated by wealth power to create almost any valuation they want temporarily! So wealth is inflated without any economic benefit at all.

Market Exploitation

So much for market manipulation, unfortunately market exploitation is even uglier. Exploitation is achieved by rigging a market so that it looks like a market but it is actually an exploitation machine! It is rigged so that one side of the supply/demand market has an inherent advantage that allows this advantaged side to use the market to ruthlessly exploit the disadvantaged side and make it appear the market did this exploitation! One of the most common types of exploitation is extortion where labor is threatened with loss of jobs unless they work for lower wages. Another type of exploitation is distortion such as used in the currency market. The global economy is a good example of both extortion and distortion on a massive scale.

Remember the discussion in topic: "The Invisible Economic Slavery". Indeed, since the free market chant and economic religion say markets are always "good", this is not exploitation at all. It is just "divine guidance to a better economic world"! Let us explore in detail two examples first for Capitalism and then for Humanism. I think this is a great way to contrast them and show you what Humanism is all about and show you how Humanism is like Capitalism and yet very different than Capitalism. The contrast will help explain the ideas of Humanism.

For this purpose let us use two examples we have already discussed somewhat, the labor market and the currency market which are the two most important markets in any nation's economy. Furthermore, remember the discussions on economic axioms. Axiom 1 clearly separates humanity from exploitation. Any market affecting humanity directly must be carefully scrutinized to avoid victimization. Moreover axioms 2, 3, 4, 5, and 6 clearly stipulate special mathematical rules including the labor markets and the currency markets. Now we will show how those markets will be enhanced to meet those axioms.

The Labor Market

The single most important market in any economy is the labor market (95%). The labor market consists of workers who supply labor to the businesses who have demand for it to produce goods and services for the greater economy. Right away you can see that this is an inherently unbalanced market that is easy to rig as a power based conflict instead.

First it balances the supply of an individual worker against a large and powerful company demand. It is easy for the powerful company to "divide and conquer" the workers one at a time. This is a huge imbalance of power at least 100 to 1 to maybe 10,000 to 1 or more.

Secondly there is an inherent imbalance in the vulnerabilities of the supply side and the demand side. Workers need to work in order to survive and keep their families alive and free from suffering. It's a human existential predicament that businesses do not have and this unbalanced vulnerability is easily exploited and manipulated.

Thirdly businesses can affect rationing of available labor demand by increasing unemployment both at the local level and through policy at the global level. The larger the unemployment, the larger the advantage is for the business side so unemployment is rationed at about 5% minimum to achieve equilibrium at the lowest pay possible. Finally, this is a zero sum game. Any reduction in wages goes directly to benefit business profits and thus management wages and bonuses as well as profit returns to shareholders. So the incentives for exploitation are high and the rewards **go directly to motivate the exploiters**. The greater the exploitation the greater is the reward. It is a perfect win-lose exploitation machine that is rigged to have a high yield payout for management and the shareholders at the direct expense of humanity!

We already know from previous discussions that what begins as a "win-lose" game quickly becomes a "lose-lose more" game once positive feedback and generative losses are accounted for. As we discussed with market manipulation notice how exploitation of the market mechanism supports a wide range of labor valuation outcomes. This "noise" is easily exploited by wealth power! The observations above were well known and well understood by the late 1800's when labor unions were first formed in a desperate attempt to better balance the exploited, manipulated, and unfair labor "market" based on power.

Prior to labor unions, we had a market consisting of a single force opposed only by resistance that had no equilibrium resulting in a persistent downward spiral of exploited wages. Yet our economists did nothing to create a fair, humane, and prosperous equilibrium! Instead they enabled wealth power to exploit the labor market to create and sustain cheap labor under the pretense of "good market economics"!

In fact it is not a market at all! It's a power based conflict rigged to look like a supply/demand market! The labor union movement provided a crude and marginal counter force to offset some of the exploitive forces but it was costly to the economy and the workers with only fractional success. The labor opposition set up a condition of constant conflict and barbaric warfare between labor and business to see who had the most brute power. It is hard to achieve prosperity in the middle of a constant power based, "Law of the Jungle" war that pretends to be a market! No wonder "fair is foul and foul is fair".

Worse yet some workers were partially protected by unions and others were not. To be an unprotected worker on this "battlefield" was like having a target painted on both sides of you. Nowhere to turn! Keep in mind that our democratic government, the privileged wealthy class, and the professional economists all opposed the unions and eventually neutralized them using the exploitation opportunities of a lawless global economy. Unions were tolerated to reinforce the market facade but they were neutralized once they were no longer needed to keep the market scam going. Does this sound to you like the path to prosperity?

The truth is that the only intention of this power struggle was to eliminate the unions and exploit the labor market so wages could be kept at the cheapest labor possible. We are now back to the Dark Ages of the 1890's without even crude and fractional equilibrium. Do you think this story will end well for humanity if you do not stand and intervene? Do you think we should just wait for this perpetual mess to magically fix itself? Will exploitation lead to good market economics?

Zinc does not laugh or cry. Zinc does not dare to die. Zinc does not get hungry or thirsty. Zinc does not need to be sheltered from the elements. Zinc does not get afraid and cannot be threatened or intimidated. Zinc does not love and care for its children or worry about their welfare. Zinc is not vulnerable to the exploitation of desperation like poverty, homelessness, and starvation. Most of all zinc does not hope and dream of a more prosperous and humane economy for all!

So why does the economic religion of wealth economics insist on extorting the human labor market the same as the supply/demand of zinc in the name of "good market economics"? Auctioning off human labor like we were bidding on zinc is exactly **human slavery**! It denies humanity the right to **inclusion** in our economy as principals rather than **exclusion** from our economy as victims! We need a better idea!

What is good economics for zinc and soybeans is **not** necessarily good economics for humans as axiom 1 reminds us! Humans are complex economic entities both rationally and emotionally so we have a much greater impact on our economy. Humans are not just another resource to be exploited. Humanity provides all the production of goods and services for our economy and we provide all the consumption of those goods and services as well. It is time for "**economics as if people mattered**" (Schumacher, 1973). Clearly humanity's role in our economy is that of a key (95%) economic principal or majority economic "shareholder" not just an exploitable economic commodity!

Why are we victims of our own economy instead of its principals? The answer I am sad to say is in the malice and greed of a few people against humanity simply because bad **economic religion allows them to get away with it**! They are enabled by bad economics, armed with the "free" market chant, and encouraged with the "what's good for business…" slogan! This malice and greed will not end waiting for evolution to genetically improved morality. Economic inhumanity to humanity has **no** limits unless **we define and we enforce those limits with metaeconomics** based on human rights and proactive axioms!

Clearly this is out of control and our economists are too corrupted by wealth economics and wealth power to fix it! We have no other choice but to intervene and modify the economic system so that inhumane treatment is inherently impossible, easily detectable, and quickly correctable proactively by the ECA! That is exactly what the 6 axioms of metaeconomics do for us. So this modification is simple, easy to implement, and highly effective making our renaissance easy to start.

What is even more profound is that the modification will have almost no negative risk impact on the current economic system because it will be implemented as a "layer on top" of the existing system at the meta-economic level. Remember the summary discussion about the meta-level change. The market system will be kept intact as is with no micro change. The only change is at the macro level above the micro market level so that the market cannot even "see" any changes or any risk!

The Currency Market

The currency market is the second most important market of any economy. This is particularly true now that the global economy is so important. In addition to the wage exploitation of cheap labor discussed above, the global economy also uses cheap currency as the primary means to achieve trade advantage and further exploitation. As we have discussed before, this market is highly rigged to the advantage of the host currency's central bank. Lawless trade makes this possible.

Each central bank can print any amount of money and sell it for other currencies thus deferring the inflation consequences. This means that each central bank can cheapen its currency at will unless another larger central bank opposes. As we discussed with market manipulation notice how exploitation of the market mechanism supports a wide range of temporary valuation outcomes that are easy to manipulate.

This situation is easily exploited by wealth power! As others have explained this is certainly a complex high stakes "poker game" that could escalate into currency wars or trade wars (Rickards, 2011). But like the labor "market" it is not a supply/demand market at all! Nevertheless the "free" market chant continues mindlessly with massive worldwide exploitation disguised as "market economics".

Well the disgusting part is over. Now let us look at what Humanism has to offer these same two distorted and extorted market situations. Both of these market situations can be tamed with a similar technique that neutralizes the manipulations and the exploitations yet keeps the powerful benefits of the supply/demand market in place. So we will embed our supply/demand market system inside an axiomatic shell.

Hybrid Markets

I described this method earlier as a hybrid market. Both Capitalism and Humanism realize the power of the supply/demand market mechanism. But only Humanism finds a way to transcend the market's limitations while maintaining the market's benefits. Before we further describe the solutions in detail, let us review some easy theoretical background ideas that can help us understand the hybrid market idea.

The hybrid market idea came from a common technique used for synthesizing electronic circuits. Suppose we wish to process an input signal and produce an output signal. One common technique is to split the input signal into two components and then process the components using separate circuits each circuit specialized for its component.

Then the processed components are recombined to produce the final output. One very common example is separating the AC (changing) signal from the DC (not changing) signal, processing them separately and then recombining them. Another common example is separating the video and audio signals, processing them with special circuits for their type and then recombining them to produce the final output.

If this explanation sounds too electronic that it becomes distracting, I can generalize these ideas mathematically and sound more economic. Suppose we have two or more entities like wages (or currencies) X and Y ... and we wish to determine their valuations. Capitalism would just use a supply/demand market and tolerate the limitations of the result. Especially if they designed the limitations intentionally! But our new Humanism suggests a different approach. So let us break this problem into two different components or valuation equations. So suppose we chose these two valuation equations as: $X/Y = A$ and $X + Y = B$.

So we have divided the problem into two separate components, the ratio and the sum. But we do not know "A" so we use the supply/demand market to resolve the ratio "A". The market resolves all of the relative ratios X/Y of all of the variables something no equation could ever hope to do – that is the power of the market!

Furthermore the market solution gives us hour by hour real-time updates so that X/Y changes are realized almost immediately. So it tracks well in the short term but it can be manipulated and exploited in the longer term tracking. If we believed in "high religion" we would just apply the "free" market chant and use the market to resolve the X + Y… = B equation as well. Especially if we want to realize the ugly exploitation we had designed in or were otherwise benefiting from!

But Humanism says no! Metaeconomics provides us with a better way. Because we have available axioms, guiding principles, and goals that can be combined with readily available data and other measurements to calculate the value of "B" very accurately and resolve the X + Y… = B equation with a measurement and a calculation, **not a market**!

The X + Y … = B equation is just our national labor income equation and "B" is our Gross Domestic Income (GDI) less corporate profits. Review Title 6 and "The Role of Profits in Humanism" for details about the Labor/Profit balance issue. That was how I chose the two equations in the first place. The calculation of the sum (X + Y = B) is not subject to the manipulations and exploitations of the market. So this embedded calculation can track the longer term macro conditions accurately without interfering with the short term relative market mechanism (X/Y = A). We refer to this combination as a hybrid.

Now let us apply these ideas to the two markets that we have been discussing. First the labor market will use the hybrid approach generalized above. To resolve the labor market we must resolve millions of relative X/Y ratios, such as: how much do doctors earn compared to lawyers, plumbers, nurses, teachers, and so on? It is an immense set of complex ratios that could never be calculated or managed in any other way than a supply and demand market.

So we use the market that we already have with only one slight macro-level change. We use the relative market to determine how much lawyers make compared to doctors (ratio) but we use a calculation to determine how much total they should make together (sum). The market resolves only the relative ratios **not** the absolute value that determines Profit/Labor balance. In fact the relative ratio market could never have supplied the correct absolute value. It's impossible! It will only supply the summation which in a rigged perpetual buyer's market gives the minimum wages and salaries humanly possible! So we embed the relative labor market inside a calculated profit/labor shell.

On the other hand Humanism demands the maximum wages and salaries possible without creating wage inflation (axiom 1 & 5). So we calculate the annual national wage and salary income that resolves the absolute value. Then we sum (measure) all the relative wages and salaries and form a scale factor. We use the correction factor to scale relative wages and salaries up or down slightly each month to track the correction formula of Title 11a. This will achieve the calculated Gross Domestic Income (GDI) less corporate profits much like we do to measure and calculate the GDP. So Profit/Labor share is not a market!

Our GDP is not determined as a market! Why should Labor wages be treated like a market when it should be treated like a measurement and a calculation formula: $W = M \times P$ or on the macro level: Labor Wages = GDI - Profits = $M \times GDP$. So our macro wages are a calculation but micro wages are a market! The difference between the rigged buyer's market of Capitalism and the no wage inflation goal of Humanism over the last 45 year working lifetime was a stunning 88% loss of income increase! And it is projected to grow to 129% over the next working generation. See "What Would Adam Smith Have Thought".

Finally we break down the calculation into ten, 10% groups and publish the deviation data once a month. We include an 11th group for management wage inflation and a separate vector of 11 groups for new hires. Employers automatically combine the two solutions into a composite solution when they do payroll by permanently augmenting each employee's current market wage rate with the published aggregate % deviation by pay group. Finally the "pay prevailing wages rule" ensures that the aggregate scaling is statistically distributed correctly for each job classification. So our relative micro-market remains as a wage market but our macro wages are corrected by macro-calculations. Review Title 11a above for details. We will actually use three different calculations for various economic cases:

1) For up to ten year periods or more we can use the differential equation $W\% = Ip\% - Iw\% + P\%$ for national income of axiom 5 in Title 11a which is that wage rates must increase by the product inflation rate plus the productivity rate excluding any wage inflation.

2) For longer periods we have the absolute value equation of Title 11 b which is that income of B90 must be greater than 70% of national income.

3) And for international and national discrimination issues we will use axiom 2 and the W = M x P equation, the equal pay rule of Title 6, and the minimum wage of Title 8.

We combine all three and calculate a small tracking adjustment every month for all ten income categories that each employer must apply to wage rates updated each month. We include an 11th group for management and a separate vector of 11 groups for new hires. Separate vectors could be used for gender and race as well.

Look at the results: no wage inflation, no wage erosion, no gender or racial bias, no wage manipulation, no wage exploitation, protects every worker, and is accomplished with a scientific methodology that does not require strikes, Pinkertons, burning cars or old tires, or any other form of barbaric warfare between labor and management. Removing this barbaric war between labor and management would result in an unavoidable boom in prosperity for all. **Economics as if people mattered**! See more in topic "The Unification of Business and Labor".

Finally let us look at the currency market. Here we will use a similar hybrid technique but we will split the currency valuation issue differently. We know that the market mechanism is highly effective for the short term resolution. So as with wages we will keep the market operational as is except that the nominal daily trading target price will be calculated by the "equal currencies buy equal goods rule" of axiom 3, Title 7 above. This local cost of the standard basket of goods and services together with forward guidance by day will be issued by every host nation and updated whenever the basket cost or the forward guidance changes. This updated info can be used by nation pairs to calculate their nominal exchange rate in real time continuously.

Currencies could be traded in pairs without a reserve currency or a reserve currency could be used for exchange so I will describe the more general method of direct exchange. For any currency pair being traded the nominal price will be defended by the pair of host central banks according to which one bank must print and sell its money to bring the price of its currency down to achieve their currency parity.

No attempt will be made to hold the nominal price rigidly but the price will be allowed to rise or fall below the nominal according to some agreed price elasticity. If the volume is light the nominal will hold. If the volume is moderate the price will be allowed above or below nominal by a moderate amount. If volume is heavy the price can deviate significantly. Once the volume returns to light, the price returns to nominal. So there are two exchange prices target and traded.

Each nation will have limits beyond which they are allowed to let their currency float as the current system does now. Nations that do not participate will exercise controls of their own choice but they may be subject to tariffs if their currency is out of range particularly if their central bank transactions seem to be manipulating the price in the unfair direction. So the new currency market will be a constant daily manipulation by central banks as it is now! The difference is that the manipulation has scientific guidance and controls intended to achieve fair currency values by treaty agreement instead of just manipulation.

This system is far less prone to currency wars than the existing system. Because the measured value is very stable compared to the market, it will help stabilize the traded market. Furthermore the system does not have to be perfect. A 5% deviation from nominal would be huge for a currency yet a big improvement over the deviations we currently have.

Notice that calculations on fair exchange settlement value and tariff rates use the calculated nominal exchange rate which is decoupled somewhat from the traded market rate so that small deviations can be absorbed and tolerated. It is interesting to note that an even cruder solution would probably get acceptable results and the cruder solution is much easier to understand and much harder to argue against.

For example by treaty agreement all Central Banks would be prohibited from selling any currency, especially their own if the current price of that currency is below the measured nominal (already undervalued, so why sell more?) and they would be prohibited from buying any currency, especially their own if the current price of that currency is above the measured nominal (already overvalued, why buy more?). Otherwise there would be no requirements to be proactive and no other restrictions. How could you argue against that?

The two ideas could be combined as well. For example the G8 nations would have to meet both requirements while the smaller nations would only have to comply with the simple requirements. The most important thing to understand is that a currency's relative value to other currencies can be measured with much more stability and less volatility than the market. Combined into a hybrid market they are much more stable and much more accurate than either one alone.

The labor market and the currency market are two important examples of how Humanism is the same as Capitalism and yet very different than Capitalism. The similarity is obvious while the contrast is striking. Clearly Capitalism demands that humanity must serve the economy, while Humanism demands that the economy must serve humanity! This axiomatic metaeconomic difference is profound.

We see that the greed of Capitalism has so badly corrupted the economy that our two most important markets are dysfunctional and exploitative. It's clear that with very little effort Humanism can restore these markets to functionality free from exploitation and manipulation. This is exactly what "free" markets were supposed to be in the first place! It's time! Why not replace **foul** economics with **fair** economics?

Natural Resource and Pollution Market

As explained in the discussion on economic axioms there is a third market area that needs to be addressed per axiom 6 and item 7 of the Bill of Rights. That market is the natural resource/pollution market. It is economically flawed with the silly idea that natural resources are "free for the taking" and that our planet is a "free dump" for pollutants.

Of course this flaw results in massive misallocation and consumption of natural resources and excessive production of "no cost" pollution on a worldwide scale. Is this intellectual failure what we expected from "good" economics? How could the Economics profession fail so profoundly to provide a system of proper valuations for profit, labor, currency, natural resources, and pollution? As with profits, labor, and currency we must ensure that the current depletion cost of natural resources worldwide truly represents their future replacement cost and that pollution costs truly represents their future elimination costs!

I believe that we have a little time left to fine-tune a solution for resources and pollution. I believe we can correct this market flaw using a hybrid depletion/pollution tax formula agreed to by a trade treaty. I hope others will join the discussion and work out the details. Global warming and other types of pollution can likely be addressed using a similar mechanism. Otherwise the ECA will be charged with identifying a solution as part of its early formation responsibilities of the Economic Trade Department. Review depletion and pollution tax ideas in "Humanistic Economic Axioms and Guiding Principles".

In Capitalism only the capitalists are considered principals of the economy. Everything else including humanity is considered to be a resource to exploit. In Humanism all of humanity is considered to be a principal of the economy in a democratic fashion. Humanity cannot be thought of as just a resource to be exploited like zinc or soybeans unless economic slavery is the goal and Humanism rejects that goal.

Axiom 1 demands that humanity is special and must be treated specially. Axioms 2, 3, 4, 5 and 6 specify special mathematical requirements for humanity that we have met by hybridizing the labor and currency markets with embedded controls and we will do the same for natural resources and pollution. We are principals of our economy, **not its subjects**. Humanity does not need any more exploitation and slavery; we need inclusive prosperity through professional Economic Engineering. Yes it is time for **"free markets as if people mattered"**!

The Role of Old Wealth vs. New Wealth

To clarify the wealth issue we must discuss wealth and its role in our economy and in our political system. Notice that all wealth is not equal. Newly created, first generation wealth is quite different from perpetual wealth our main topic. Newly wealthy people are almost always from middle class or poor families and their upbringing has no hint of wealthy behavior or mentality. They are wealthy because they were successful; not just successful because their family was wealthy!

These two situations are almost the complete opposite! Almost without exception, new wealth was driven to perform by a vision of a product, or service, or an idea, or a goal they wished to achieve. They are seldom motivated by greed. In the beginning they see money as only capital to achieve their goal and later they see money as only a way to score their achievement. They have no goal to be rich, only successful.

New wealth opportunity and new wealth achievement are extremely beneficial to the prosperity of our economy! So we must keep alive the hopes and dreams of wealth achievement. The increase in recycled capital deployment and small business capital support of Title 9 should increase new wealth opportunity and achievement substantially more.

There is a key difference between new wealth and old wealth. Old wealth tends to perpetuate itself using money to make more money absent any economic investment, while new wealth does not have capital inflation as an option. New wealth is almost always acquired through successful economic investment. On the other hand old wealth is just passed on from generation to generation like the "golden spoon" of privilege without any criteria for achievement or accomplishment.

Another difference is that the idea of personal wealth is strange and uncomfortable for the newly wealthy and most take all of their lives to get used to wealth. When forming their wills they have mixed emotions as to whether passing wealth to their children is a good idea or a bad idea. They usually do so knowing their children would not forgive them if they did not pass most wealth on to them. Even then many newly wealthy see inherited wealth as so dangerous that they risk alienating their children by minimizing their family inheritances.

Perpetual wealth is quite another matter. Perpetually wealthy are born into wealth and so were their parents for some generations. They know nothing but wealth and they expect it to perpetuate indefinitely. They are usually greedy and take family pride in passing on more wealth to their children than was passed to them. That custodial goal of perpetually expanding their family dynasty becomes their vision and their definition of success. This old idea is a carryover from feudalism.

With few exceptions they are taught to think privilege, act privileged, and expect privileges as their feudal birthright. Our goal here is not to judge them because we do not "walk in their shoes". Yet our goal is to determine what their role is in our economic and our political democratic system and how it should be changed to achieve and ensure prosperity of all mankind in the future as dictated by axiom 1.

The perpetual wealth issue can be summed up with one simple question: what have the perpetually wealthy done for humanity that would warrant such a profound perpetual privilege? The privilege is clear but the justification is quite obscure. Excess capital has no value to our economy. So economists "cheerleading" for the wealthy usually argue that wealth benefits the economy without separate consideration of whether they are discussing the new wealth or the old wealth.

In this tricky sly way economists are able to justify all wealth using the significant contributions of the newly wealthy. When the two groups are considered separately, economists usually have to argue that the "trickle down" from the perpetually wealthy provides necessary capital for the economy. Unfortunately there is never good data showing who trickles, how much they trickle, when they trickle, or where the trickle ends up. And we never consider new ideas that eliminate trickle at all.

In particular how much trickle ends up in economic investing and how much trickle goes to non-economic investment, wealth assets, and wealth consumption? I can only presume that if the data were collected it would be embarrassingly small or non-existent. There are other trickle issues as well. How dependable and reliable is the trickle? During boom times we hardly need more trickle. During risk times does the trickle continue in the face of risk? Or does it frivolously turn to a dribble or stop altogether while the perpetually wealthy hide "under the bed" or "leave town" until the recession or crisis passes?

It seems during our recent 2008 crisis that 10 years later in 2018 the wealthy are still "under the bed". Perpetual wealth has increased substantially since 2008. Yet we still have insufficient economic investment deployed to grow out of the crisis. Something is terribly wrong! Never in the history of economics has "so much capital, in the hands of so few, did so little, for so many". How could our economic professionals and institutions give us such an unreliable, ineffective, unscientific, and inefficient capital formation system and hold their heads up in public? The perpetually wealthy are the only ones who benefit. Frivolous, "now you see it, now you don't" capital is unstable and dangerous for our economy. We need stable sources of capital!

Our "cheerleader" economists also fail to discuss or come up with better alternatives for capital formation. In Title 9 above we proposed that national retirement funds be directly invested in economic capital deployment. These funds are invested with 100% efficiency (no fractional trickle) so that all the funds **go to and stay in** economic investing. So it is stable and reliable **all** the time not just in good times.

On the other hand the trickle-down funds are probably between 1% to 5% or less of wealth principle. That means that fractional trickle-down requires up to 100 times more wealth to get the same economic investment deployed into our economy. How convenient for the perpetually wealthy? Yet it is not an efficient way to manage capital!

In recent years I hear fewer and fewer arguments presented that justify wealth perpetuation. It has probably been abandoned as a lost cause? It seems the current trend is to boldly go on the offensive and argue that wealth accumulation and wealth perpetuation do not hurt the economy so why complain? So privileged perpetual wealth is now a birth right!

This type of argument says that it cannot be proved that the 85 achieved their wealth at the direct expense of the 3,500,000,000. The 3,500,000,000 are just lazy and do not want to work hard like the 85! Why punish the 85 for their "success" when you should have punished the 3,500,000,000 for being "lazy". Ugly greed conquers all problems!

If they were not lazy they would be willing and eager to work longer hours for even less pay! Some do not even have jobs because they are unwilling to "find" them in the "labor Easter egg hunt". This idea is based on a wealth economics theory that I call the "Easter Egg Employment Theory". It says that persistent job seekers can "find" jobs that are "hidden" by the 85 and their 1% friends like Easter eggs!

The implied supposition is that there are more than enough "Easter eggs" for the lazy job seekers to find. If they do not find one, they are just not looking hard enough. This is a great way to obscure deliberate job rationing using interest rates to drive down wages and make it appear to be the "lazy" worker's fault instead of the **failed economic**

governance that it is! If we are dependent on the 85 to lead us out of this darkness, we are blind and we are forever doomed to the yoke of perpetual economic exploitation justified by the feudal birth right of privilege and the right to never ending perpetual economic aristocracy!

Perpetual wealth privilege is the antithesis of wealth opportunity. Wealth must be recycled to create a continuous opportunity for new wealth creation generation after generation. Without new wealth opportunity our economy will stall and collapse under the stagnation and privilege of perpetual wealth. Perpetual wealth privilege is a doomed idea we must abandon with glee otherwise we will be doomed with it! Instead we need a new idea: "**wealth as if people mattered**".

Perpetual wealth has no legitimate role in our economic or political democracy. While new wealth has a very prominent yet restricted role in our economic and political democracy. Recycling wealth continuously to provide new wealth opportunity for each new generation is extremely important to avoid the stagnation of perpetual wealth and achieve the prosperity we so deserve as defined in axiom 1.

However even new wealth is not without restrictions. For example the balanced voice mandate demands that new wealth must be restricted from being used to upset the natural balance of political power that our political democracy and our political Constitution dictates especially "one man one vote", "equal opportunity", and the Economic Bill of Rights. Humanism has a much better idea about the role of wealth in our economic democracy and even in our political democracy as well.

Perpetual Wealth is Perpetual Power and Perpetual Corruption

If it is possible that slavery never ended, maybe it is possible that aristocracy never ended either? After all they are two sides of the same "coin" of privilege. The $85 = 3,500,000,000$ formula certainly looks like aristocracy and privilege to me! In fact it looks like the privilege of aristocracy of aristocracy of more aristocracy! We have been told repeatedly that wealth is power. Even the "cheerleaders" tell us wealth is power. Indeed they insist labor valuation is just a power struggle because they claim brute power is a key guiding economic principle!

One of the key principles of Capitalism is the Golden Rule: "those with the gold rule". There seems to be general agreement on this idea that wealth is power. Yet this is exactly what is wrong with wealth concentration and wealth perpetuation. They corrupt our political system, our economic system, our financial system, and our economic professionals and institutions. This corruption attacks our nation at its very core and it will eventually destroy our political democracy too!

Let us look at our political system. The golden rule idea is in direct conflict with the democracy idea. The two ideas cannot coexist indefinitely. I recently heard on national business news that a wealth proponent (Benen, 2014) had proposed that we change our political system from "one man, one vote" into "one dollar, one vote" so that the wealthy could have their "proper" political power and privilege.

Apparently the privileged class realizes this incompatibility as well and they are anxious to resolve this conflict by replacing democracy with "dollacracy"! See also (McChesney, 2014) for a broader concept. We have managed to struggle with this coexistence until now by having a democratic government and a non-democratic economy. But as the wealth becomes more concentrated and more perpetuated, the conflict is growing to a breaking point I called a dichotomy at the start.

Let us look at another political crisis; I call it the "representation crisis". It is caused by wealth corruption in our political system so that the idea of democratic representation is defeated. Almost everyone I know is aware of this problem and many complain that no matter whom or how they vote, they end up without political representation.

Here is how it works. The privileged economic class uses their wealth power to control the candidates so that all the financially viable candidates are minimally acceptable to represent **them** on the issues of **their** interest. Then they are more than willing to let the voters choose which of the candidates will actually represent the privileged class because all candidates are acceptable. The voters make their choice but they never actually get representation on the issues of interest to the privileged economic class. It is a lot like a "bait and switch" scheme.

The hot issues that "bait" the voters include: gay marriage, abortion, immigration, racial equality, and gender equality. These are the issues that the privileged class does not care about even if they pretend to care as part of the scheme. They will accept any outcome on these issues preferably no outcome at all so that these issues can be reused again as bait in the next election! All the while both candidates quietly agree to satisfy the status quo issues that the privileged class does care about by keeping them off the table such as perpetual wealth taxation, fair trade, fair wages, or other economic reforms we have discussed!

I believe that the feeling of many voters that they are disenfranchised is correct and that this is a symptom of the conflict and corruption discussed above. If the majority became more disenfranchised who became more enfranchised? Of course the wealthy did especially the perpetually wealthy. They assert and maintain their political control using wealth power and opaque representation hidden from view.

I call this representation by a "whisper and a wink". After we elect officials, they get a "whisper or a wink" from the privileged class agents. They get a whisper if they are off-key and a hoodwink if they are on-key. We never know who represented who but they surely did not represent us! So we are left without any representation at all!

Perpetual wealth has corrupted our economy and our financial system as well. We have already discussed the many aspects of economic and financial corruption in the above topics. One aspect that is new to the scene is "too-fat-to-fail". This idea states that if big money gambles on "fast buck" schemes and they fail, it is the taxpayers who must take the loss because these investors are too fat, bloated, and pampered to fail.

In the recent TARP case in 2008, Wall Street had figured out a scam to hide doubtful mortgages invisibly inside AAA rated mortgage backed securities and pocket the quick profit. How brilliant and ingenious! Yet the scam backfired and made all AAA rated mortgage backed securities doubtful – DAH! Billions of humans were harmed substantially on a worldwide scale and yet it was the taxpayers who picked up the bill! Even worse nobody but Bernie Madoff went to jail.

Greed conquers all problems? This AAA rated mortgage scam is a great example of Wall Street greed. The truth is that greed makes you stupid and the greedier you get the more stupid you become. But greed also intoxicates you with superiority so you cannot see how stupid you really are! Every religion on our planet teaches us how dangerous greed is yet Wall Street, business journalists, and economists know better so they persistently glorify it with the chants: "greed is good" and "foul is fair". Clearly wealth economics is morally bankrupt!

This new TARP concept seemed to come out of thin air. This new concept appeared in October 2008 with no prior consideration, debate, or scrutiny that I could find as a concept or economic theory. How could a new concept like this suddenly appear and be totally accepted by our political system in a matter of hours or days? If you're in doubt, this is exactly what corruption looks like, sounds like, and feels like.

How many more concepts like "too-fat-to-fail" are awaiting us in the future? What is stopping "dollacracy" from being approved after a few hours of debate at midnight with a voice vote (no record) to "save" our economy from destruction? Is "dollacracy" that much worse than "too-fat-to-fail"? We are all at grave risk to lose the "war on democracy" that many of us didn't even know had already started. Be forewarned!

The perpetually wealthy want to resolve the conflict by the elimination of our democracy. Humanism intends to resolve the conflict by eliminating perpetual wealth, continuously recycling wealth opportunity for every new generation in the future, and implementing a democratic axiomatic economy based on first principles. Wealth stagnation and atrophy are clogging our economy and destroying the dreams of new wealth opportunity on which our democracy was based.

We intend to recycle this wealth into new economic investment making it available to new entrepreneurs with new ideas for **perpetual prosperity** instead of perpetual wealth. Moreover we will use the excess capital to pay off the economic mistakes of the past and achieve an exciting future for all of humanity. We will use this excess capital to refinance social security, retirement medical care, and eliminate our national debt as well as institute affordable health care and education.

This contrast and difference is clear and distinct! Title 5 and Title 9 describe exactly such a recycle, reinvestment system. The voting decision will be yours provided we act before our democratic government is destroyed and transformed into an aristocracy of the privileged wealthy class. It's time to start our economic renaissance!

The Renaissance of Economics as a Science

One aspect of corruption that needs more discussion is the corruption of wealth power among our economic professionals and our economic institutions. One symptom of this corruption is humanity's total lack of economic representation. Another symptom is the constant promotion of wealth economics instead of prosperity economics. This is a special kind of corruption that I call intellectual corruption. It is very unusual in world history. There are few historical similarities that I can think of and none on the scale we are facing. Here are some similar situations:

1. Global Warming or Resource Depletion, *An Inconvenient Truth*
2. The Cold War Propaganda
3. The "science" of Alchemy
4. Copernicus vs the Church
5. The "Emperor's New Clothes" or an "Elephant in the Room"

These are all situations where some overwhelming power forces the collective majority to openly deny an obvious truth because the truth is not perceived as convenient for the goals of the overwhelming power. Then one day a child says: "the economic Emperor has no clothes"!

Our economic community is severely conflicted by this situation. On one hand they wish very much to satisfy the demands of the wealthy ruling class because they are in constant fear of their power. They fear that their income, their careers, their tenure, and their academic institutions are at risk if they do not stay "on-key". They know they must promote and sponsor wealth economics instead of prosperity economics or they stand to lose $ billions in donations each year. In some cases the wealthy elite have even put their own dynasty's name on the School of Economics so everyone will know who has control.

Consequently our economists have **forfeited their own voice** in the field of wealth economics to wealth power! Instead they have become cheerleading victims of their own abdication! They no longer claim responsibility for our economy. If anything goes wrong it's always Washington's or Wall Street's fault. On the other hand prosperity economics through the new ECA will provide a new professional voice and political authority guided by axiomatic principles open to **all** economists to be heard and have a proactive responsibility **to guide us to prosperity**. It's a true renaissance in economic thinking and action!

Many economists pursuing wealth economics sense that something is very wrong although they are afraid to find out what it is. So they are left to a dangerous dance in between two conflicting urges that has been called "cheerleading". This dance consists of the constant use of slogans and chants that are known to be safe for wealth economics mixed in with a kind of economic "mumbo jumbo" that sounds like complex scientific reasoning but is actually divisive and deceptive.

For example the "free" market chant is one of the most common. But we know now that "free" actually means: free to manipulate, extort, and exploit the market with unrestricted brute power. Yet this is the exact opposite of the: free from manipulation, exploitation, and extortion that it should have been! **So "free" isn't free at all**. This deliberate and deceptive terminology is exactly intellectual corruption in action. It is part of the "fair is foul and foul is fair" double talk! Our renaissance will finally correct this so fair is **fair** and foul is **foul**!

Likewise the most common slogan is "what is good for business is good for the economy". As first discussed in Title 14, the idea of this slogan is that no one, not even economists, need to worry about what is good for the economy because businesses guided by greed and corruption inherently do what is best for the economy automatically!

Thus economists are freed from their professional economic responsibilities to pursue full-time "cheerleading" for wealth economics instead. I will list some of the exceptions we have discussed but a complete list would be impossible since new items would be added daily. These are some of the many things that greedy businesses and management do that are **not** good for the economy.

1. Paying dividends is not good for the economy.
2. Stock buybacks are not good for the economy.

3. Excessive advertising is not good for the economy.
4. Excessive marketing and sales costs are not good for the economy.
5. Low debt/equity ratios are not good for the economy.
6. Consumer credit is not good for the economy.
7. Excessive legal costs are not good for the economy.
8. Excessive cash accumulation is not good for the economy.
9. Unrestricted management wage inflation is not good for the economy.
10. Capital inflation is not good for the economy.
11. Pressure to drive down wages is not good for the economy.
12. Unemployment is not good for the economy.
13. Low productivity is not good for the economy.
14. Low efficiency is not good for the economy.
15. Low "quality" products are not good for the economy.
16. Excessive consumption of natural resources is not good for the economy.
17. Pollution is not good for the economy.
18. Non-economic investing is not good for the economy.
19. Gaming the financial system is not good for the economy.
20. "Fast buck" schemes are not good for the economy.
21. Currency manipulation is not good for the economy.
22. Constantly pampering and mollycoddling wealth power is not good for the economy.
23. $85 = 3,500,000,000$ is not good for the economy.
24. Economic slavery is not good for the economy.

This idea that "what is good for business is good for the economy" is clearly false! The truth is that only science can determine what is good for the economy and science can only accomplish that goal through the guidance of a rigorous axiomatic system of metaeconomics such as that which we have proposed. This system must be free of greed, manipulation, exploitation, and corruption not swimming in it! Furthermore what is good for the economy is not difficult or invasive for a business and it is well within what is reasonable and consistent as a win-win accommodation for both businesses and our joint prosperity.

So we must conclude that "what is good for our economic goals" is inherently what is acceptable for businesses in the aggregate long term. Furthermore any individual "junk" business whose interests are contrary to "what is good for our economic goals" should be absorbed or replaced by those businesses that are compatible. Instead, deliberate rationing of employment created an artificial shortage of jobs that then could be used to justify this ugly capital and labor mismanagement.

We were told that "junk" businesses were better than no jobs at all. How divisive and deceptive! On the other hand Humanism tells us that there is **no** shortage of businesses and that we can **pick** and **choose** with taxes those that are best for our economy and our prosperity while continuing 100% full employment at maximum possible wages! Recall that Humanism proposes this simple economic model in Title 15.

This model shows that there are many more businesses that can be imagined and capitalized than our labor capacity will support. So why waste precious labor, natural resources, and capital on "junk" businesses that are incompatible with the common good and prosperity of the majority? Instead we could have imagined and capitalized businesses that were compatible using the same labor, the same natural resources, and the same capital consistent with item 6 of the Economic Bill of Rights. So our economic dichotomy is just **Truth** vs **Power**.

The use of chants like "free market" and slogans like "what is good for business is good for the economy" are underlying symptoms of the collective dishonesty and intellectual corruption that is prevalent in the economics profession. These underlying symptoms are like big "turds" proving the presence of a powerful "elephant in our economic room".

Maybe Humanism can disrupt and provoke the economic community into having a momentary intermission from the insanity of the "dangerous dance" long enough to collectively realize that the "economic emperor has no clothes"? Maybe then we could begin the renaissance of economics as a disciplined axiomatic science of democratic and sustainable prosperity instead of constantly pampering and mollycoddling big wealth, big banks, big business and big Wall Street. Then we could focus on achieving **big prosperity** for all of humanity! For the first time in economic history fair will be **fair** and foul will be **foul** as a hallmark of our metaeconomic renaissance.

The Academic and Professional Challenge

I have another challenge for economic professionals. But this time I wish to challenge the college age youth studying economics and other technical professions that wish to contribute to our inclusive prosperity quest. We will be glad to have you as our economic professionals. Don't allow yourselves to get stuck in the trap of defending the indefensible corruption of the past! The future as you can see is a fascinating field ripe with new opportunity and no apologies are needed. The advent of axiomatic metaeconomics, the economic Bill of Rights, and HERA will revolutionize economics and you will be at the forefront of our quest for the economic "moon"! What an exciting time for you! But special opportunities come with special responsibilities.

The future of institutional economics and its relevance to humanity must be debated throughout our country and the world. This debate must take place in a protected sanctuary free from political and authoritarian interference. Only our colleges and universities offer that sanctuary and sometimes even they fail to protect academic freedom.

This is even more likely when our institutions are threatened with loss of $ billions of perpetual wealth donations that they have become dependent on. Yet the debate must take place and it must take place during your time as students. Unfortunately it will take place in an environment that sponsors the economic religion of wealth economics over the science of prosperity economics, and prefers perpetual wealth over perpetual prosperity making a legitimate debate difficult at best.

If an honest debate does not take place, your profession will be locked into a debilitating controversy that will make your economic careers painful at best. You will in effect inherit a gigantic perpetual mess! You may not be able to avoid this mess but if you make the debate clear from the beginning you can gain the moral high ground and the opportunity to lead us out of the mess! As with all humanity, this choice is yours. I can only hope that you have the courage to stand.

Capitalism has not been challenged with reform or improvement since Communism and the challenge from Communism was almost entirely political and military not economic. This book proposes an economic grassroots movement starting with our colleges and universities to change economics into a science of democratic sustainable prosperity called Humanism. This grassroots idea is expressed with our slogan: We don't need a savior and we don't need permission! Our democratic government already entitles us to our democratic economy now.

So our youth and our universities must lead the grassroots way out of our Economic Dark Age if we are to make the changes needed! The fate of all mankind is dependent on the courage and inspiration of our youth. These infantile ideas must be debated and scrutinized in an environment free from the corruption of power and wealth. Academic freedom is needed to bring these ideas to the forefront of intellectual scrutiny and debate so they can become a reality for all mankind. The fate and course of our democratic ideas is up to you; only you can hold them safely in your hearts and minds until they see the light of day!

This book can be used as a template for that debate. Most of the issues are discussed here in enough detail to start the debate. We should start with the Economic Bill of Rights and the 5 key axioms. We must force the economic establishment to either accept these rights and axioms or successfully argue against them with overwhelming international conviction including an even better set of axioms. They will not be successful in arguing against them! And they will not propose better axioms. So they will try to avoid the truth by avoiding the debate. Likewise HERA speaks for itself. The establishment must accept and endorse HERA or propose a better and more comprehensive reform package. The status quo is unacceptable! There is one fundamental issue that should begin and end the general debate. It is the role of Capitalism and democratic Humanism and the transition from one to the other. So I would like to help you start this discussion example.

Let us look at the simplest model for our global economy. There are three players in this model, 1) Natural resources, 2) Humanity (labor and consumption), and 3) Capitalists (capital and management). There is only one goal, the sustainable prosperity mandated by axiom 1. Notice that humanity is on both sides of the supply/demand equation.

We have been referring to this as our **duality**. Humans supply all the labor on the supply side and all of the consumption on the demand side. Business to business economics is only intermediate. Moreover in Humanism, humanity supplies a significant portion of the base capital through retirement fund investments. Furthermore this capital is deployed with 100% efficiency and in a reliable and stable fashion.

So it is, and always was true that the economy is of humanity, by humanity, and for humanity. Our economy is inherently democratic and prosperity is inherently democratic. It always has been democratic and always will be democratic. It is undeniable! Capitalism is simply withholding and defying an inalienable truth in the same way that King George III or King Louis XVI did during our quest for political democracy. This power based defiance does not represent a viable argument but rather the lack of it! Power does not lead to truth. It never did and it never will. Instead it obfuscates the truth indefinitely!

Yet Capitalism sees only the powerful elite capitalists as principals of the economy and it sees all of humanity as mere natural resources to be exploited by brute power obtaining maximum perpetuated wealth for the capitalists as the definition of prosperity. This is an amazing, unnatural, and narrow interpretation of our true economic process.

This narrowness is contrary with the very meaning of broad scale prosperity! Even the exploitation of our natural resources has come into serious question such as discussed in Title 4. But the exploitation of humanity was always unnecessary, undesirable, and inappropriate; it must end now! And it will end as soon as our renaissance begins.

As we discussed in Title 18, the profit paradigm of Capitalism is based on assumptions that might have been partially true in 1850 but these assumptions are glaringly irrelevant and untrue for the next working generation and beyond. Global economics has matured drastically and the idea that capital or capitalists are in short supply in the developed economies is laughably untrue. Indeed the current excess capital has been sufficient to already capitalize the developing nations as well.

On the other hand, the availability of capital in the developing nations is just a temporary transient issue that is well underway and nearing completion. Soon these developing nations will be able to provide their own ongoing capital creating an even greater excess. To complete this transition successfully to a fully developed world economy, we need guiding principles and assumptions that are consistent with our future **not** our past! If we set our future goals based on the past, we will probably end up stuck in the past forever! In fact excess capital chasing after speculation and diminishing yield is threatening our financial stability already as first discussed in Titles 24 and 25.

Clearly the only shortages in the future will be labor, natural resources, and antipollution so this truth must be debated, resolved, and included in any vision of our future. Indeed once speculation is harnessed to prosperity there will be a flood of capital and capitalists. "Throttling back" investment and "mopping up" the excess capital will be a full-time job for the ECA and its international counterparts worldwide.

Old guard capitalists know this is true and they will do anything in their power to maintain regression to the 1850 heydays of the profit paradigm of Capitalism. Wealth economics teaches us that the only shortage in economics is capital so we must constantly pamper and mollycoddle the capitalists mindlessly so they will not "hide under the bed" or "leave town". What a self-serving, antiquated idea designed for capitalists and endorsed by our economic professionals. No wonder they hold onto the past with a death-grip and fear preparing our future!

Similar to the academic challenge there is an implied professional challenge as well. Those in the fields of engineering, science, and mathematics are in a unique position to contribute substantially to the wellbeing and prosperity of all mankind. Never in recent history have your professions had such a monumental opportunity to contribute so much for humanity. Your conventional professions are quite mature.

In general they are all focused on completing the last 5% of their knowledge base and the opportunities for profound contributions are limited. However the emerging fields of Economic Science, Economic Mathematics, and Economic Engineering are relatively new as is metaeconomics. So the opportunities for significant contributions are vast and exciting. The economics profession sorely needs your involvement and humanity sorely needs your help. Join us in changing the field of Economics into the new science of democratic prosperity and sustainable life. The benefit of our renaissance for humanity will be truly enormous for us, our children, and all our future generations.

In this regard these outside professions could help considerably with the debate issues discussed above. We could form a panel of twelve of our nation's finest professionals from the fields of Science, Sociology, Mathematics, Engineering, Philosophy, and Political Science carefully chosen to be free of any influence from big business, big banking, big wealth, Wall Street, or any other form of wealth power or influence.

We could then use this panel to create a national forum for the debate. The issues discussed in this blueprint could be discussed and debated by wealth economists, prosperity economists, and other interested parties. This could be a floating forum where public meetings would be held at major universities throughout our country. Then the panel could conclude with a report to the nation on its findings and recommendations. This idea could be easily replicated on a worldwide scale. The challenge is clear. Help us achieve the economic "moon" for all mankind the same way your professions did for the real moon!

The Role of Labor Efficiency

Once we have sufficient economic investment and economic profits, combined with streamlined and highly competitive businesses, ready to compete in fair and unexploited markets, we are ready to achieve prosperity for all mankind. The keys to achieving prosperity are to continuously improve **labor efficiency** and **business efficiency**. We have already discussed business efficiency in titles 14 – 21 and other discussion topics. Regarding labor efficiency there are three separate factors that make up labor efficiency: 1) Employment Participation rate, 2) Underemployment rate, and 3) Productivity improvement rate.

Employment Participation Rate

The employment participation rate measures that percentage of working age citizens that are actively employed or between jobs. It is a measure of the percentage of working age that attempt to **try** to work. Imagine economics making work conditions and pay so draconian that many don't even try! And some of those that do try end up defeated as homeless. This percentage is usually around 67% to 68% but due to "economic progress" it is currently (2018) down to about 63%. Like welfare low participation rates diminish our prosperity substantially because those that do try to work must support those who fail. You could think of this added burden as being added to the minimum cost of living contributing directly to reducing the prosperity index.

Furthermore if the minimum wage were implemented as we recommend and flexible underemployment was substituted for unemployment so that ample good paying jobs would become available, the participation rate could exceed 70% or more. If more effort could be directed to accommodating and facilitating disabilities and homelessness further improvements could be achieved. We have a lot of work to do but the elimination of unemployment, the advent of a true minimum wage, and fair international labor rates will improve this measure drastically during the first ten years of our economic reforms!

Underemployment Rate

The underemployment rate is the new replacement for the old unemployment rate as discussed in Title 12. A 2.5% unemployment rate would correspond to a 2.5% underemployment rate or an average of 39 hours for a week. While a -2.5% rate would correspond to an average of 41 hours for a week. This range spans our business cycle.

Because underemployment is proportional and has excellent labor elasticity it will be easy to maintain rates of 0% and even negative percentages if needed. As the rate approaches 0% there is no reason for anyone to be involuntarily unemployed; many jobs will be unfilled. Although currently (2018) our unemployment is near 4.0% this is an anomaly because our normal unemployment is about 5% at best. So we should be able to improve employment by more than 5% on the average. This will be possible because the ECA will have direct control of wage inflation at 0% as discussed in Title 11a and Title 23.

Consequently there is no reason to ration underemployment at 5% anymore because of fears of wage inflation. So there is no need to increase interest rates higher and higher to force our economy into a "quasi stall" just to reduce employment forcing cheap labor. The ECA can measure wage inflation and simply subtract it from the wage growth mandated by axiom 5 using monthly corrections as discussed in Title 11a and implemented in the correction formula $W\% = Ip\% - Iw\% + P\%$. Then the ECA can reduce underemployment until the monthly correction becomes excessive or full employment is reached.

Equilibrium might take a few years but businesses will adapt quickly. Initially businesses may respond to the shortage of labor by bidding up the price of labor but they will quickly learn that increasing productivity is less expensive. Improvements in the control system discussed in Title 23 will make this equilibrium easier to maintain.

100% Full Employment

Furthermore the improved labor elasticity of the flexible workweek discussed in Title 12 will make the inflationary pressure of full employment much lower and much easier to compensate. Full employment will no longer act like an abrupt "brick wall". Instead it will be a smooth linear continuum. At full employment the flexible workweek can still be easily varied +/- 5% or more without generating any significant inflationary pressure on the correction mechanism. So wage inflationary pressure will be much lower than our current Central Bank interest rate system stabilizing and lowering interest rates.

Moreover the ECA's wage measurement and correction mechanism of Title 11a can compensate for wage inflation pressures that are 10 to 100 times larger than the old Central Bank interest rate system could hope to compensate. The old system was very indirect trying to control the economy by offsetting one delayed tendency (wage inflation) by inducing another delayed tendency (unemployment). Instead the new mechanism directly measures any wage inflation pressure and subtracts it out of wages and salaries directly and immediately using a mathematical monthly correction formula by 10 percentile category.

So even though the wage inflationary pressure is very high by conventional standards it can still be compensated directly and mathematically eliminating any wage inflation from the aggregate wage growth of axiom 5 with no instability. In addition wage inflation shows up with new hire wages and salaries first and foremost. So the new hire compensation vector (11 categories) will more directly and stably target the onset of any wage inflation tendency without risking any instability in general wages and salaries (lead will offset lag).

Where would all the new jobs come from? For one example, look back to the previous discussion in Title 16 about the employment created by the 7% tax reduction on businesses and other streamlining. It is important to understand that, contrary to the scary propaganda that we are told, employment is easy to create because employment creates more employment; it's generative. Each job created then helps to create a major fraction of another job and so on magnifying jobs.

As discussed in Title 12 unemployment is very inefficient compared to underemployment. Each unemployed person continues to consume at 60% or more of their employed norm but their productivity drops abruptly to 0% so they abruptly produce nothing. This results in a spurt of reduced productivity that reinforces the recessionary tendency prolonging the unemployment. On the other hand full employment with a flexible work week is proportional and does not suffer this fault.

Unfortunately our understanding of employment issues has been clouded and confused because this issue is extensively manipulated by economic propaganda in a deceptive manner much like a two handed "shell game". On one hand at the macro level the Central Bank keeps employment in a constant throttled back, quasi stall condition using interest rates so that they can maintain the lowest wage equilibrium possible in the name of cheap labor and "fighting inflation". We referred to this earlier as rationed employment at about 5% minimum.

On the other hand at the micro level, businesses constantly justify every scheme or scam they come up with as a way to "create jobs" and they avoid any idea that they do not like under the guise of "saving jobs"! Isn't it amazing that they have been "creating and saving jobs" for hundreds of years on a massive scale but we still do not have full employment even though we only needed a tiny 5% improvement!

This is collective intellectual dishonesty on a flagrant scale! Which profession should be held responsible for instituting and perpetuating this sly, deceptive, and manipulative behavior? Indeed why is "sly, deceptive, and manipulative behavior" a part of economics at all? It is not part of any other science! If we can avoid this kind of ugly harmful behavior in Chemistry, why can't we avoid it in Economics as well?

Notice how rationing employment and its scare tactics over many years have caused us to be so over sensitized to jobs, creating jobs, losing jobs, saving jobs, finding jobs, improving jobs, and keeping jobs, jobs-jobs-jobs. Obviously we have been brainwashed into believing that there is actually a shortage of jobs threatening us. The threat is very real but the shortage is not! The truth is that the rationed "shortage" was manmade to drive down and harm wages. Beware of any proposal from the "left hand" of business that claims to "create or save" jobs because the "right hand" of the Central Bank will eliminate them promptly to keep labor cheap. Now you see it; now you don't!

Let's end this economic shell game once and for all with full flexible employment and seamless job transitions of Title 12 maintained indefinitely in a **perpetual boom**. No more need to "create and save" jobs because they are created and fully utilized by the full employment sub mandate and managed automatically by the control system of Title 23 transparently for all to see. Once cheap labor is eliminated as an economic concept and wage inflation is controlled directly by a separate mechanism, it will be easy for the ECA to simply allow fuller employment by using less throttling and less risk of unstable stalling. There is absolutely no "degree of difficulty" in this achievement at all!

Our new full employment, higher productivity world will be quite different from our current rationed employment, cheap labor world. Businesses will no longer be "creating and saving" low productivity junk jobs because there will be no labor available for such jobs. Instead businesses will be constantly eliminating these jobs and replacing them with higher productivity jobs that have employment available. What a conceptual change! This is truly a renaissance.

Employees will be treated with respect and dignity. Indeed managers who treat employees poorly will be demoted instead of promoted! There will be a constant shortage of workers especially at the entry level and a constant increase in productivity all the way up the pay scale. Businesses will quickly learn that the only way to meet their labor needs is to increase the productivity of their current employees.

Furthermore they will offer free on-the-job training programs to achieve this higher productivity. Businesses that rely on trying to pay exorbitant wage rates instead of upgrading productivity will degrade their profitability. Eventually they will be revamped or replaced by efficient businesses that are successful with increasing productivity and coping with full employment. This is truly a world we would all prefer to live in. Review Titles 14 and 15 to refresh these ideas.

Full employment is a new mindset and it will take a little time for businesses to get used to it. Most businesses will have continuous open requisitions for new employees although there are rarely such employees available. Consequently businesses will make do with the employees that they already have focusing on increasing employee productivity rather than bidding up the wage cost of new hire wages.

Conventional wealth economics has taught us that we should not have open requisitions for which there are no employees available. Instead wealth economics teaches us that businesses should always have long lines of unemployed (5% min) waiting endlessly for any junk job that might become available as a way of pampering and mollycoddling businesses with instant and excessive employment availability! To reinforce this propaganda wealth economists even decreed that this 5% condition be called "full employment" to disguise their real intentions!

On the other hand prosperity economics shows us that an abundance of open and unfulfilled requisitions is **normal and healthy** for our economy and should not be avoided. There is no need for draconian unemployment lines! It is perfectly ok if open requisitions go unfulfilled on a large scale perpetually. Nothing bad will happen to businesses or our economy. Instead this condition will motivate businesses to increase productivity and efficiency to meet their needs.

Initially we may find that the wage inflation correction mechanism becomes too high to achieve 0% unemployment immediately without risking instability. Using a separate correction vector for new hires will help target the inflation correction mechanism and achieve better stability. Over time businesses will learn how to manage in a full employment, limited labor equilibrium and full employment will be achieved and maintained. To help, the ECA can provide the CEOs and management who don't get it with free on-the-job training as well!

This improvement in average underemployment (5% or more) together with the improvement in participation rate (7% or more) would be a very significant overall (12% or more) improvement to labor efficiency! Review Title 23 for a detailed example of how to manage full employment stably and "Near Term Global Economic Outlook" for more sources of new high productivity employment. The path from *profits* to *prosperity* is clear, easy to understand, and ready for action!

Labor Productivity Rate

Finally this brings us to the productivity improvement rate which is the year to year percentage improvement in labor productivity at full pay. Productivity could be measured on the macroeconomic level as GDP/Total labor hours. In general the cost of a product is the labor hours it takes to produce it. If fewer labor hours are required for the same product, its currency cost will be reduced if labor rates are equal.

However according to axiom 5 and Title 11a) the labor rates should eventually increase by the productivity improvement rate, so currency cost and thus the cost of living will be unchanged but labor earnings will increase. Prosperity will increase by the same percentage as the productivity improvement since the prosperity index is determined by the M80 average income divided by the standard cost of living.

For this reason, productivity is the key to achieving steady-state ongoing prosperity. Unfortunately productivity improvements require intense cooperation between labor and business management in a win-win fashion. Capitalism and its profit paradigm have destroyed trust between these two groups after years of war-like, brute power based, exploitation by management and union retaliations from labor.

This war-like, power struggle situation is hardly a good environment for trust and cooperation! Why didn't our economists come up with a better idea than this flaw? As Humanism becomes more of a win-win game, labor and business will realize that they are on the same side of this issue and their cooperation will result in persistent productivity improvements year after year benefiting everyone indefinitely.

The ECA will be a very positive force as well because they can help broker a better relationship between labor and management since they are trusted by both parties. In time management will start to trust the productivity suggestions made by labor because labor has the best visibility over productive opportunities when their jobs are not at risk.

In time labor will cooperate fully because they trust the ECA to provide and maintain full employment so that their employment is **not** at risk. All labor is guaranteed 100% full employment by sub mandate. Then labor can really cooperate with the elimination of jobs that productivity improvements require knowing that the ECA backs and provides full employment at higher productivity and higher salaries.

For the first time labor will trust that new higher paying jobs will be provided without interruption of employment. Rather than the false economic promises of the past like NAFTA that ended up substituting minimum jobs for high paying industrial jobs drastically reducing productivity and prosperity. As stated in Title 2 the ECA should have subordinate mandates for 0% wage inflation, employment participation greater than 70%, underemployment less than or equal to 0% (100% full employment), and productivity improvements greater than 2%. So labor will be directly protected from misapplication of robotics and AI.

The prosperity tax ideas of Title 16 and the bonus incentives of Title 21 together with the minimum wage will provide another positive motivation for business management to focus directly on productivity. In fact many of these ideas are directed exactly towards improvements in efficiency and productivity with bonus incentives. Instead of being the victim of greed, we can harness some of its appeal to management and direct it towards improving efficiency and productivity instead.

Is it any surprise that a new win-win system can provide what the old lose-lose more system has destroyed? Instead of Robotics and AI being a threat to humanity they will become a godsend for humanity. Productivity improvements will launch us into constant improvements in prosperity. When this is combined with direct improvements in participation and underemployment rates we will be on our way to a much more prosperous world for rich, middle class, and the poor!

Beware! Economists, Greed & Productivity

Beware! Economists, greed, and productivity make for a toxic combination. What an amazing situation! The most important single metric of economics, productivity, is overtly and consistently mismanaged by economists with very few exceptions! How could such an outrageous statement possibly be true? How could it even be a little bit true? Let me cite two examples in detail that are profound and directly relevant to our general subject, prosperity by metaeconomics.

The Minimum Wage

First let us take the issue of minimum wage or as I prefer "minimum job". We discussed this issue a little in Title 8 above. The minimum job idea is to put a floor in the labor market that establishes a minimum productivity that a wholesome job should have. This minimum job is a (P,W) point on the W = M x P line of Title 6. By specifying a minimum wage, we send a clear message to business management to stop creating "junk" jobs whose productivity is below the minimum job. If they continue they will have to pay the difference out of their coveted profits because the productivity of the minimum job will be less than the corresponding value of the minimum wage!

As we discussed in Title 8, the gap between the current minimum wage and the minimum wage of Axiom 4 is a national embarrassment created to increase profits and decrease wages! The minimum wage should be managed properly as we have suggested in Title 8 by using a formula that would automatically increase the minimum wage as the minimum cost of living increases. It would be easy for businesses to make slight improvements in productivity year after year that will keep the minimum job productivity well above the fair minimum wage.

The minimum wage is all about improving productivity at the basic minimum job level. This puts upward pressure from the floor forcing improved productivity all the way up the labor pay scale. The previous recommendation in Title 8 to make the minimum wage increase with years of economic service, makes the floor in effect much wider and therefore a better "platform" to push up productivity at the higher pay scales. Furthermore once we have average productivity data for each 10 percentile income group, the equal pay axiom will ensure that any increase in productivity will be reflected continuously at the higher linear productivity levels using the correction mechanism of Title 11a.

As we discussed in the previous topic, productivity is the most direct way to improve efficiency and therefore our prosperity. Also as we pointed out above increasing productivity always results in temporary local increases in unemployment or underemployment because of the very definition of productivity. In other words the same product is achieved with fewer labor hours so somebody must work less until increased demand compensates with higher wages and prosperity.

This is a temporary transient condition because economic growth created by the increase in productivity will create replacement jobs at even higher wages. Prosperity creates more prosperity. Moreover when this is a continuous process making small improvements each year, last year's productivity improvement produces growth that provides for increased employment to cover next year's employment productivity shortfall. When properly managed, in the steady-state there would be **no** net unemployment or underemployment even temporarily! Review Title 23 for a detailed economic control example.

Every year it seems a proposal comes into national news exposure to increase the minimum wage. And every year economists come to the news front and shout it down! Most economists oppose the minimum wage almost unanimously because they are "cheerleading" for businesses that want cheaper and cheaper labor so they can pocket the profit difference. How noble! Why can't they represent us instead?

In 2014 they used a technique that I could not remember seeing before. It was a scare tactic that warned that increasing the minimum wage would increase unemployment at a time when we were fatigued with persistently high unemployment. This deceptive ploy came equipped with data and analysis from the Congressional Budget Office, no less.

It showed that there would be an increase in productivity and a corresponding increase in unemployment (Davis, 2014). How sly and manipulative! Yes the fear of further broad scale increases in unemployment swept our nation and once again the minimum wage increase was defeated! It was defeated again in 2015, 2016, 2017, and 2018 the same way. So "Sly deceptive greed conquers all problems!"

Yet not even one economist came forward and pointed out that productivity improvements always result in a temporary increase in unemployment and that is why we strive to accomplish productivity improvements! So not one economist came forward and pointed out that arguing against the minimum wage increase is the exact equivalent of arguing against productivity improvements in general.

For an economist to argue against productivity improvements because they would cause unemployment is the medical equivalent of a Doctor arguing against curing disease because it would increase world population! This is "collective dishonesty" on a huge scale and it actually happened in 2014 right in front of our eyes (Davis, 2014) and it continues. This is truly disgusting. If our Doctors were like our Economists we would all be **sick or dead already**! I ask again: if Biology or Medical Science does not need this kind of manipulative sly deception why does the field of Economics need to indulge in it?

The Global Economy

Secondly let us consider the development of the global economy over the last 30 years or so. As you can see from the previous discussions, productivity (prosperity) is the greatest achievement any economy can ever accomplish. It is a precious achievement that leads directly to prosperity and higher standards of living. But apparently economists do not agree? During this 30 year period the American middle class was systematically decimated by transferring **high** productivity jobs in American industry into **low** productivity jobs in emerging nations.

Simultaneously we replaced those high productivity jobs in the USA with **lower** productivity jobs. This transfer and substitution was massive, it continued for at least 30 years, and it continues now! This represents a direct attack on productivity resulting in broad scale, long term destruction of productivity and its prosperity! How could such a harmful transition be endorsed by the community of economists as "good trade economics" when it was so harmful to productivity and human prosperity? Oh yes, "fair is foul and foul is fair in economics"!

So the answer is that the global economy was a "fast buck" scheme intended to exploit workers in the emerging nations and then use that exploitation as an extortion threat to further justify continuing ongoing exploitation of workers in the USA in a downward spiral, ratcheting back and forth. The goal was simple: to pocket the quick profits of cheap labor and currency for big business, big banks, and big Wall Street. Of course the "cheerleaders" endorsed this as good economics!

Under Humanism and HERA such a transition would have had **no** financial incentive. The equal pay for equal productivity rule would have produced equal product cost in both situations. For example if the productivity in the emerging nation was 3 times less than the USA then 3 times more workers would do the same work each for 1/3 less pay and the product's currency cost would be **exactly** the same. There would be no profit benefit and no motive for manipulation, extortion, and exploitation just fair economics. Review the Title 6 & 7 discussion to refresh the ideas of wage linearity and the $W = M \times P$ equation.

In order to make the scheme work, currency values were set unfairly low, violating axiom 3. Furthermore the emerging nations' workers were forced to work for wages well below the equal pay for equal productivity rule, violating axiom 2 & 3. Combined together these distortions allowed cheap products to have a much higher labor hour cost and therefore higher economic cost but a lower currency cost!

This was a great step backwards for productivity that caused major dislocations for both economies that will take generations to fully recover. Now the USA is stuck with the trade imbalance, personal debt, and sovereign debt required to finance this scheme. In addition the emerging nations are struggling with conversion of their emerging economies from export heavy to balanced trade. Yet big business, big banks, and big Wall Street made their quick buck and that is all that matters! HERA would have made this sad scheme impossible because of fair currency values and the equal pay for equal productivity rule.

The ECA could have achieved the global economy in a much better way (Title 6 & 7). They would have represented humanity and insisted on a more balanced trade growth approach that could have kept trade more balanced and productivity achievements intact. They also would have been a strong force to make a rapid and aggressive transition out of these subsidized economic situations. See discussion in "It Is Time for a New World Order" and "Near Term Global Economic Outlook".

Nobody is in Charge!

In traditional wealth economics who is in charge of our economy? Who is in charge of our prosperity? Who is in charge of productivity? Who is in charge of national income? Who is in charge of the national distribution of income and wealth? Who establishes our ongoing economic goals and monitors and manages their achievement? Who enforces the Economic Bill of Rights? Who verifies compliance with our axioms? Who monitors trade agreements to make sure they are fair and represent good economics? Where is our technical representation?

Where is our economic "NASA" that could professionally lead us and technically guide us to our economic "moon"? We have lots of ugly manipulation, exploitation, and corruption with plenty of authority but no responsibility and no accountability. Apparently there is literally **no one** in charge of our economy! The other possible explanation would be that an undefined, secret, opaque, and corrupt entity is in economic control but that thought is even more outrageous! See the next topic.

The possible exceptions are the Central Bank and Congress. Congress has clear and abundant authority in economic matters but they are a **legislative** authority not a **management** authority. It is impossible for Congress to professionally manage our economy. They only get fully involved when there is a crisis, like TARP in 2008. Yet they only get involved long enough to deal with the immediate crisis and then it is back to "gay marriage", "immigration", "abortion", or "haggling over the budget". So we have little management authority for our economy!

The Central Bank was originally created because Congress realized it did not have the ability to professionally manage on a continuous basis. But only monetary policy was addressed which is not sufficient to encompass the full scope of our economy. So the Central Bank has some authority over interest rates but otherwise their hands are tied. Recall from Title 23 how weak, inaccurate, and slow interest rates are.

No wonder our economy has performed so poorly for the vast majority of us, violating axiom 1 and the other axioms as well. It is like trying to go to the moon without a NASA! Can you imagine our Congress debating what rocket fuel to use? The Corn Belt states would insist on alcohol and the ranching states would want to use cow dung. So we would end up with the political compromise of "dungohol" which turns out to be nonflammable! No wonder because good economic governance is not just a political issue. It's a scientific issue as well!

The profound importance of this economic deficiency may not be that obvious. So let's look at this in more detail. Over the last 50 years we have heard frequent economic news reports about how wages, salaries, and prosperity in general are substantially and consistently under-performing while corporate profits, wealth, and GDP are expanding rapidly. However this chronic disparity is never fixed or resolved.

Hardly a month goes by without some new report to this effect, year in and year out such as (Greenhouse, 2013). However these reports never tell us what is going to be done to fix or correct the problem because there is no "NASA" to recommend or implement a proactive fix. In fact this deliberate silence, repeated monotonous, is designed exactly to brainwash us, without actually admitting to us, that there is nothing that can be done about the economy because **no one** is in charge!

This propaganda tells us that the economy does what it does like a volcano and we must accept the outcome as willing victims of sacrifice. Our economic volcanologists decree that the "natural flow" of this economic volcano is to move wealth from the middle class to the wealthy in order to appease the economic wealth gods. This anarchy is justified as a "free" market controlled by the wealth gods.

Any thought of a fix, correction, or compensation is considered uncooperative, heretical, and could disrupt the "natural flow" of our economy upsetting the gods causing disaster. How could economic religion be explained as anything but brainwashing extortion on a global scale? And what profession facilitates, implements, and sustains this intellectual corruption and "high religion" on such a vast scale?

Instead we need a full-time professional management authority that is responsible and accountable for our economy delegated by Congress! This authority must be transparent, independent, and apolitical. We must be able to see exactly what they are doing, how they are doing it, and what the results have been so far. This authority must be charged and chartered with constitutional rights and axiomatic first principles that mandate institution and support of our democratic metaeconomy.

Moreover the ECA must have tools for monetary, fiscal, tax, and investment policies together with specific performance criteria. We need 24/7 year-in and year-out measurement and management of our prosperity, productivity, underemployment, employment participation, national income, distribution of wealth, international trade, and any other national economic goal that affects our prosperity. It's time for professional proactive Economic Engineering to achieve our goals.

That is exactly what HERA proposes in detail; it's exactly what the ECA is intended to achieve. This is a simple yet powerful idea whose time has come. Let's complete the debate – a democratic scientific economy is no longer negotiable! It is a necessity for our renaissance!

It is time for **action** to make this a reality so we and our children will benefit for generations to come. We are proud of our forefathers for having had the courage to institute a political democracy and our children will be as proud that we had the courage to institute an economic democracy. On the contrary they will be equally sad, sorry, and disappointed if we leave them this ugly unsolved perpetual mess!

It is Time for Economic Law and Order

Continuing the ideas of the previous discussion on a slightly different plane, it seems that the current development of our economy is very similar to the primitive conditions of the "Wild West" era associated with our open range development in the USA. During this period there was no law and order. There was only one rule "those with the gold, and therefore the guns, rule". They make the "laws" and enforce the "order" according to what suits their power, privilege, and preference.

What suits them is unrestricted (free) lawless privileged exploitation! Moreover they hire the "guns" (economists) as henchmen to achieve their goals. Open range Cattle Barons insist that lawlessness (free of laws) must prevail in order for the privileged to be willing to continue the exploitation they call "progress". We banded together and ended that era using democratic principles! It is time for us to do it again!

The "Cattle Barons" sound like Wall Street espousing on "Laissez-faire". The "Laissez-faire" idea has been seriously corrupted over the years to try to justify the exploitation and corruption. It was originally a democratic idea that challenged feudal corruption and control. Now it is used to justify Wall Street's corruption and control which is the exact opposite of its original meaning! "If greed can't spin it, maybe corruption will"! The "free" trade/market idea now actually means lawless trade and markets free of laws that would protect our economy from the corruption of excessive wealth power and its privileged exploitation of humanity. This is economic anarchy not law and order! And it's justified using the "fair is foul and foul is fair" mumbo jumbo.

Until now Wall Street has had the perfect scam! So Wall Street insists that "nobody" (but invisible them) should be in charge of our economy so that they can take control whenever they feel the need. Most of the time they get what they want by privilege. The rest of the time they have to intervene using the "Invisible Hand" of market manipulation, distortion, extortion, and exploitation. Therefore Wall Street always gets it their way and they have no responsibility and no accountability!

Best of all, if anything goes wrong it was the "Invisible Hand" that is always to blame but never accountable! After all if nobody is in charge it must have been caused by an "economic volcanic eruption" - right? If you object to this scam, thousands of economists will be "gunning" for you so they can keep their perpetual wealth donations and their perpetual scam going with perpetual anarchy, power, and privilege!

It is time for economic **law and order**! It is time to put the Wild West of 1850 behind us. The "Cattle Barons" need the Wild West but our economy does **not** need the "Cattle Barons" any more if we ever did! Our economy needs law and order. The axioms and guiding principles together with the Economic Bill of Rights and HERA represent that new body of law and the ECA represents the law enforcement of that order. Our economic "moon" is full and clearly visible. Grasp it tightly and don't let go! Even though the ride will be rough, our democracy will prevail and our children will rejoice with pride and prosperity!

Trickle Down "Magic"

The most common argument against any kind of economic law and order or economic reforms is a scare tactic that goes something like this: the perpetually wealthy are the only humans who know how to do the magic that causes trickle-down crumbs to fall from the table of the perpetually wealthy and then trickle-down to make capital formation. Apparently knowledge of this "capital magic" can only be passed on by genetic bloodline, a new version of the old "blue blood" idea. Title 9 provides us with a very different idea of the power of public capital.

Yet wealth says without this magic our economy would crumble and die from a lack of economic capital. So "You better watch out! Better not pout" because the perpetually wealthy are coming to our economic town! If you do not constantly pamper and mollycoddle them they will abandon us in favor of some other economy that will give them the privilege and indulgence they so magically and perpetually deserve!

This divisive scare tactic sounds a lot like an economic fairytale or an economic nursery rhyme and that is exactly what it is! It seems to derive its "validity" from the generalized golden rule. They with the gold, rule. In other words, they with the gold are above the laws of humanity and they can do whatever they want as a kind of economic exclusion of wealth power to law and order. We must live in constant fear that their patronization could be removed or withheld. They claim to have the power to hold our jobs, our lives and our economy hostage.

There seems to be three separate fallacies that combine to give this scare tactic its power: 1) that we are dependent on perpetual wealth as the primary source of economic capitalization, 2) that the perpetually wealthy are free to remove their wealth outside the jurisdiction of their nationality with impunity, and 3) that there is some new jurisdiction available inside of which they are free to hide and protect their wealth from law and order. Let us look at each of these ideas in more detail.

First the idea that we are dependent on perpetual wealth as the primary source of economic capital is just false. Perhaps there was some prior era like 1850 during which this was partially true but it is in the distant and dark past. In fact public corporations provide the vast majority of all new capital through retained earnings and there is such a chronic excess and surplus of such capital that they have to pay dividends and stock buybacks to avoid the excess cash piling up. So our future is much different. Look at the special features of HERA that we have already discussed that provide new sources of significant economic capital in addition to the excess abundance that we already have now!

1. The new National Fund of Title 9 will provide many $ trillions at maturity directly invested in economic investment with 100% efficiency and 100% reliability instead of the fractional "crumbs" of trickle-down inefficiency and privileged frivolous liquidity.

2. Elimination of dividends and stock buybacks of Title 17 will make large amounts of economic capital available for reinvestment by businesses from retained earnings our most powerful investment.
3. Economic investment tax incentives of Title 23 provide a strong control that will make economic investing more attractive than speculation and other forms of non-economic investing.
4. Business taxes on excess cash and low debt/equity ratio in Title 16 will force reinvestment of surplus cash and working capital.
5. Huge amounts of corporate offshore profits will be returned from the international arena once corporate income taxes of Title 16 are eliminated.
6. The improved capital gains tax of Title 24 will encourage economic investing over speculation.
7. In a minimal growth (productivity only) mature economy no capital is needed beyond depreciation replacement, productivity improvements, and business revitalization. We no longer need this excess capital. The heydays of 1850 Capitalism are long gone!

The combination of these improvements alone will likely require the ECA to throttle capital investing back even more to avoid overheating the economy because there is not enough labor, natural resources, and antipollution available. So there will be no shortage of capital for economic investing even in the distant future since the ECA has even more future options than those listed to manage economic investing.

Indeed the looming problem facing us in the very near future is how to deal with huge surpluses of capital inflation chasing after limited yield that were injected into our economy in an effort to stabilize it after the 2008 crisis. Furthermore how do we re-absorb the huge surpluses of capital return we no longer need for the emerging economies? We will need to find an orderly systematic way to "mop-up" huge surpluses of excess capital liquidity (QE) in order to maintain stability and avoid inflation. Thus we will pay off our national debt, refinance sustainable retirement, and refinance Medicare retirement. We will use excess wealth and capital as solutions for our economy, not just problems!

Secondly the idea that the perpetually wealthy are free to remove their wealth outside the jurisdiction of their nationality with impunity is a fantasy at best. As indicated in Title 5 any attempt to avoid paying inheritance tax by terminating citizenship will trigger the inheritance event before any impunity. So only the after tax funds can be removed.

In a simple sense the inheritance tax is a liability that must be satisfied before termination of citizenship can begin. The net worth tax on the after tax amount would likely be considered a liability as well. Since the wealth was accumulated in our economy over time it has an obligation to be taxed as an investment in our economy for a period of years proportional to the time of the accumulation. In other words, you can't "play and then not pay"! Wealth accumulation has obligations.

Finally there is no place to hide. There is only one global economy. Nations that trade must not thwart each other's laws. Our USA authorities have had no difficulty clawing back funds from all sorts of offshore accounts. Even if capital could be hidden it will quickly diminish if it cannot be invested in the world's economies. With the advent of HERA the USA will likely continue to be the country with the greatest investment opportunities. Those of wealth will likely want to stay right here because that is why they were here in the first place.

The key question to expose this issue is: what have the perpetually wealthy contributed to humanity that would warrant such a profound perpetual privilege? Economic professionals answered this question when I went to college using the trickle-down theory discussed above. Over the ensuing years they have been embarrassed by the fairytale to the point that they no longer use the name but they continue to use the scare tactic concept when needed in sort of a "now you see it - now you don't" fashion. So the above question now goes without an answer unless you press hard and then you get some disguised version of our favorite fairytale. Could fairytales really guide us to good economics?

No! It is time for an economic "Declaration of Independence". We do not need the perpetually wealthy as our economic privileged class! They need us! Furthermore the perpetually wealthy are not above the laws of humanity even though they strive for and demand this privilege. There is no "magic". It is all a façade to make us believe that we cannot and should not have a democratic metaeconomy and that we must subjugate our economic **truth** to the **power** of perpetual wealth. So let us get started with a paradigm that will provide **perpetual prosperity** instead of perpetual wealth. Our future depends on it!

It is Time for a New World Order!

Understanding international trade should not be hard except that it has been distorted, extorted, and manipulated with exploitation to such an extent that wholesome economic trade is "lost in translation". Let us begin by identifying some common types of trade situations and trade terminology that we can then use to better understand the current trade situation and its future outlook under the metaprinciples of Humanism.

The Background

1) **Mandatory Imports:** This is trade primarily in natural resources where the importing economy cannot produce the resource or commodity and there is no substitute. For example crude oil is a mandatory import in Japan. This forces other exporting countries to supply the mandatory resource or commodity as a mandatory export.
2) **Optional Exports:** This is trade in commodities, components, or finished goods that are produced locally and are available for export if efficiency is high enough to offset added trade costs. In some cases these exports are natural resources that could satisfy other nation's mandatory imports.
3) **Local Assembly:** This is assembly where the majority of resources and components are available locally and the final product is consumed locally. In this case there is little or no international trade and the economic efficiency is the highest because there are no trade related costs added.
4) **Import/Assembly:** This is assembly where the majority of resources and components are imported because they are not available locally. But the final product is consumed locally.
5) **Assembly/Export:** This is assembly where the majority of resources and components are available locally but the final product is exported, usually because local wages are too low to afford local consumption.
6) **Import/Assembly/Export:** is the most inefficient trade where resources, components, or subassemblies are imported,

assembled, and then exported. These are usually called "economic zones" but they should be called "exploitation zones". In many cases multiple levels of zones, shipping, and reshipping are involved first as components, then subassemblies, and finally as finished products. The concept is simple. Move the natural resources and components to wherever the labor is most vulnerable and desperate. So cheap labor can be easily extorted and exploited and then ship the product to its final destination where some consumer still has high enough wages to afford to buy such products.

In many cases the components and subassemblies are made in a different "zone", further compounding the inefficiencies in a quest for cheaper and cheaper labor and currency exploitation. In most cases the producing company has no commitment to the zone since it only subcontracts the facilities and production management. So the prime producer is free to move assembly to another "exploitation zone" with only a few months' notice to exploit a cheaper labor deal there. This is truly an ugly cheap labor and cheap currency "exploitation machine".

NAFTA is an example of this exact situation. The exploitation zone was on the Mexican side of the border with the USA. Components were shipped in mostly from the USA, assembled, and then shipped back to the USA and Canada for consumption. Because of the close proximity, special open door border, and round trip trucking transportation this structure had greater efficiency than most exploitation zones. The NAFTA exploitation zone appeared to be virtually "inside" the USA but used exploitable foreign labor – the perfect exploitation combination providing an exploitation "heaven"!

This more efficient scheme seemed to work well for the first 10 years or so but gradually the Mexican government could no longer extort labor to work for less and less each year because illegal immigration to the USA was a competing labor option along the border. So eventually the assembly was moved to more vulnerable and desperate labor sources such as East Asia and Indonesia where illegal immigration was not an option. This left behind empty Maquiladora plants, a sure sign of bad economics. This is a great example of how the profit motive in international trade trumps efficiency with vulnerable desperation!

The Projection Forward

So in an effort to understand what international trade should be, let us put aside the current sad state of affairs. So we can project forward to what international trade will become under the axioms of meta-economics in general and specifically the equal pay mandate of axiom 2 and the equal currency mandate of axiom 3. The simple idea here is to project a steady-state solution of future equilibrium based on our guiding principles and then work our way back to the current situation. Then it will be easy to see a transitional plan to get from where we are now to where we want to be in the near future. This transition can then be considered in three sequential and partially overlapping stages of competitive trade: "emerged", "balanced", and then fully "developed".

In order to "jump start" the emerging nation's economy the emerging nations have been allowed to have a subsidized trade situation. Their currency values are deliberately undervalued violating axiom 3, and their wages are deliberately undervalued violating axiom 2. Combined together this exploitation creates a situation where the workers in the developed nations are economically forced to subsidize economic development in the emerging nations by buying products whose currency cost is artificially low, unsustainable, and deliberately unfair.

Consequently the emerging nation's workers are forced into "working poverty" caused by unfairly low wages and unfairly low currency values. Quickly this race to the bottom ratchets back and forth, driving down wages in the developed nations as well to spread ugly "working poverty" throughout the world. This unsustainability is characterized by workers making products that they could not possibly afford to buy and export surpluses. Yet it is justified as "good market economics".

On the other hand the developed nation's workers that do buy these products rely heavily on unsustainable debt at the sovereign level, unsustainable debt at the trade balance level, and unsustainable debt at the personal level. This trade subsidy situation is usually referred to as an "Export Led Economy". Review the topics, Title 6 and "The Role of Profits in Humanism" to refresh Humanistic ideas on transitioning emerging economies with wage linearity and the $W = M \times P$ formula.

This subsidized unsustainability mandates that the transition to "emergence" take place quickly and aggressively under a strictly monitored plan. Otherwise this artificial, fake economy becomes addicting to **both** sides. The addiction motivates continuing the "drug" rather than making the transition to a sustainable economy that is not dependent on subsidies! So an emerging nation's international trade has "emerged" when it complies with the "no subsidy" requirements.

- Emergence requires compliance with the equal value pay for equal productivity axiom 2 nationally and internationally.
- Emergence requires compliance with the fair currency axiom 3 that equal currencies must buy equal goods.
- Notice that Emergence does not require high productivity. Low productivity and a low standard of living are acceptable, fair starting points for emergence that will still be able to produce competitively priced products for international trade without any extortion or exploitation! Review Title 6 for analysis of the benefits of wage linearity based on the $W = M \times P$ formula.

An emerging nation's international trade has become "balanced" when it complies with the following requirements.

- In equilibrium all nations under consideration have "emerged" and all have sufficient infrastructure to manufacture any product that they may need locally excluding natural resources and they have the investment needed to do so.
- In balanced international trade each nation should have imports = exports.
- In balanced international trade the majority of the national investment for a nation should come from the local nationality and the investments should be approximately balanced. The

nation's investment in foreign countries = the foreign investments nationally.

A nation's international trade has started to "develop" once balance is achieved. A "developed" nation is an ongoing achievement that complies with all the axioms and has no conclusion. During development certain general principles should be operative.

- The trade/transportation costs including export, lading, international shipping, import, inspection, unlading, national shipping differential, amortized trade startup costs, and other trade related costs add **no** economic value to the products and must be absorbed by some forfeiture of profits that the product had or could have had nationally. Axiom 2 and 3 specifically **prohibit** exploiting labor wages or currencies lower just to offset these added trade costs! Review the discussion in Title 6.
- So these costs represent a natural barrier to trade because most businesses would not have sufficient profits even if they were willing to forfeit them. Consequently only the most efficient producers will be able to be successful at international trade and local production will always be naturally preferred. Furthermore product dumping will be easy to detect as a direct violation of (ISO) compliance documentation. Review Title 16 for discussion about streamlined taxation for optimum trade.
- Where natural resources must be imported, efficiency dictates that they be imported in a form that has the lowest shipping cost and should not be refined and then re-exported. These resources should only be imported for local consumption. For example efficiency dictates that a nation that does not have iron ore resources locally should not be a general steel exporter.
- An emerged and balanced nation in the process of developing does not need to have high productivity or high prosperity or a high standard of living. It may take many years for their economy to become fully "developed" as each nation strives to achieve its highest prosperity and some succeed more than

others. In addition every worker will have equal access to the international market no matter how high or how low their productivity may be! Furthermore every nation will have equal access to natural resources that they do not have locally.

Earlier in a previous discussion about lost productivity in the global economy, we made the claim that the ECA could have represented humanity and helped to manage this transition more effectively with better balance. Review the discussion in "The Role of Profits in Humanism" for ideas to use the W = M x P linear formula to standardize transitioning emerging economies. Now we have the background information to further explain our previous claim.

Suppose we had passed HERA and formed the ECA and further assume that the ECA supported by the developed nations encouraged the WTO (World Trade Organization) to adopt similar mandates for international trade. Then the WTO with the help of the emerging nations would have instituted a comprehensive emergence plan. Using China as an example, this approach could have achieved complete and total emergence by 2012 or sooner. Yet China has still not emerged!

During the recent 8 year period from 2003 to 2011 China had average real GDP growth in excess of 10% annually (after inflation) and this is only slightly higher than previous periods (Wikipedia, 2013). This is the growth characteristic of a subsidized economy on steroids! Clearly no economy with such a high growth rate should be operating on subsidies. No economy needs this kind of growth rate to accomplish emergence! Yet it persists with no end in sight justified as good trade.

Clearly the economic forces driving this hyper-growth should have been redirected towards making the "emergence" transition that would have ended the subsidies as unnecessary by the end of 2011 or sooner. China's wages could have been increased shifting growth from exports to local consumption while currency rates could have been gradually adjusted upward towards fair axiom value ending labor exploitation.

It is important to understand that China is not necessarily the culprit here. Other emerging nations were in the same situation. The developed nations were in the leadership role prior to and during this period. After all Capitalism was Wall Street's creation not Beijing's! The developed nations were "hooked on" the same "steroids" that "drugged" China in the form of artificially cheap products that could be sold for artificially high profits. There is every reason to believe that China, the other emerging nations, and the developed nations all wanted the transition to occur. As far as I know, only Wall Street benefited from the cheap labor and cheap currency procrastination!

Looking at these principles for each stage: "emerged", "balanced", and finally "developed", we can easily conclude that the majority of the trade that is going on presently will be gradually eliminated as inefficient or exploitive! Let us look forward to this new equilibrium. As mentioned above there are two kinds of trade, mandatory and optional. So it is only natural that any nation with mandatory imports would balance them with their most efficient and profitable optional exports with the lowest trade/transportation costs. Only the most efficient products will be profitable enough to overcome the natural barrier of these costs and local production will always be preferred naturally because of its efficiency compared to international trade.

This then represents a "minimum trade equilibrium" condition. Each nation offsets their minimum mandatory imports with optional exports that ideally are another nation's mandatory import with the balance provided by optional exports of convenience and demand. We are not proposing that this trade minimal balance is necessarily the most politically popular but it is the most economically efficient. So good economics leads to good trade and bad economics leads to bad trade.

In economics efficiency usually "wins the day". From Humanism's point of view, we will strive for maximum worldwide prosperity and we believe that maximum prosperity is very close to, if not exactly equal to **maximum efficiency**. The prosperity paradigm of Humanism together with axioms 2 and 3 provide an international blueprint for fair trade to accomplish for the first time "**trade as if people mattered**"!

Notice that this minimal trade concept guarantees every nation equal access to natural resources through international trade sufficient to meet their national needs. Furthermore these trade concepts denounce the idea that "more trade is inherently better trade". To help clarify this we can summarize the primary purposes of trade as twofold:

1. Provide all nations with access to natural resources to meet their national needs.
2. Achieve maximum global efficiency through specialization.

Expanding trade beyond these two goals is inefficient and self-defeating expansionism growth. So that it is only fitting that the natural barriers discussed earlier should discourage trade outside these boundaries. Moreover it should be clear that the current level of trade activity is well beyond the efficiency and access goals stated above. So "trade war paranoia" or not, inefficient international trade will need to be decreased to support increasing international business instead.

Let us look at the political aspects of this optimal trade equilibrium idea. The failure of global economics has created some serious conflicts in our understanding of political sovereignty. As our trade dependence increases, our sovereign independence decreases. As a world we have yet to achieve any effective progress with international governance that works reliably. So to become economically dependent under these circumstances would be destabilizing at best. As examples, look at the problems that Argentina is having with sovereign debt and a New York court, or Greece and Euro debt, or Brexit as recent examples (2015+) of this international conflict.

So economic efficiency or not, it is unlikely that the world's nations will continue to further forfeit their sovereign independence for doubtful economic benefits. The risks of political backlash like Brexit make it mandatory that we substitute trade science based on win-win ideas for the failed economics of global exploitation. Trying to make exploitation "fair" is an impossible oxymoron because both ideas are mutually exclusive! To continue the benefits of trade we must achieve international "law and order" based on international axioms and metaprinciples that are inalienable and indisputable for all nations.

We must be careful to avoid confusing minimal trade equilibrium with any kind of restriction or protectionism on product or service availability. Widespread economic availability of products and services is absolutely necessary for successful worldwide prosperity. Remember our discussion under Title 19 about how macroeconomics is all about "finding supply-supply-supply". The trade equilibrium issue is about how to deliver the supply efficiently, not restricting it.

The equilibrium suggested above will likely be accomplished by local production of international business rather than trade. Businesses will use temporary, less efficient trade to test and establish a viable market for their product (remember, identify demand-demand-demand) and then switch to more efficient local production as a way to satisfy the bulk of the market demand efficiently. Thus we will likely have many more international businesses and much less unfair international trade.

Exploitive trade policies have over emphasized the importance of international trade and drastically under-emphasized the importance of international business. We should have had much **more** international business and much **less** international trade. For example the USA should have invested in starting more businesses in China that produce products in China for Chinese consumers. That kind of international business development instead of exploitative trade would have avoided the creation of the "working poor" and made the transition to balanced trade much easier to achieve. See next topic for further discussion.

The Current Outlook

Now let us return our consideration to the current situation. First we should ask: since the global economy has been underway for more than 30 years, have the "emerging" nations emerged yet? If not, why not? What was the plan? Are we ahead of the plan? Or are we behind in the plan? If we are behind in the plan, what did we do to catch-up? And what do we plan to do in the future? Has China emerged yet? Why not? All that is required is compliance with the two axioms. What is China's schedule? Has India emerged yet? Why not? What is India's schedule and benchmarks? How about Russia? How about Indonesia, South America, and Africa? Couldn't we answer all these questions by simply consulting the "Master Global Economic Plan"?

No, not exactly! It seems that our economic professionals did not insist on having a "Master Global Economic Plan". Thankfully they were not in charge of going to the actual moon! It would have been yet another humiliating embarrassment like the minimum wage! There was no plan agreed to by each emerging nation. By modern standards of professional conduct this is a medieval economic deficiency! How could such a deficiency be explained or tolerated? How could we achieve good economics with such bad professional methodology?

Maybe "the plan" was to exploit as much of humanity as possible, for as long as possible, and for the greatest profit possible. And then abandon the mess to move on to some new exploitation scheme or scam all in the name of "good market economics"? You would not want nor need a "Master Plan" for that would you? It would be self-incriminating for the crime of economic rape! Furthermore you would not need an exit plan for exploitation if you never planned to exit!

So we have a rather ugly current condition with global trade. Easy labor exploitation makes very inefficient international supply chains profitable in the short term even though they are not economically viable in the long term. As long as exploitation is an option, there is no motive to wring out the supply chain inefficiencies. Instead we just offset the inefficiencies with cheaper labor and cheaper currency to maintain the appearance of profitability that is not actually sustainable!

This is clear in the NAFTA example above where the profit motive trumps efficiency with vulnerable desperation! It is also clear from the data of the China 2003-2011 period. This data shows that no matter how high the growth rate becomes exploitation and inefficiency continue to expand. So exploitation generates the need for more and deeper ongoing exploitation! Does this sound like an exit plan to you? No! It's a trap! As long as there is a profitable demand for human exploitation there will be a supply – an "endless" human supply!

A Brave New World?

What "Brave New World" has been forced upon us under the guise of the "good" economics of cheap labor and cheap currency? All that is needed to facilitate an "endless" supply of cheap labor and cheap currency is "endless" and ever increasing human desperation. Many of our international political institutions appear to be more than capable of providing endless desperation even when it is not profitable! Can you imagine how easy it is when there is a strong profit motive? They achieved broad scale hunger, broad scale disease, and broad scale poverty. What is stopping them from adding broad scale desperation to their list of "accomplishments"? Yet cheap labor and cheap currency are not an accomplishment; they are a dangerous house of cards.

Let us look at an example scenario. Suppose international profits are waning and there is a need for a new plateau of even cheaper labor to rejuvenate profitability and continue exploitation worldwide. We would need a new "advanced" exploitation zone that would extort a new norm of vulnerable desperation that would provide even cheaper labor and even cheaper currency. And we could call it "competition"!

This new norm could then be used as a standard to ratchet down labor rates globally in back and forth extortion and exploitation to achieve the new lower global plateau. We have already established that this is the exact case when we discussed the wealth economics' concept of "working poverty". How much "investment" (bribes) would be needed to arrange a rebellion or a Coup d'état that could provide the increased desperation needed for a new lower plateau of an exploitation zone?

It is just economic supply and demand. Once we create the demand for exploitation, the supply of exploitation will follow if the profits are large enough! And the profits will be large enough if the exploitation is deep enough. We probably do not even need a rebellion? For the right "investment" any warlord, dictator, or military junta would be happy to accommodate the needed economic "reforms" for a more "advanced" exploitation zone by adding bribes to the inefficiencies!

A Ponzi Trade Scheme

Ultra-high unemployment is easy even for economic idiots to achieve and it is usually sufficient to provide the necessary desperation. For example look at the ultra-high unemployment of youth in France, Spain, Greece and Venezuela. Worse yet these are supposed to be developed economies! No dictator or military junta yet? Do not be so sure. The entrepreneurial spirit is large when the profits are larger. It should be clear that this desperation "market" has **no bottom**. There is no amount of desperation too high to stop even more desperation. Even "working starvation" would be viable because parents would work to their own starvation death in hopes of feeding their starving children! Without sound metaeconomics there are **no limits** in wealth economics no matter how ugly and draconian the exploitation may be.

Human exploitation is providing the profit incentive for unbalanced and inefficient trade. As long as exploitation is available as an option, the "emerging" nations will never emerge! They cannot afford to emerge! As long as it is profitable, exploitation will continue and even increase if necessary to offset the inefficiencies so that we can continue with **bad economics because it is temporarily profitable**. It is like a giant global economic "Ponzi scheme"! In the end, bad economics will dead-end by breaking the back of humanity with "endless" desperation. Thus "working poverty" will transition to "working homeless" that will in turn achieve "working starvation".

There will be no stable way out, causing collapse of the worldwide economic system. We are digging a large international trade "hole". The deeper we dig the harder it will be to find an exit! We must stop digging, intervene, and secure international commitments to achieve the equal pay for equal productivity axiom and the fair currency axiom on an aggressive yet stable transition schedule. This will buy us time to follow with an aggressive schedule for balanced trade and finally a fully developed world economy complying with all our axioms.

In the early days of the global economy most nations were insulated from each other because the percentage of international trade was small. The exploitation of one economy by another seemed to have benefits without any significant negative consequences. But all the world's economies are now intertwined and dependent. Everyone is now a customer and/or a producer for everyone else. This idea that we could exploit one another to achieve common prosperity is idiotic!

Indeed this lawless ("free" of laws) trade exploitation provides us with a form of international economic **anarchy** forced on us in the name of "good trade economics". We were told by our economists that lawless trade based on cheap labor and cheap currency exploitation would lead us to prosperity but it only led us to exploitation and economic anarchy. As with the other developed nations, we went from a nation where national commerce (trade) was conducted under law and order to an international anarchy where lawfulness must "compete" with greedy lawlessness. It's no surprise who is "winning". Not humanity!

It should be obvious that the market cost of lawlessness will always be less than that of lawfulness not because of efficiency but because of the ease of economic exploitation and extortion afforded by anarchy. For example in the USA we have laws regarding pollution for all producers but these laws are easy to thwart by moving production offshore where vulnerable desperation provides more accommodative lawlessness. **This is foolish anarchy** not trade science. So in the name of greed we exported pollution to China as a malicious substitute for good economics! Clearly the USA lost and clearly China lost, so who won? Not humanity! Yet Wall Street has a big smile on their face!

Instead we need a systematic methodology for international trade that is based on irrefutable win-win ideas that constitute a new trade science. And these win-win ideas will be much easier to implement than we have been told. Agreeing to the axioms is easy because they favor humanity – all humanity equally without privilege! We will achieve a truly unifying idea for metaeconomic common prosperity.

Once a few key nations agree to the new principles of trade the remaining nations will have a "no brainer" choice to join the new or continue with the old exploitation trade group. The old exploitation trade group will then be able to continue exploiting one another as a means for mutual prosperity! But without willing exploitation losers there will no longer be exploitation winners. Just losers who are exploited in turn the more they exploit others in an endless downward, dog-eat-dog nightmare. Which trade group would you want to join?

Win-lose trade concepts are near their demise. We have been told by our economists that bad trade is better than no trade at all. This is a sly and deceptive argument intended to scare us into, and perpetuate, bad trade situations because these ugly situations benefit wealth power at humanities' expense. This argument is based on the fallacy that our choices are limited to bad trade or no trade. Yet good trade is clearly an option in Humanism and it is preferred by all people and all nations.

Unfortunately good trade is not preferred by the wealth power of Wall Street, big business, big wealth, and big banking because it is more difficult and less profitable. The absence of the extortion, distortion, manipulation, and exploitation to produce cheap labor and cheap currency slavery diminishes quick and easy profits. This goes against the primary premise of wealth economics: that pampering and mollycoddling wealth power is the only path to common "prosperity"!

Moreover it should be clear that good trade cannot even be achieved if we embrace the idea that bad trade is better than no trade at all. It is harder to recover from bad trade than it is to recover from no trade. So we have been led into a "bad trade trap". It seems to us that we cannot achieve good trade without returning to no trade at all. But this is a delusion because trade science based on the axioms leads directly to good trade and the transition is easier than returning to no trade at all. With these flawed, **foul** ideas no wonder our economic professionals failed to provide us with a systematic, scientific, **fair** trade alternative.

Instead they have provided us with a kind of "trade war paranoia". In this fear phobia mere mention of fair trade ideas immediately invokes warnings of protectionism, trade wars, and eminent worldwide economic disaster if we try to reform bad trade. This phobia is partly a deliberate divisive scheme to perpetuate exploitation. Furthermore it seems plausible because the global economic Ponzi scheme discussed above **does** make our international trade into a fragile "house of cards" that could collapse at any time. So this scare tactic fear seems justified.

Yet this "house of cards" is not caused by trade reform but rather it is caused by the lack of it! Under these circumstances trade science is our only workable solution. So trade protectionism will no longer have a motivation because open and reciprocal trade will be encouraged in a systematic scientific way. The longer we dig the exploitation hole deeper, the greater the danger of collapse. Review Title 6 to refresh the technical foundation for these ideas of **linear wage based prosperity**.

The necessity of international trade science is also indicated by the current proliferation of ad hoc "trade deals" like WTO, NAFTA, TPP, TTIP, and EEC. This "alphabet soup" of trade is not the solution rather it is a symptom of the underlying problem. The idea of international trade inherently includes the idea of mutual agreement but not divisive agreements to gain privileged advantage over other agreements in some kind of grand agreement-counter-agreement power-play scheme.

Truth or **Power** which will guide us? Trade science must be based on axiomatic first principles that are self-evident, inalienable, and irrefutable. Furthermore **all** nations must have the choice of inclusion equally without special "deals", preferences, or privileges. For example NAFTA tries to get a special deal for North America and the

EEC promises a special deal for the European Community. Do you think that more privileged "deals" like this will improve international trade? Trade science based on truth of first principles is our only hope!

We need **one,** good, scientific, and fair "new trade deal" based on inalienable axiomatic principles that are open and free of any non-reciprocal tariffs or trade restrictions that include no privileges and exclude no nations except those that wish to be excluded! Furthermore international economic prosperity and coexistence are too important to allow petty political sanctions to be introduced for political reasons. Short of a declaration of war the only trade sanctions allowed are for economic axiomatic noncompliance. International political issues must be resolved by some other political organization and methodology such as the UN, not the WTO and trade sanctions. Trade science must be given an international economic sanctuary free from international political interference so good metaeconomics will prevail worldwide.

Bad trade economics based on cheap labor and cheap currency "competition" has collateral damage as well. One of these collateral damages is the worldwide harm caused to product quality. For example almost all electronic manufacturers have drastically cut their quality programs because they simply cannot afford to compete with cheap labor and cheap currency trade while maintaining quality programs. Even the most basic inline quality testing has been eliminated as indicated by the common experience of buying products that fail out-of-the-box on first use because they were never tested.

Basic inline testing just adds costs to find defects that cost even more to investigate, correct, and improve. So why not just ship the defects directly to the end user and let him test them! Greed conquers all problems! This way there are no factory defects, no testing costs, and no need for any quality improvement programs. The consequences of this loss of quality are increased lifecycle costs and decreased product value that decrease prosperity. On the other hand competition on a level playing field, provided by trade science principles, would give the quality producer a distinct competitive advantage. What a change!

It is time for a New World Order! The WTO is a good candidate for a reformable organization to establish a single, consolidating, worldwide trade agreement free of all non-reciprocal tariffs and restrictions that will schedule a transitional compliance with these economic axioms on an agreed to plan. We proposed a systematic transitional plan based on linear wage prosperity and the $W = M \times P$ formula in Title 6 and topic "The Role of Profits in Humanism" and fair currency values proposed in Title 7. There is no reason this "emergence" cannot be fully accomplished in most cases within 8 years or less. Balanced trade will follow soon thereafter. Final development may require a lot longer depending on productivity improvements achieved by each nation.

This is a win-win situation based on axiomatic concepts that are inalienable and indisputable for all nations. There are no losers in this New World Order only winners! No one can deny that political democracy has had a profound effect on the world as a whole. So it is likely that economic democracy will substantially expand this effect by providing a new concept of economic prosperity for all mankind.

Furthermore axiomatic economics and its trade science open up a clear path to **worldwide unity and peace**. We have struggled for many millennia to find a unifying idea for political worldwide unity. Political Democracy is the best idea so far. Unfortunately we have still failed miserably! It seems that the political diversity required to truly represent all of humanities' races, creeds, ethnicities, and political imagination cannot be unified sufficiently. So without economic democracy, political democracy alone is insufficient to provide the complete governance solution that we so desperately need and deserve.

Instead we could shift our effort to democratic, axiomatic economic compliance on a global scale that would support the worldwide unity and peace that we strive for without necessarily requiring political democracy. The sooner we get started with our economic democracy the sooner we will accomplish worldwide prosperity. Once we do democratic prosperity could unify us instead of mere politics! Who knows? Maybe a new plateau of democratic politics will follow also!

Near Term Global Economic Outlook

The previous discussion looked at the past term global economic strategy and condition for the last 30 years or so. We also projected a steady-state trade equilibrium based on application of our axioms to trade economics especially axioms 2 and 3. Now let us look at the near term transition from the old exploitation trade system into the new Humanistic version of international trade over the next 10 years or so.

Let us also focus our attention away from the global economy and just concentrate on the two most important "poles" of the global economy which are the emerging nations led by China and India and the developed nations led by North America and the European Common Market. The rest of the global economy can easily be understood by comparison and contrast of future trade with these two general cases.

Emerging Nations

First let us look at the near term transition in the emerging nations particularly China and also India. Both of these nations have been in the emerging stage for some time now. They are characterized by large well developed manufacturing capacity and, particularly in the case of China, large, out of proportion, imbalanced trade favoring exports.

They achieved and maintain this export heavy trade imbalance by underpaying their workers and undervaluing their currency so the currency cost of their products is artificially low and attractive to foreign markets particularly North America and Europe. Unfortunately the economic cost of these products (labor hours) is actually too high and inefficient making this scheme into an economic trade trap.

Both nations have strong public political commitments to achieve more balanced trade yet they are stuck in a vicious trap. Their "working poverty" consumers do not make wages that will justify purchasing the products that they manufacture! This has caused the chronic worldwide deflation that we have experienced since 2008. Their "working poor" are willing and able to work for less and less out of greater desperation but they are not willing **much less even able** to buy the products they produce! So there is a dangerous disconnection or gap between production and consumption causing unbalanced trade.

Thus product prices drop forcing deflation and even lower wages in a downward, self-perpetuating spiral. However lower prices do not help because lower wages just maintain or even expand the production-consumption gap. Guess what? Central Bank strategies like zero interest rates and more QE bond buying do not help either. They only treat the symptom not the root causes: cheap labor and cheap currency.

Worse yet this production-consumption disconnect could be fatal as "working poverty" continues to spread further back into the developed nations as well. Indeed the broad scale concept of workers making products for wages too low to buy the products that they make, is inherently economically unsound and intellectually disgraceful! Remember the discussion under "The Invisible Economic Slavery" about the greedy factory owner that never figures out what is wrong?

Luckily the way out of this trap is simple and easy to understand. All workers must be paid enough to afford to buy the products that they make! So they need to implement the two economic axioms discussed above in an aggressive but stable fashion with a pre-agreed compliance schedule. Eventually they will be able to comply with all of the 5 axioms. They already have the manufacturing capacity in place. Large scales of further investment are not needed and are well within their capacity. All they need to do is shift this capacity to locally demanded products. In addition they could consider a temporary export tax selective or general to help them manage the transition temporarily.

This temporary export tax would be more useful if it were capable of being either a tax or a credit if necessary. Then currency values and wages could be increased in a way that is best for the local economy while the export tax/credit could adjust trade temporarily to meet international goals. For example, suppose that the optimal currency values and wages are achieved locally but they are too high to support the international export requirements and exports drop faster than desired. A temporary export credit could help achieve equilibrium during the economic transition to a common linear wage prosperity.

China and India are different and each of them will need their own plan, their own schedule, and their own careful measurement and monitoring. Unfortunately in this case, procrastination will not lead to stability while "digging the trade hole deeper". So it is important to be aggressive and yet carefully monitor results for a stable transition. The beauty of the current situation for all emerging nations is that they are all on the verge of entering a golden age of rapidly increasing human prosperity that will last for many generations and beyond. What a hopeful and exciting outlook they will have if only they can demand that their economies make these changes and implement this transition. Let us hope for the sake of all humanity that they have the courage to make this change now before some catastrophic economic collapse!

Developed Nations

The developed nations including North America and Europe are facing a somewhat different and more demanding challenge from this same global trade situation. All developed nations and in particular the USA must embark on an ambitious re-industrialization program of major proportions. In order to allow emerging nations to make products for their own economy, developed nations must return to making their own products nationally instead of borrowing money to buy them abroad. Axioms 2 and 3 discussed in Title 6 and 7 make this possible.

The emerging nations have only to shift production from one product destination to another. But the developed nations must invest in new capital infrastructure that no longer exists. It rusted away in the "rust belt" so to speak. This is both a difficult challenge and a unique opportunity but it will require a lot of capital, labor, and productivity.

Luckily the developed nations have access to the capital investment needed for this transition provided they adopt the reforms described in HERA above. The more difficult problem is having enough labor for all the new high paying, high productivity jobs that will be needed! Once again the reforms described in HERA will save the day. The sub-mandate for increasing the employment participation rate from 63% to above 70% and the sub-mandate to improve underemployment from 5% to 0% will provide a quick source of 12% added labor resources.

Moreover immigration skill reforms, affordable education programs, and job skill training could easily provide the balance. Furthermore the wage compensation system of Title 11a ($W\% = Ip\% - Iw\% + P\%$) will ensure that there is no wage inflation or wage deflation during the transition. In the longer term the central prosperity mandate will strive for and provide continuously improving productivity and that is just what the "doctor ordered". The path forward to prosperity for all is clear and obvious once we abandon this idea of cheap labor slavery.

The best opportunity of all comes from the biggest problem of all; our old infrastructure is gone! Luckily the old infrastructure has already been written off. This means that we will have the "opportunity" to build new, from the floor up, manufacturing facilities with the most advanced robotics, automation, AI, and other productivity tools to provide productivity that we so need and so want for our prosperity! Furthermore the axioms will make this automation **safe for humanity**. It is an opportunity for a second industrial revolution using 100% full employment automation as we accomplish our economic "moon"!

It should be reassuring to find that once the reforms that we specified in HERA are also enacted at the international level that those reforms provide exactly the changes we need to support finishing the reforms at the national level for both the emerging and our developed nations. This demonstrates a kind of conceptual "completeness" or "closure" where the results reinforce and help to fulfill the original requirements. It is a way to prove the feedback loop is positively reinforcing before we close the loop. It shows how a win-win solution should match up when the loop is closed. It sets our nation and our world on course for an economic renaissance realized with our Humanistic first principles.

International Prosperity

This is not just a hopeful and exciting time for emerging nations. It will be an equally hopeful and exciting time for the developed nations as well for many generations ahead. What a truly amazing contrast this situation presents! Without reform our current outlook is dismal at best and probably catastrophic. Yet with just a few very easy to understand axiomatic reforms at the systemic level our outlook suddenly becomes hopeful and exciting beyond belief! What a change and there are no losers just winners! Metaeconomics by the axioms makes this possible.

No wage or currency exploitation is needed and all workers of all nations are mathematically guaranteed the maximum salaries possible based on their own productivity. Moreover all businesses of all nations compete fairly with equal labor cost for equal productivity. Therefore all nations, from highest productivity to lowest productivity, will be guaranteed equal access to international markets and equal access to international resources no matter how high or low their productivity may be. So protectionism will no longer have a reward or motivation!

The International Challenge

Not so quick! This positive outlook is based on the assumption that we have the courage to stand and make the changes and reforms needed. Will we? Or will we let others stand and wait to see if we are really needed? Will we just wait to see if the old system will magically fix itself? That is what the paid professional "experts" will tell us to do!

If we wait, big business will do nothing. Big politics will do nothing. Big economics will do nothing. Big trade will do nothing. Big Wall Street will do nothing. Big banks will do nothing. Big wealth will do nothing. And if we are very lucky we will just get **nothing**, the best we could ever hope for from wealth economics. However it is far more likely that we will get nothing for a while and then suffer an ugly catastrophic collapse from which there is no recovery for many generations crushing our children and grandchildren into poverty!

We will suffer the demoralization of knowing, and knowing our children and grandchildren know that we failed to stand and make a difference when we had the opportunity. I do not have the heart to describe this ugly outcome further! It seems to me that we have had more than enough ugly already? Instead I want an exciting future based on prosperity and security for all peoples and all nations where equal performance produces equal rewards for everyone, guaranteed!

However if you are motivated by ugly, there are many "gloom and doom" authors with an abundance of scary details that will make you sick with fear and loathing. The chronic lack of free, reciprocal, and balanced trade will eventually force the USA to abandon its sole role as the world's "free trade maker" and the house of cards will collapse. Nations whose trade practices end in trade wars should not be trading!

What began as a "fair trade fantasy" will end as a "foul trade fiasco". The trade science of Humanism is our only workable solution. For my part I am far more motivated by the positive than by the negative. So I want maximum prosperity for the vast majority of mankind worldwide whether or not there is a threat of "gloom and doom". **Prosperity is our economic destiny**! Why should we strive for or accept anything less? We deserve this and we are long overdue. I am ready and I know most of us have the courage to stand! What about you? Are you ready?

What Would Adam Smith Have Thought?

Most economists would claim that Adam Smith was the father of economics. It seems interesting to me to ask the question "how would he react to the ideas of a democratic, axiomatic, proactive economic control system for metaeconomics?" We should look at each of these ideas "democratic", "axiomatic", and "proactive" economic control and see if we can imagine how he would react as a reasonable guess based on his writings and the context of the economic situation in which he lived. So let me give you my simplistic interpretation of his work *The Wealth of Nations* and his era in regard to these questions.

Economic Democracy

His work was to a great extent motivated as a reaction to the then current state of market control. In his time markets were under the control of the feudal system, the same feudal system that the Dutch, French, and Americans were rebelling against politically. You might say that he was leading the economic rebellion against the same economic feudal system that we were rebelling against politically.

At that time all market decisions about product pricing were made by the kings and queens with some advice from their courts. As you can imagine this feudal control system was an insane asylum of corruption, chaos, and power inspired ignorance. There was only one guiding economic principle: "the larger the king's commission the better the price"! This advanced economic "principle" was an early forerunner of the later version I have been calling "greed conquers all problems".

This corrupt situation had persisted since the beginning of recorded history with the possible exception of the Greek's short experiment with democratic governance. What is not recorded in history is the immense pain and suffering that all humanity incurred generation after generation, millennia after millennia. Humanity could not rise up and throw off the yoke of this insane asylum for something much better!

Why you might ask? I wish I knew for sure but I suspect that we find it much easier to follow the lead of powerful personalities rather than following the lead of powerful abstract ideas. Powerful personalities mesmerize us and then exploit us while powerful ideas require our democratic participation. Or maybe powerful ideas are just hard to come by? In any case it was Adam Smith's powerful ideas that lead us out of that feudal market darkness into a systematic market idea.

Market Valuations

His most important idea was that a systematic supply/demand market mechanism could be used to establish the price of any commodity or product. This would negate the need to "make a deal" with the king or queen to set the price. In keeping with his era his idea was strongly democratic since any buyer could buy and any seller could sell. This system gave equal access to everyone. What a breakthrough idea: that the price could be achieved automatically by a systematic continuous bidding process between buyers and sellers and this would free the market from the insane asylum of feudal corruption and control!

Our economic reality has changed a lot since Adam Smith's time. He could not possibly have known that it would be possible to manipulate, corrupt, distort, extort, and exploit his market system to the extent we have now achieved. He believed that this would be impossible. He did not realize that the economic environment surrounding his market mechanism could itself be corrupted. He could not have imagined the $ billions that would be donated each year by the perpetually wealthy to our academic economic institutions to sponsor and ensure wealth economics is taught and promoted instead of prosperity economics.

He also could not have imagined how harmful it would be under these corrupt circumstances to apply his market ideas to the human labor market or to the currency market without a safe, embedded guiding principle. He did not realize that he needed to apply his ideas as well to the meta-level of economics to provide a safe systematic structure for his market mechanism to maintain its freedom from corruption.

Axiomatic Superstructure

The axiomatic ideas we are proposing are the same kind of ideas as Adam Smith's but recursively applied to our modern day meta-level problems. We need a modern system to "free all of economics" the same way that Adam Smith "freed the market". We need a superstructure that will free economics from the insane asylum of corruption and control of Wall Street, big banking, big business, and perpetual wealth. They should serve humanity by providing prosperity rather than rule humanity by providing higher profits for themselves!

We need a systematic meta-structure that will support, protect, and keep Adam Smith's free market mechanism safe from manipulation, extortion, and exploitation. While at the same time we need this new meta-structure to provide a democratic superstructure for economics that will maximize the prosperity of the vast majority of mankind as collective principals and collective beneficiaries of **our** economy!

Let us look at a specific example. According to a New York Times article (Greenhouse, 2013) derived from the book *The Big Squeeze* (Greenhouse, 2009), "From 1973 to 2011, worker productivity grew 80 percent, while median hourly compensation, after inflation, grew by just one-eighth that amount (10%), according to the Economic Policy Institute, a liberal research group. And since 2000, productivity has risen 23 percent while real hourly pay has essentially stagnated (0%)".

You do not even need a calculator to determine that according to axiom 5, wages between 1973 and 2011 should have risen by 80% while they only rose by 10%. If we compound this 70% loss over 38 years of income out to the 45 year average of one working lifetime, the difference would be 88% more pay increase during your working life.

That 88% differential was your money that went into someone else's pocket! The euphemism for this loss is usually called "wage erosion" but it would be called "wage robbery" in a world of economic law and order! Title 11a defines a simple embedded compensation mechanism together with a wage compensation formula ($W\% = Ip\% - Iw\% + P\%$) by which axiom 5 should be implemented. Together they would ensure that this wage robbery could never possibly happen again, never again for you, your children, or grandchildren, or any future generation!

Our economic journalists give us reports like this all the time. They are quick to report harm to us as if it was our proper lot to be perpetually harmed. The media just wanted to keep us updated on our most recent harmful economic exploitation. Yet they **never** suggest we should correct the harm much less stop the harm from possibly occurring in the first place. We are **presumed to be victims of our own economy**!

Why? Because that is exactly the way invisible economic slavery must be dealt with in the news media; you can't fix what is invisible but you can report the losses! You cannot discuss the invisible "elephant" in the room but you can discuss the "giant turds" left behind. Foul economic slavery is considered fair and unavoidable like a volcanic eruption yet the losses caused by the eruption can be duly reported!

The report above was not a report of a volcanic eruption that wiped out 88% of our pay increase over the last 45 years. It was a report about real and massive harm caused to humanity by a minority of other real people who were motivated by greed and corruption and enabled by bad or totally lacking economic science! These are manmade problems and they do have easy manmade (engineering) solutions. If some evil men can break it; other men can fix it and keep it fixed indefinitely!

This is why civilization created law and order and how law and order helped civilization in turn to flourish! Do you see the inherent power of axiomatic economics to prohibit harm ideologically, axiomatically, and proactively at the outset while maximizing and protecting our ongoing prosperity with a very high degree of accuracy, and certainty?

What would Adam Smith think? You can decide for yourself. My imaginary hero would vigorously applaud our ideas. He would firmly and fully support our democratic ideas as an extension of his own democratic, objective, market mechanism. He would loudly cheer the mathematical systemization of our axiomatic ideas as a teacher would, whose students grasp his idea so well that they then apply it, to his surprise, to the meta-level encompassing his own market subsystem recursively. He would champion "**markets as if people mattered**"!

Avoiding Greed and Corruption

He spent his whole life trying to wrench market control away from the feudal system and its insanity of greed and corruption. Would he not shout support for our efforts to wrench economic control away from the insanity of greed and corruption of Wall Street, big banking, big business, and perpetual wealth? He was opposed to controls under the power of the feudal system in particular and in general he opposed controls by what I paraphrase as the "good faith of powerful men". He understood that **power without principles** is economically dangerous!

Instead he wanted controls by a systematic, objective methodology that could be evaluated and scrutinized by anyone without reliance on the trust in the "good faith of powerful men". I am sure he would advise us to get started right away while we still have the will and resources to do this! And he too would wonder what took us so long?

Of course Wall Street and their entourage will be quick to claim that Adam Smith was against a controlled market and that they are saving our economy from the controls to which he so objected. This is like Wall Street saving us from rain during a drought. They propose to ensure security for our "hen house" by hiring their "fox". They would propose avoiding controls by the "good faith of powerful men" by substituting the corruption achieved by the "good faith of greedy men" instead! They propose that greed can lead the way to prosperity for all!

So somehow bad economics becomes "good" because it trumps bad politics! The hypocrisy and collective dishonesty of the "free" market chant is truly appalling! Wall Street, big business, and big banking including the Central Bank and our economic professionals all worked together to rig the labor market with 5% minimum unemployment and other strong market biases discussed previously in "The Role of "Free" Markets in Humanism". Would he approve of this sly market rigging?

These controls and manipulations rigged an unbalanced, perpetual buyer's labor market to have a very strong, overwhelming employers' market advantage. The goal was to drive up profits and to drive down wages and salaries and keep them in equilibrium at or near their lowest sustainable levels possible just short of violent backlash and rebellion.

These deliberate market exploitations so biased and distorted the labor market that 88% of your wage and salary increase over these 45 years got "redirected" from your paycheck into business profits, salaries and bonuses for management, and the balance passed on to the privileged wealthy class shareholders instead! This indicates that our pay increases were underpaid by 1.45% of GDP each year compounded for 45 years while corporate profits were overpaid by the same 1.45% of GDP. It may seem small, but not when it's compounded over your life.

How convenient this is for wealth power. And the wage robbery has increased substantially since then making the annual loss 1.9% since

2000! If we compound this projected loss over 45 years it would be a 129% loss of generational income growth. So the wage robbery is getting progressively worse as we wait to correct this abuse. Do you really think that waiting is the correct strategy? The Central Bank could have easily reduced its unemployment target to achieve a wage equilibrium that would have included this annual loss but wealth economics ruled and prosperity economics was defied or ignored.

The five axioms would have mandated prosperity economics and the Central Bank would be **forced** to proactively comply as the new ECA! And we could confirm their performance independently with public measurements and calculations of their compliance. What a profound difference in economic governance from the old system where your exploitation is the preferred option to a new system where your exploitation cannot even be an option! It's a night and day difference!

Economic Hypocrisy

Why do you suppose the market was deliberately rigged **against** humanity instead of **for** humanity? Title 11a shows a simple correction mechanism ($W\% = Ip\% - Iw\% + P\%$) that allows paying maximum wages, including the full 88% lost to corruption, without causing wage inflation at all, guaranteed by measurement and simple subtraction! And the $W = M \times P$ formula stops the need for most of this correction.

Obviously Capitalism is rigged in the extreme and mindless favor of the privileged wealthy class. When markets are biased, controlled, and manipulated to benefit the privileged wealthy class this is called a "free" market. Yet when the exploitation and manipulation controls are removed for the benefit of humanity and replaced with an axiomatic, scientific, mathematical system then this is called an "anti-free" or a "controlled" market. Oh yes "foul is fair and fair is foul in economics". Yet it is hard to tell with this draconian mumbo jumbo weather it is "good" foul or "bad" fair because we will always lose either way!

If greed can't spin it corruption will. This situation could only "make sense" in an insane asylum! Do you think this insane asylum will magically fix itself if we do not intervene and stop the harm? Clearly this is way out of control and our economists are way too corrupted by wealth power to fix it! It is time for a change. We have suffered enough! Guided by the axioms, the Economic Bill of Rights, and HERA, the ECA will wrench control of our economy from Wall Street the same way Adam Smith did with feudal control. Good riddance!

Yet we will **not** return it to the control of the "good faith of powerful men" but rather to the control of technicians, engineers, and scientists operating as a verifiable mandate to the democratic axioms of Economic Geometry. The head of the ECA is just the chief economist acting consistent with the axiomatic economic system the same way the chief geometrist would for Euclid's Geometry. He does not rule.

We define the principles; **they** comply. The ECA does not rule Economic Geometry; we do because we can all independently verify proof of **their** compliance with **our** axioms. We do not have to rely on the good faith of anyone! It is truly a democratic system that is open and transparent to all. It is a system that is not controlled by anyone. It's democratically controlled by the collective majority of everyone.

I have had enough long ago; I am ripe and ready for a change! I am ready for a mathematical, scientific, and democratic system that will produce economic law and order by changing economics into the science of democratic prosperity and sustainable life. How about you?

Justice in Economics

Could there be justice in economics? What a daring idea! I thought there was a law in economics that says you cannot use the word "justice" in the same sentence as the word "economics"? When I do a search for sentences that contain both words I receive few meaningful matches. Maybe that is what Keynes meant when he discussed why we must **pretend** for another 100 years that "fair is foul and foul is fair in economics" (Keynes, 1931)? I think our 100 years will soon be up and we are still not ready for the honest truth. Foul is not the path to good economics and it never was! They say there is "no crying in baseball" (Hanks, 1992) and so I guess there is "no justice in economics" either! Can't you just imagine Tom Hanks playing the coach of Wall Street while espousing his theory that there is "no justice in economics"?

Volcanic Voodoo

Why you might ask? Well now as Tom would explain: it is because there is no law and order in economics that would or could support it! Furthermore, you can't hold a volcano responsible for the damage of its own eruption can you? So the voodoo of the "volcanic theory of economics" plays an important role in our imaginary theater that tries to rationalize the absence of any human justice in wealth economics.

On the upside what if human economic exploitation was a felony offense? What if failure to pay prevailing labor rates was a felony offense? What if market manipulation and "gaming the system" were felony offenses? What if it was a felony offense to use personal, corporate, or institutional wealth as a political privilege to advocate harm, obstruct, reduce or interfere with or exert unreasonable control or influence over the democratic rights of others especially "equal opportunity", "one man one vote", and the Economic Bill of Rights?

What if political contributions were regulated so that the voice of the populace was kept proportional to the voice of wealth power? What if conspiracy to commit these economic crimes was held in special contempt like the RICO laws? What if whistleblower laws were extended to support financial reward to help prosecute these crimes?

What if "Certified Public Economists" were required to take and keep a Hippocratic type oath including the commitment "to do no harm" and the requirement "to represent the prosperity of the vast majority of humanity in economic matters"? What if these economists could be sued for the harm caused by malpractice like doctors? Our economic health is just as important as our medical health. So why are financial and economic criminals not actually prosecuted and then sent to jail?

Our economic culture would change from a culture of greed, privilege, corruption, and exploitation to a new culture of democratic prosperity. For the first time in economic history "scientific economic practices" would prevail over "greedy business practices". Over a relatively short period of time our lives would be transformed into a new dimension of prosperity previously unimaginable! I hope you can see clearly that economic justice, our democratic prosperity, and our economic moon are clearly visible and within our technical and engineering grasp!

On the downside Justice may become democracy's last bastion of defense? Our political democracy is now under the most direct, merciless, and lethal attack of its entire history and this attack comes from within. This attack is facilitated through the wealth power of economic greed, exploitation, privilege, and corruption rather than by some external military threat! We are confronted by a stark reality and a clear threat: that either we expand our idea of political democracy to include economic democracy as well or we will lose **both** facets of our precious democracy to wealth corruption and economic aristocracy!

If we are not successful in making this transition politically, then our last line of defense will come from our political Constitution and its interpretation by our Supreme Court. Our final burden of defense against total loss of democracy may be placed on the Scale of Justice. Can she withstand this merciless attack? Can she stand strong where the institutions of politics and religion have tried and failed to stand?

I believe our democracy will prevail because of the strong support of our grassroots effort but without this support our democracy and our planet are in grave danger! I hope that for the first time in history mankind will throw off the yoke of greed, exploitation, privilege, and corruption by Wall Street, big banks, big business, and perpetual wealth. These visions will become a reality because the axioms of economics, the Economic Bill of Rights, and HERA will provide the legal groundwork to support achieving law and order in economics.

Furthermore the ECA will become the enforcement agency with the power to ensure compliance and they will provide the professional economic representation we have been deprived of for so long. The "volcanic theory of economics" will be exposed for what it is: a crude and divisive attempt to obscure the responsibility and accountability of corrupt and greedy people from the legal consequences of their toxic, injurious, and harmful actions and economic crimes against humanity.

Pay Discrimination

Let's look at racial pay discrimination and its counterpart gender pay discrimination as relevant issues that are also indicative of the economic failure and injustice issue in general. I would like to speak directly and personally to these two issues as a white male. Early in my college youth, fifty years ago these two problems were clearly identified, analyzed, measured, confirmed, debated, and a national consensus proclaimed loudly for all to hear and agree with **fair pay**.

So the vast majority of males along with almost everyone else insisted that female pay discrimination was a travesty and should be corrected forthwith. Likewise the vast majority of whites along with almost everyone else insisted that non-white racial pay discrimination was also a travesty and should be corrected forthwith. It seemed that there was then, and is now, "**no one**" who advocates these inequities! Who advocates racial pay discrimination? Who advocates gender pay discrimination? **Nobody**! Yet they still persist on a massive scale!

So as a white male I presumed that these discriminatory practices would be corrected at least thirty years ago or sooner. I was made aware of legislation and court cases that reinforced that presumption. My profession like most of you focused on other matters equally important to mankind. We trusted our politicians and economists to implement this social consensus while we invented integrated circuits, sequenced our genome, went to the moon, developed personal computers, created the internet, explored space, cured diseases, invented smartphones, and much more! **We did; they didn't!**

Science, Mathematics, and Engineering succeeded brilliantly while Economics, Politics, and Justice failed mankind on a profound scale! Their list of economic "accomplishments" during this same period would include: pollution, resource depletion, economic devastation of the middle class, widespread homelessness, unfair and failed global trade, unaffordable health care, unaffordable education and student debt, a defunct national retirement and Medicare system, out of control public debt destroying us, a massive concentration and perpetuation of wealth, and finally chronic economic gender and race pay disparity!

Capitalism sponsors economic slavery through cheap labor and cheap currency. Yet it is hard to eliminate one kind of slavery (racial/gender) while sponsoring another more basic (economic)! So fifty years later we find only a little measurable progress has been made on these pay discrimination issues or general issues of prosperity as well! What a breach of professional confidence! How could this corruption and betrayal exist and perpetuate itself on such a vast scale for so long?

To begin to understand how these travesties of pay discrimination have perpetuated we must grasp the false and divisive explanation for their perpetuation. We are led to believe that these issues have perpetuated because of the perpetuation of prejudice and malice in the hearts of mankind, in this particular case whites and males. Thus this easy explanation is plausible especially for the victims, non-whites and females, so we must dig deeper to understand the real root cause.

First and foremost we must understand that both of these problems are innately and inherently **economic failures driven by greed** not just social, political or moral issues. How could these problems ever be solved without a **specific economic solution mechanism** designed and engineered carefully to proactively correct the problem? Yet no such economic solution mechanism was ever proposed much less executed.

No wonder the social, political, and moral progress noted above was insufficient to achieve a real solution! In order to better understand the economics of these problems let's use a technique popularized in the Watergate scandal called "follow the money". After all both of these discriminations involved businesses redirecting money from one group to another. That is the inherent nature of economic discrimination.

In Capitalism businesses are fundamentally and directly responsible for salary administration. Businesses found that extorting vulnerable females was easier and much more lucrative than just attempting to further extort males. Likewise they found that extortion of vulnerable non-whites was easier and much more lucrative than just attempting to further extort whites. Both of these new groups were more vulnerable and businesses were quick to exploit this desperation advantage because exploitation of the vulnerable is considered by economists to be "good market economics". Whatever is good economics for zinc and soybeans must be good enough economics for humanity – right?

In both cases females and non-whites historically entered the workforce later than white males and they were targeted by businesses to work for substantially less as a prerequisite for entering the employment market. This wage robbery was one of the greatest crimes in the history of economics! Yet it was justified as "good economics". Can you imagine if these underpaid funds were clawed back over the last 50 years how large the total would be? Can you imagine if these funds were paid out to the victims as lump-sum compensation? Can you even imagine "**economic justice as if people mattered**"!

Where did the money go? It did not go to white males who were already exploited to the greatest extent possible for hundreds of years! It went where it always had gone before: directly to the business's bottom line of the Income Statement where it was used for management bonuses and salary increases to reward the exploiters and to pay dividends for rewarding shareholders or Retained Earnings to improve the Balance Sheet and reward the owners. In general the money went to reward capitalists for their exploitation of the vulnerable and desperate consistent with "good market economics"!

This was a direct and intentional exploitation where the exploitation proceeds went directly to reward the perpetuating exploiters. Why? Simply because they could since they were supported by the "free market" chant and the "what's good for business ..." slogan. Furthermore they will continue as long as economics allows and encourages businesses to exploit workers with the lowest wages attainable and reward the exploiters with the proceeds of the criminal exploitation! Yet what is good economics for zinc and soybeans is **not** necessarily good economics for humans as axiom 1 clearly reminds us!

During this time capitalists, CEO's, and their management entourages knew full well about the discrimination and they knew full well of the social mandate to make corrections. Yet their greed motivated them to simply continue to perpetuate these economic discriminations for their own benefit! They justified their exploitation by saying that "good economics made them do it"! They were already paying white males the lowest achievable wages. There was no elasticity left to pay white males even less to achieve wage parity with non-whites and women.

So the only opportunity for wage parity correction was to pay equal wages to women and non-whites avoiding exploitation. But this was not an option because it would reduce the corporate profit opportunity for the exploiters. That is exactly what Humanism proposes! Female and non-white wages and salaries will be increased each month gradually until the wage parity of axiom 2 is achieved and then maintained indefinitely. There will be a proactive wage correction mechanism (Title 6 and Title 11a) at the aggregate national level for the ECA to enforce the fair wage axiom nationally and internationally **without** depending on the good faith of business management!

Social, political, or moral progress does not automatically achieve good economics and without good economics first and foremost we will not be able to resolve these injustices. Axiom 2 is a first principle that clearly disallows such economic injustice proactively at the ideological, metaeconomic level, at the outset. Our only hope for a resolution of these toxic issues and many others is the institution of axiomatic scientific metaeconomics to provide economic law and order through subsequent economic reforms discussed previously. The path forward is clear and concise. Let's take the challenge on now!

Loss of Democracy

There is one final aspect of injustice in economics that should be discussed even though it is painful. This issue is kind of a "skeleton in the closet" type of issue. It centers on a widespread loss of faith and hope in our political democracy that goes unexpressed and undiscussed because it is so painful to admit the possibility that our political democracy could have been hijacked and **lost already**! Moreover this situation is much easier to perpetuate if it is never discussed, left to fester and grow in the darkness of the hopelessness that it sponsors (see internet: Citizens United and Move To Amend).

I think the best way to bring this issue to the surface is to pursue a simple question repeated throughout this book. We outnumber the 1%'ers a hundred to one and we outnumber the 85'ers by much more so how could we not have enough democratic votes (51%) to institute these reforms in our political democracy? How could it be possible that the USA, the world's leading proponent of democracy, has already lost its own democracy to wealth power and wealth corruption?

Merely asking the question presents an insulting, horrifying, and humiliating image. One possible explanation is that humanity does not want prosperity and reform! But that idea is so preposterous that it is laughable. Another possibility is that wealth corruption has "stuffed the ballot box" defeating our votes. But that is unlikely on such a large scale and with easy detection and correction. So there must be a better explanation for this profound inequity and perpetuated injustice.

A more plausible explanation comes from the wealth power and wealth corruption of our democratic representation system. In this system we only get to vote on our representatives and they in turn vote our wishes (we hope). If the voice of wealth power is much greater than the voice of the populace then we lose our representation because our representatives only hear the stronger voice. Our voice is drowned out by the voice of wealth power until it is totally inaudible. The concept of "one man one vote" becomes meaningless and the system becomes hopelessly corrupted ending democracy without any fight.

We never have a choice to elect representatives that will represent us; it is never even an option because it is not an election problem but rather a representation problem. The corruption paid for during the election process becomes effective during the representation process. This certainly explains why we keep voting to fix the problem but the problem never gets fixed no matter who we elect! Review "Perpetual Wealth is Perpetual Power and Perpetual Corruption" and "Title 5: Freedom from the Economic Privileged Class" to refresh these ideas.

There is no doubt wealth power is trying hard to corrupt and destroy our democratic system. And our economists will not help us. So the only question left is whether our situation is beyond hope? Once the majority succumbs to hopelessness, democracy is lost permanently and replaced with a kind of "pretend democracy" instead. Our government pretends to protect and enhance democracy while we pretend to enjoy and cherish it out of fear and dread of the scary and unthinkable truth!

I meet so many young people who have abandoned all hope and are no longer willing to try to reform the system. They think it is impossible and their only option is to avoid the pain of trying again (Bernie Sanders, 2016). They cannot tolerate the possibility that they could try to hope again. Their plight is that they started before we were ready. The fear of more disappointment is overwhelming for them. To them I would say: "your democracy was hijacked without a fight"! You didn't lose it; we never fought for it! That fight is now at hand. Join us now. Armed with this economic blueprint we will be successful this time!

Maybe our democracy has already been lost or maybe it is still functional enough to support these reforms? I believe the latter but in any case, I am sure of one thing. Now is the time to force this issue and find out so we can take appropriate action in either case. We must challenge this issue before it becomes the accepted constitutional truth.

Now is the time to find out if our democracy has been lost to economic aristocracy already? There is no benefit in waiting in the darkness for this question to be answered by history, only grave danger. It's our history and our answer; let's shout it out! The new civil rights law for the balanced voice mandate suggested in Title 5 and included in the authorizing legislation is a simple first step that we can all agree will force this ugly issue out into the open where justice can deal with it.

The Unification of Business and Labor

Capitalism and its profit paradigm forced business and labor to be polarized in antagonistic opposition to one another in a barbaric, war like, power based conflict. The economic goal in this conflict was to find a way to determine the correct valuation price for human labor in an economic system. The valuation price of human labor is the most important price in any economy and the price balance between labor and profits is the central and most important issue in all of economics!

The Economic Unification

So our economists come up with the idea that, instead of just letting businesses use their wealth power to cheat and exploit the workers ruthlessly, it would be more "sporting" to let the workers throw rocks and burn old tires in retaliation! This silly tit-for-tat conflict could masquerade as a "bid-ask dynamic" and would help economists to pretend that this power struggle insane asylum was a "market" seeking equilibrium! So they could exploit the workers using standard market mechanisms appropriate for zinc or soybeans but totally inappropriate for human labor! In fact this "crazy power war" was not an economic market at all. It was rigged as a horribly unbalanced, power-play scam.

Greed conquers all problems! This barbaric idea to use power based conflict and a pseudo-market to rig the price of labor at the lowest level possible was well below the previous standards of intellectual corruption set by alchemy! Collective bargaining is somewhat less barbaric but no more sane. Power based local negotiations "beg the question" of value in economics; 2 + 2 does not equal 4 because we were forced by brute power to compromise and agree to it! The "Law of the Jungle" has **no role** to play in the quest for truth or the quest for fair economic valuations either. If we are going to collectively argue, let's collectively argue about the wholesome axioms of economics!

After that argument is over the axioms will permanently determine the correct valuation for labor in our economy and many other important economic valuations and questions as well! Apparently no one considered the possibility that such an important economic price should be set scientifically and mathematically based on inalienable and irrefutable first principles such as axioms 1, 2, 3, 4, 5, and 6 combined into a science for metaeconomics instead of brute power.

No one noticed that if wage inflation is directly compensated to be zero, it becomes easy and safe to let wages rise up to their natural equilibrium instead of depressing them to their artificial minimum! No one noticed that the $W = M \times P$ equation and the $W\% = Ip\% - Iw\% + P\%$ equation answer this labor price valuation question exactly and precisely in a scientific manner with proactive engineering guidance!

Just over the last working generation humanity's losses to this insane war between business and labor are tens of trillions of dollars in the USA alone and they are even more mind boggling for the world as a whole. As we have already discussed this polarization is characterized by businesses constantly focused on mindlessly reducing labor rates while labor unions are mindlessly trying to increase labor rates. Neither of these poles had any particular goal in mind or any particular system or science of equilibrium to achieve. Instead one pole wanted labor rates to go down for ever so they could pocket the profit for ever and the other pole wanted to get even for previous never-ending losses.

As citizens of our economy we became used to this never-ending war between labor and business. We grew to accept this antagonistic dog-eat-dog nightmare as the "natural order" of our economy. Our economic professionals did little or nothing to dispel this bad idea and they certainly did not propose an alternative form of metaeconomic equilibrium that would guide us to a less **foul** and more **fair** system. It is time now for professional economic representation for humanity!

On the lighter side this situation comically reminds me of an old engineering professor in college. He taught techniques for solving difficult equations. He always started his introductory class with a joke he liked. He would say: "the first key to equation solving is to make sure you know which are the "variables" (things to solve) and which are the "constants" (things that are already fixed). Otherwise you will end up in the embarrassing situation of wrongly solving the equation for a constant!" There were always a few students who did not laugh. I just assumed that they did not like his joke. Yet, now looking back, I think maybe they were economics majors taking a technical elective?

Indeed the sad economic truth about labor rates is that they are a **constant** for business and labor **not a variable**! Labor rates should not be decreased by business nor should they be increased by labor even if they have the brute power to force it. **Power** does not help the economic valuation or the resolution. It impedes and distorts it! What a profound realization after all these years of economic strife, turmoil, and conflict! Wage rates are "fixed" by a continuous mathematical adjustment mandated by axioms 1, 2, 3, 4, 5, and 6 as embodied in the economic axiom formulas: $W = M \times P$ and $W\% = Ip\% - Iw\% + P\%$.

As axioms, the relevance of these principles is ascertained and "fixed" **outside of and above economics** at a higher metaphysical level. It is at this metaeconomic level that Capitalism and its profit paradigm failed humanity and it is at this metaeconomic level where we must fix it. We will fix it by making everyone a capitalist and a principal in our democratic economy and we will end this conflict between business and labor unifying them with the true idea of Capitalism: **Prosperity**!

Both business and labor must turn their attention from labor rates to the real variables of economics such as scientific valuations, scarcity, prosperity, productivity, efficiency, full employment, economic investment, fair and open trade, product improvement, product quality, product performance, customer support, and many other important economic and business challenges. True economics is not primarily about labor rate exploitation, wealth, or about capital or capitalists.

They are all of secondary or less importance. The fundamental reason our economy exists is to serve humanity in facilitating our inclusive worker/consumer duality by achieving maximum prosperity for the vast majority of mankind! Its purpose is certainly not to facilitate perpetual wealth, big banking, big business or Wall Street who motivate business and labor with the challenge: "let's **you** and **him** fight" so **we** can maximize our profit extortion and exploitation!

Once we understand the real reason for our economy the war between business and labor simply evaporates as unnecessary confusion and ignorance. This war becomes silly like the alchemy of times past or "solving an equation for a constant"! Businesses are the engines that generate prosperity by facilitating the workers to satisfy the consumers with maximum **humane efficiency**. There is no conflict between the workers and the consumers because the beauty of this duality is that the workers and the consumers are one and the same: **humanity**!

Business owners, shareholders, and business managers are not economically privileged and separate! In fact the economically privileged no longer have any need to be privileged or separate if they ever did. Their privilege is a dark artifact of our 1850 past like the feudal system or alchemy. Privilege might have been necessary once-upon-a-time but that dark time is long past. It's time to move on from foul to fair, from wealth to efficiency, and **from profits to prosperity**! So instead "these privileged" are just specialized humans operating with the same motives as all other worker/consumers to earn income to satisfy their consumption. They are fully included. Moreover because their productivity is high their incomes are high as well ($W = M \times P$).

Title 9 shows us how to make all worker/consumers into capitalists as well further ending the ideas of privilege, exclusion, and separation. Capitalists, shareholders, and business managers are no different than other specialists and experts like economists, accountants, astronauts, engineers, doctors, or so many others. In our modern economy the only legitimate shortages are labor, natural resources, and anti-pollution. Capital and capitalists are in excess abundance and always will be in a Humanistic economy. In Title 21 we already discussed the "great management shortage" that never was and never will be! Or the great "king and queen shortage" that never was. Of course the self-appointed elite always want to self-glorify their own indispensability!

Economic investment will always be available in a constant "throttled back" condition more or less to avoid overheating the economy. Boom or bust, the ECA will always ensure by professional mandate that there is more reserve capital ready for deployment than is actually deployed. Moreover they will ensure capital deployment matches full 100% labor utilization even if they have to inject emergency capital to get it.

Humanism promises that if we all work together with cooperation then prosperity will become a win-win achievement much larger in magnitude than could ever be achieved by acting selfishly or in an exploitative or antagonistic elitist manner. Review Title 23 for an example feedback control system to manage capital deployment and labor utilization successfully under all conditions even a major crisis.

In the future workers will be convinced that maximum achievable fair wages will be guaranteed by mathematical axioms and formulas that they can understand, that they can agree with, and that they can verify independently. Likewise businesses will understand that they compete on a level playing field which mathematically guarantees that labor productivity costs are the same for every competing business no matter how high or how low their productivity may be as discussed in Title 6.

Then business and labor can turn away from the "wage war" to the "prosperity peace". The Yin & Yang of economics will be in balance and harmonious. As mentioned in previous discussions once labor and business begin to cooperate, productivity will become easier and easier to achieve so the prosperity that Humanism promises will be realized, maintained, and could become the key idea for worldwide unification.

The Political Unification

Can you imagine a world where labor and business are unified by our common prosperity goal? It would have fundamentally positive effects that would reach far further than just economics or prosperity. It would permeate our daily lives with an absence of fear and a sense of faith, hope, empowerment, and wellbeing. These powerful human emotions will energize our collective human spirit to produce a vibrant global worldwide economy. Even more important this common prosperity of economic democracy could unify the entire world in the same way that we always hoped political democracy would someday. So we hope the impact reaches far further! We hope that economic democracy can provide this worldwide unification based on worldwide prosperity.

For example, look at our two party political system characterized by our Democrat and Republican parties. This two party system is based almost exclusively on the business/labor polarization to provide their political identities. Worldwide other political systems like the parliamentary system have the same polarization such as the Labor/Tory parties in UK. Global Capitalism forces this ugly polarization.

Indeed in recent years both parties' identities have morphed beyond the business/labor polarization into an even more negative antagonism! In this more negative antagonism, Democrats become anti-Republicans and Republicans become anti-Democrats. In effect both parties become "once removed" from the original business/labor polarization into a new antagonistic polarization. One symptom of this new level of antagonism is the increase in retaliatory rhetoric and legislation exemplified recently during the Trump administration.

For example suppose both parties are engaged in a heated issue. In a democracy one party will "win" and one party will "lose" and then both should move on to the next most important political issue and repeat the process. But instead the "loser" institutes new retaliatory legislation whose sole purpose is to punish or harm the "winning" party and get even for the previous "loss". As you can imagine this "getting even" can build on itself quickly until the real issues facing our nation are never addressed because we expend all of our political energy on retaliations and counter retaliations! This is exactly the dysfunctional divisive politics that we have had in recent years!

Under these circumstances we should wonder how HERA will be received by this dysfunctional political polarization and how HERA will affect that polarization. Could the advent of economic democracy further reinforce our political democracy to reach a "more perfect union"? I think so! Looking back on a previous discussion "Is a Humanist a Democrat, Republican, or an Independent?" we can see that HERA is very appealing to Democrats, Republicans, and Independents. It is overwhelmingly a win-win situation for all because it is such a win-win for both business and labor on a worldwide scale.

Prosperity is extremely attractive for constituents of both parties! Yet the initial reaction of both parties at the institutional level will likely be negative! Why? Because "win-win" does not have enough "lose" or "punishment" to satisfy either party's retaliatory instincts! Neither party is satisfied with just "winning" benefits for their constituents. Instead they want humiliating "losses" for their opponents as well!

In fact HERA is so win-win that it would be impossible to tell which party was the "winner" and which party was the "loser". There simply is no loser! Neither party would want to expend considerable effort and risk for a political result for which they could not declare political "victory" and humiliate the losing opposition. These institutions do not even begin to try to represent you until after they satisfy their own institutional instincts for punishment, retaliation, and self-glorification!

So the initial institutional reaction will likely be negative. This is one of many reasons why the Prosperity Party (EHP) is needed. However after the institutional reactions are over each party's individuals will vote according to their own self-interest. This will determine the final outcome. For example imagine a self-employed voter who currently pays the 6.2% tax twice because she is both employer and employee even though she has no hope that she will ever see any retirement benefit at all much less twice the benefit that she pays for already!

Do you think she will be swayed by her party telling her NO on HERA? She does not need permission and she will not tell anyone how she is voting. She will not change political parties either because she likes her party. She will recognize that this is a once-in-a-lifetime referendum type opportunity that is outside of political parties and she will vote for whichever candidate seems most supportive of HERA! And she will keep voting this way until HERA is finally approved.

Clearly we could come up with many examples just as poignant as this one. Look over the list of 37 goals and pick out your favorite vote deciding benefit. Is it elimination of income taxes or twice the retirement for half the cost? Is it a 20% increase in income or a 27% increase in wealth or return of the 88% of income lost to corruption? Or the 129% we can expect to lose in the next generation. Or is it elimination of sovereign debt, or a balanced budget, or streamlining business, or elimination of unemployment, or elimination of racial and gender bias, or so many others? The total benefits to the average Democrat or Republican are estimated at from 131% to as much as 172% increase in earnings prosperity just over the next generation!

HERA speaks for itself. It does not need a Democrat or a Republican voice! Nevertheless it will likely get both voices eventually once it becomes obvious that both parties need to try and claim victory with this reform legislation or risk losing constituents. Then you will see not one HERA but two versions of HERA one for Democrats and one for Republicans and our Prosperity Party (EHP) will see to it that the right compromises are made to fully accomplish our unified goals. I can only hope to live long enough to see this become a reality. And I hope you will join me in knowing that we can do this if we just join together and implement these ideas for the benefit of all mankind.

Understanding the Power of Design

We Engineers are by profession comfortable with the idea of design but the majority of people do not understand the power of top-down design. It is no coincidence that it was the power of top-down design that got us to the real moon! So it should not come as a surprise that the same kind of top-down design will be needed to get us to our economic "moon" as well. Maybe it would help to explain top-down design by considering and contrasting the alternative approach which is usually called an "ad hoc" or a "piecemeal" solution approach.

Politicians love piecemeal solutions! In a piecemeal solution each problem is attacked separately as if they all were independent from one another. This makes the solutions easier and each problem can be considered one at a time with separate legislation until they are all solved. Unfortunately the ease of this approach ensures that it is overused until the only problems left to be solved are interlocked in a grid or mosaic that ensures that none of these problems can be solved without solving all the others in unison. This situation is exactly the situation we now face. Our current economy is gridlocked in a mosaic of unsolvable problems using piecemeal solutions. So we are stuck!

Our only option for economic reform is to stand back and look at the economy from the top down so we can understand all of its systemic and core problems. Only then can we envision core solutions that will break the deadlock of insolvability. So we must be brave enough to have the intellectual courage to ask the key question: what is wrong with Capitalism and its wealth economics and what can we do to fix them in a humane way providing "**economics as if people mattered**"?

Remember the previous discussions about Capitalism having attained the status of "high religion" and the corresponding intellectual corruption. Under these circumstances asking the key question could be hazardous to your health! Not to even mention facing the honest answers! So is it any surprise that our problems have gone on for so long without solutions? It is time for this blueprint to stand strong as the answer to that key question using a top-down design approach. Here is a summary of our most important economic core problems:

- Our government is not in charge of the management of our economy, so wealth power is in default control instead.
- Capitalism is not democratic, humanity is exploited the same as zinc or soybeans. We are victims of our economy not its principals.
- Perpetual wealth is perpetual corruption of our political and economic system. We must proactively end this corruption.
- Taxes are poorly designed only for revenue not to achieve prosperity. Yet taxes are our best control for achieving prosperity.
- Businesses are motivated to maximize profits and revenues not to optimize prosperity. It's time for a prosperity paradigm instead.
- Businesses, the engines of our prosperity, need streamlining and tax reform. We need lean, clean, productivity machines.
- Unemployment is an unnecessary curse against humanity.
- Wages are deliberately exploited in a downward spiral.
- International trade is a lawless exploitation of humanity worldwide that will collapse as a "house of cards" without reforms.
- Perpetual sovereign debt is taxation of future generations without representation. It's a time/money trick to destroy posterity.
- Our Social Security and Medicare Retirement Systems are flawed in design and they will eventually fail without reforms now.
- The imbalance between economic and non-economic investment does not favor growth. Yet we wrongly depend on it.
- Our current economic system depends on continuing growth that cannot be achieved in the future. It's unstainable already!
- Overpopulation to achieve this impossible growth threatens to destroy our planet and our human life that depends on it.
- The true cost of labor, profits, currency, resource depletion and pollution are flawed; they are not economically valued properly.

- Profits and labor must be balanced proactively to achieve optimum prosperity. The "Laissez-faire" idea is not enough.
- Axiomatic economic science must replace mindless regulation.
- Racial and gender economic discrimination continue unabated.
- Business and Labor are needlessly polarized in a power war.
- There is an absence of economic law and order to achieve justice in economics. We need an axiomatic control system.
- The representational voice of wealth power drowns out the voice of the populace threatening our political democracy as well.
- The economic privileged class is winning its "war on democracy"! If we do not act soon we will lose our political democracy as well as any hopes for an economic democracy.

Here is a summary of new ideas we need to fully understand in order to achieve an economic renaissance and its resultant prosperity:

- Conventional "wealth economics" is Capitalism based on a profit paradigm. We have proposed a prosperity paradigm instead.
- Our new "prosperity economics" is Capitalism based on a prosperity paradigm instead called Humanism.
- Humanism's idea of prosperity includes wealth but Capitalism's idea of wealth does not include prosperity!
- Proactive economic Engineering is made possible because the axiomatic nature of prosperity economics is based on formulas.
- Our economic renaissance will shift from a profit paradigm to a prosperity paradigm changing Capitalism into Humanism.
- Imagine selecting from all possible businesses the "most prosperity efficient" first until 100% labor utilization is reached. That is the mathematical formulation of our humanistic economy.
- "Defensive prosperity" can be replaced with proactive "offensive prosperity" because the axioms of metaeconomics provide us with an Economic Geometry to guide us to our collective economic destiny using engineering methodology.
- Optimum national profits for a mature humanistic economy are only about 5% of GDP far less than we have been told before.
- For the first time in the history of economics humanity will have economic representation from our economic professionals.
- Speculation is just "capital inflation" that we do not need.
- Humanism will achieve "**economics as if people mattered**".

- In mature Humanism with a prosperity paradigm there are no economic shortages of profits, capital, capitalists, management, businesses, products, services, jobs, wealth, or the wealthy.
- A successful economic system must produce, manage, and sustain equilibrium with a never ending shortage of labor, natural resources, and antipolution as its **only** scarce economic resources!
- Maximum prosperity will be achieved by focusing the scarce labor resources and the scarce natural resources on the most economical, prosperity efficient products **not the most profitable**!
- Foul is not fair in economics nor is fair foul. This double talk is intended to justify unlimited greed, corruption, and privilege in economics. Yet there is no need or benefit for greed or privilege in economics at all. They are just ugly human faults to be minimized.
- Economics is a "confidence game" so a robust capital based retirement system is a requirement to achieve a stable economy.
- Wage inflation can be directly controlled with a separate mechanism so wages and salaries can be controlled by our axioms.
- Wealth and Corporate taxes can provide a feedback control system far more powerful than our current Fed interest rate system.
- Our prosperity paradigm is based on our future, not our past.

We will address these core issues and ideas with key axioms, sub mandates, and national economic goals for a comprehensive solution:

Guiding Axioms:

- The Central Prosperity Mandate
- The Equal Pay Mandate
- The Equal Currency Mandate
- The Minimum Wage Mandate
- The Wage Increase Mandate
- The Pollution/Depletion Mandate

Performance Sub Mandates:

- The Full Employment sub Mandate
- The Participation Rate sub Mandate
- The Productivity Rate sub Mandate
- The Inflation Rate sub Mandate

National Economic Goals:

- The Budget Mandate (14% GDP)
- The Sovereign Debt Mandate
- The Profit Rate Mandate (5% GDP)
- The Perpetual Wealth Mandate
- The Distribution of Wealth Mandate
- The Balanced Voice Mandate
- The Public Capital Mandate
- The Pay Prevailing Wage Mandate
- The Ongoing Prosperity Optimization Mandates

Our top-down solution, HERA, directly addresses these core issues and key ideas with comprehensive mandates at the systemic level. Any attempt to address these issues in a piecemeal fashion would be doomed to failure. To be successful these issues must all be addressed in unison as part of a comprehensive top-down reform package design. In this package design we carefully choose solutions that solve multiple problems simultaneously while maintaining support and compatibility with other such solutions in an axiomatic manner.

We must not try to "cherry-pick" the solutions we like politically and attempt to avoid the solutions we do not like politically. If we do, we will inadvertently "pull the rug" from underneath our own "cherry" goals. If we try to avoid a win-win reform solution we will end up with a lose-lose reform disaster instead! It is time for the political courage to stand and face the issue of economic reform squarely and honestly without political bias and division. We will be shouted down by wealth power again and again. Yet we must continue until we are successful.

A Legislative Road Map

The top-down design approach must be used to synthesize a complete economic reform package. The difficulty of getting such a large package architected and then approved by Congress and the President seems daunting. Yet we must avoid a procrastination piecemeal approach consisting of a thousand "baby steps" over the next thousand years. To make matters worse once the popularity of the reforms become apparent both the Democrats and the Republicans will "cherry pick" the legislative idea into two separate unworkable political packages. One consisting of all the Democrat "cherries" and the other consisting of all the Republican "cherries". So this is why we need our Prosperity Party (EHP) with street support from our grassroots effort to organize, plan, and achieve this very difficult legislative challenge.

Phased Approach

I believe we can "crack" this complex problem and achieve our goals by using a phased approach that will accomplish our comprehensive legislation package in two phases that are much more politically manageable and yet do not degrade into a "baby step" procrastination approach. This idea is to start with the structural formation first and foremost and then use the new structure to support finally achieving the detailed authorities. Here is a description for these two phases:

The first phase will not require any commitment for any of the legislative Titles herein except for Title 2 and only those items which are structural. None of the new authorities of the ECA as discussed in HERA will be included in the first phase! So this first phase will result in the creation of a "Supper Central Bank" with **no new** authority called the ECA with 6 new shell departments: Central Bank, Economic Management, Economic Taxation, Economic Labor, National Fund, and Economic Trade. They will be charged by the Phase I enabling legislation to propose to Congress a new organization, economic reforms, and new authorities. This will achieve democratic economic reforms consistent with the guidelines of the formation legislation.

A sample for the Phase I formation legislation is supplied in the Epilogue discussion "Phase I: ECA Formation Legislation". The Economic Bill of Rights and the key axioms will provide the guiding principles for this legislation. Moreover the civil rights law of the balanced voice mandate discussed in Title 5 will be included. This will guarantee that our voice of the populace will be in proportion to the voice of wealth power during the critical formation and reform stages.

Otherwise there will be no commitment to any of the legislative ideas discussed in this book. In this way Democrats, Republicans, and Independents including the EHP will all have equal opportunity to have their proposals included in the final Phase II ECA legislation so that the ECA will be enabled to plan and **architect their own destiny**!

The new Central Bank Department will be only a shell for the future department like the other new departments. The actual Central bank function will continue exactly as is now. Only the old Central Bank will have any authority and the Economic Labor department shell would be new and totally independent from the existing Labor Department which would continue temporarily unchanged as is now.

When the second phase is completed the two Labor departments will be merged into the new authority. The new Central Bank Department will become effective at this time as well freeing the board by delegating work to the new department so that the board will have more time for their new and broader responsibilities. This transition could start sooner informally if the board chooses to get an early start.

The current board Chairman and 6 board members of the current Federal Reserve Bank would be given the opportunity to resign but they would be encouraged to continue as is now. They would all be excellent choices for board members of the ECA. If they resign they will be replaced under the old authority but with the idea of their new role in mind. If they do not resign they will be considered as a default candidate for the new board as specified in the new Phase II legislation. All of the funding would be handled within the current authority so there would be no budget commitments or budget burden.

Once the target board is in place with replaced members as needed, the board will use its current authority to approve department heads for the 6 shell departments. To get the universities involved the board will ask for recommendations from all the universities who wish to participate. The board will also make its own recommendations through a committee available for public recommendations and scrutiny as well.

The transitional department heads chosen will be specialized for the formation tasks that require special expertise different than the future department heads. At the conclusion of Phase II, the new operating heads will be installed using the authority and methods agreed to in the final department authority approved by Congress and the President. For the first time our economists will proactively lead our economy!

Once the transitional department heads are in place they will each formulate a plan for staffing to produce a proposal for their departments which includes organization and Congressional authorities and supporting legislation that they need to fulfill the goals of HERA. Their staffs will reflect this legislative goal including constitutional legal experts and legislative experts while their future staffs would not require such extensive legal and political expertise.

In addition the board will identify special authorities it needs separate from its departments and prepare its own legislative proposals. In this way the total effort is subdivided into 7 different projects each of which can be approved by Congress and the President sequentially. Simultaneously with this plan, Congress will identify 7 bipartisan sub committees, one for each of the various projects. Each subcommittee will work with the department heads and board members towards a committee recommendation on authorizing legislation by project.

Notice that the legislation that authorizes Phase I involves very little political commitment except to a general concept of the ECA and a general concept of HERA that should be politically acceptable to all. The initial political issue is not trivial by any means but it is contained to these two issues: can we benefit from governmental economic controls and can we benefit from democratic economic reforms consistent with the key axioms and the Economic Bill of Rights.

If both parties are willing to "cherry pick" this proposal, the answer must be yes, as long as they have it their own way. So agreement on these two issues is achievable even though Republicans and Democrats have very different "cherry lists" and very different ideas on what HERA is, what the ECA should do, and how they will do it.

Phase II involves submitting and achieving approval for each of the 7 different authorization plans one at a time. The Phase II political issues are much more partisan and complex but we have the organizational power of a dedicated ECA to lead and sponsor the effort subdivided into 7 separate department projects and each department leads its own definition and formation. Furthermore the cost of implementing this does not impact the Congressional budget! With good choices for department heads, this two phased approach with structure first and then substance will be successful in achieving these ambitious goals.

Timeline Plan Summary

- During the Pre-phase I stage, the Prosperity Party (EHP) will be responsible for architecting and achieving approval for the Phase I structural legislation that authorizes Phase I ECA. A first draft sample of this legislation is contained in the Epilogue. The EHP with street support from the grassroots movement will be the driving force during this stage. Likewise during Phase I & II the EHP with ongoing street support from the grassroots movement will be needed to ensure our goals are achieved. The greatest challenge may occur during the Phase II efforts. See detailed discussion in "Epilogue Discussions".
- During the Pre-phase I, the current Central Bank board members will be forced to establish their position on the issues raised in this book especially the concept of a democratic, axiomatic economy and the reforms required in HERA.
- Phase I, the new ECA will reshuffle its board as needed based on pre-phase I rhetoric and posturing including Phase I personal preferences. Sorting out board members will be the first effort in Phase I and it will begin in the pre-phase I stage.
- Phase I, the ECA will call for nominations for 6 department heads. Then the ECA board will approve the transitional department heads chosen; no confirmation by the President or Congress will be required since these positions are only transitory. The operating department heads will be installed later in Phase II. Simultaneously Congress will establish 7 sub committees to deal with each of the 7 projects.
- Phase I, the department heads will prepare plans for their departments working close with Congressional subcommittees and seek approval from the board. Phase I is complete when the board has approved all department plans including its own.
- Phase II, once approved by the board the department plans will be presented to their Congressional subcommittee for approval.
- Phase II, once committee has approved, the board and department head will present the legislation to Congress for debate, modification, and approvals one by one until all departments are approved. The board will probably lead by presenting its authorization legislation first. No legislation will become effective until all departments have been approved.

- Phase II, once each department plan is approved by Congress it will be presented to the President for approval sequentially.
- Phase II, once all the department plans are approved including the board itself, Congress and the president will approve activation legislation to initiate the ECA based on those plans.
- Phase II, the activated ECA will present its recommendations for final department heads consistent with the rules specified in the Phase II authorizing legislation. Transitional department heads will serve until the new appointments are approved. These appointments may be staggered as recommended and will be confirmed by both Congress and the President. The transitional department heads could serve in the new positions provided they are re-submitted through the new appointment process. Transitional board members will serve until their terms are complete. Their replacements will be filled according to whatever new rules are specified in Phase II legislation.
- A new golden age of prosperity will begin and our children will rejoice with pride. There will be a big national celebration with international support and a new holiday – **Prosperity Day** eventually replicated worldwide like Independence Day!

Backup Plan

In case we are blocked on the direct legislation approach discussed above because of legislative gridlock or blocked by a judicial override, we will consider an alternate backup plan amending our Constitution. If we are forced to amend our constitution I would recommend that we not waste this complex, difficult process for only a single reform.

Instead I believe we should use our existing Constitutional amendment process to enact the Economic Bill of Rights, the 6 axioms, and the equal voice mandate applying either the Congressional method or the Constitutional Convention method. In addition we should institute an amendment for national referendums. The people's referendum would be put on the national ballot once a majority of states approve the measure as either a legislature resolution or a state referendum if legal.

It would be much easier to get the approval for the amendment to add referendums than to get approval for an amendment to add direct authorizing legislation to our constitution for economic reforms. Instead the amendment for referendums could then be used to enact economic reforms directly and other future uses as well. Once on the national ballot, the referendum could be passed with a simple majority.

So a 26 majority of states would be required for the ballot measure and a simple 51% majority of popular votes would be required for approval. These requirements are less stringent because Congress would be granted the authority to modify or override any such legislation with a $2/3^{rd}$ majority with Presidential approval or $3/4^{th}$ majority with veto. This would provide an achievable referendum process with substantial cross checks and balances for security.

Understanding the Political Challenge

Before looking at the political challenge facing us, let's be sure we understand to the fullest extent possible the tremendously positive impact and benefit of the reform ideas being proposed herein. These axiomatic based reforms will benefit you, your children, your grandchildren, and our future generations to an extent never proposed before in the history of economics with almost no instability or risk!

The Benefit

To understand this we must be sure we grasp a common theme presented throughout this book both as a positive goal and as a negative issue to fix. Good scientific economics matters to humanity first and foremost, and bad economic alchemy harms us more than any other aspect of our human lives! Our economic viability is the single most important factor in achieving successful lives on this planet; it's more important than religion or politics because it sets the stage for both. Indeed each week we spend 1 hour at church but 40 at work.

Also we can see this by comparing the impact of bad economics compared with bad politics. Let's imagine the average family unit worldwide. Then we can ask a simple question. What harms this family unit the most bad politics or bad economics? The answer is clear. The average family does not need political governance much at all. In many emerging nations there is almost no political governance at the family level. In fact it seems that political governance needs the family more than the family needs political governance. On the other hand look at how dependent each family is on its economic viability and success. Clearly good economics comes first and foremost!

Another way to understand the importance of good economics is to look at the global issues of racial, ethnic, gender, and religious discriminations. These inequities are at the heart of our worldwide conflict and turmoil. These inequities primarily manifest themselves through economic discrimination, unfairness, and foul exploitation.

For example if all races had equal access to employment and were paid equally for equal work then the impact of racism would be drastically reduced! So if Rosa Parks had had economic equality she would have "sit on the bus" 50 years sooner! The same is true for ethnic, gender, religious, and economic discrimination. Furthermore equal pay and equal economic stature lead us to **equal mutual respect** that provides the social basis for the complete human solution. So good economics comes first and foremost! Moreover it could be the path to worldwide human unification and common good that we so need and so deserve!

Politics and religion help us tolerate and survive under the draconian greed, exploitation, privilege, and corruption that destroy prosperity. On the other hand Humanism directly prohibits these negative factors axiomatically, ideologically, and proactively at the outset using first principles. So there is no need to just tolerate and survive anymore! For example in Title 4 we discussed the profound idea that good earth science cannot be achieved without good economics first and foremost. In the trade discussion we considered the idea that without economic democracy, political democracy alone is insufficient to provide the complete governance solution that we so desperately need.

Likewise in the discussion on "Justice in Economics" we observed an equally profound idea that without good economics first and foremost, we cannot even achieve the justice that we are already entitled to morally, politically, and constitutionally. So we can have no justice without economic justice as a basis first and foremost! We discussed other similar examples as well like economic slavery, international trade, and the unification of business and labor. Look at automation, robotics, and AI. In predatory Capitalism they are a grave threat to humanity while in Humanism they are a godsend to humanity. Also recall the discussion on the ultimate human travesty: being forced to leave our planet earth or suffer extinction because of bad economics!

The high cost of bad economics is mind-boggling. We now see clearly that wealth economics has systematically failed to provide the economic governance necessary for proper economic valuations. We are confronted by the stunning realization that the corruption of wealth economics has deliberately mismanaged and misvalued: profits, labor, currency, natural resources, and pollution. These are the 5 most important key valuations of any economy. Yet they are **all** misvalued and mismanaged on an inconceivable scale! The scope and depth of this intellectual failure in economics is beyond human comprehension!

The high cost of bad economics for humanity is not just monetary. No other factor in our lives so diminishes our "life, liberty, and pursuit of happiness". So let's look at the impact that bad economics has on our health and wellbeing. Without economic viability we don't have access to affordable health care or affordable education to break the yoke of working poverty and poor health. Worse yet look at the never ending and overwhelming, **chronic stress** forced into our lives by financial and employment insecurity; it's debilitating and deliberate!

Look at the rise of homelessness over the last 20 years in the USA. It indicates a catastrophic breakdown of successful economic life caused by some overwhelming weight, pressure, and oppression that we all try desperately to carry and endure. However growing numbers of us are not successful and their "backs break" crushing them under this heavy oppression. This causes homelessness, an economic dead-end trap from which there is no known systematic exit. Our only hope is that persistent broad scale prosperity will eventually undo this ugly harm.

These unsuccessful are like "canaries" in our economic "coal mine". Prosperity economics explains this as the unavoidable consequence of creating and expanding the new concept of "working poverty". Worse yet this concept will soon be succeeded by the next stages of draconian economics: the concepts of "working homeless" and eventually "working starvation". This is exploitation of bad economics that forces intentionally high unemployment at a minimum to accomplish the desperation needed to maintain and expand cheap labor slavery. Of course the draconians of wealth economics try to explain this as mere laziness obfuscating the chronic economic failure that it represents!

Imagine the full employment, minimum wage, fair and open trade, fair and equal pay, and maximum prosperity world proposed in this blueprint. The debilitating daily stress and anxiety in our lives would all but be eliminated. Jobs would be plentiful, many open requisitions would be unfulfilled, working conditions would be inspirational, and retirement would be secure, prosperous, and fulfilling for everyone. Also part time work would be a viable choice so each person could make their own "work week vs quality of life" choices. They could choose to pursue their prosperity and their happiness, their way!

Threat, extortion, stress, and fear would be replaced by confidence, wellbeing, creativity, empowerment, and exhilaration. These powerful emotions would be inspirational in seeking economic success for ourselves, our families, our employers, our businesses, our industries, our regional economy, our national economy, and our global economy worldwide. Everyone wins at every level! The draconian oppression and fear forced on us by wealth economics would be eliminated. Fear does not encourage prosperity; it destroys it with unhealthy economic stress and desperation required to maintain ongoing economic slavery!

Yet we have been deprived of the professional economic guidance and representation that would have provided us with an economic science for sustainable prosperity. After all we have been told that whatever is good for wealth power is good for our economy so humanity automatically gets good economics from this greed-voodoo without needing representation - right? It's time for real representation now!

We are well aware of the vast technological progress that has been made in the fields of Science, Mathematics, and Engineering to benefit mankind! It's amazing! Yet when we study the field of Economics we find **no** such vast technological progress. We find no economic "moon" for humanity because the field of Economics openly strives to be a self-proclaimed non-science intended to benefit wealth power at the expense of humanity by making Economics into a power struggle. It is time to reform economics with a humane idea for economic life. It's time Capitalism changed into "**economics as if people mattered**".

Instead this religious, non-science produces greed, exploitation, privilege, and corruption on a flagrant scale perpetuated mindlessly like economic alchemy without the benefit of economic science or economic engineering! Our vision to start an economic renaissance based on axiomatic metaeconomics is clear and concise. It will have a more profound effect on our lives than the political renaissance of our democracy started by our 1776 revolution! What are we waiting for?

Indeed without this economic renaissance our political renaissance will also succumb to the same exploitation, privilege, corruption and greed. This will inevitably lead us to the failure of our beautiful and precious experiment with political democracy just like the ancient Greeks suffered. Without an economic renaissance we will lose the political war on democracy. If we don't go forward we will certainly fall back!

The Challenge

With this perspective in mind let us look more closely at the scope and depth of the political challenge facing us. Just reviewing the 37 goals listed in the opening summary at the start, one can easily become dizzy. Any one of these 37 goals would be "heavy lifting" by our conventional economic and political standards. So the combination of all 37 seems vast and overwhelming. However the goals are more proportional to the size of the accomplishment rather than proportional to the size of the effort or the change required to achieve these goals.

This characteristic of a large far reaching accomplishment achieved with a relatively small change is exactly what we should expect from a fundamental paradigm shift. It is a common experience that when a basic core problem is understood and then the proper core change is implemented, many different problems and symptoms get solved with the same solution. That is the basic idea of a renaissance. So a single conceptual enlightenment occurs and thousands of improvements fall into place and continue to fall into place for many future generations!

I have also aided and abetted this dizziness by deliberately providing a large amount of details in the form of examples, suggestions, analyses, proposals, and other specifics. I am after all an Engineer proposing a scientific based axiomatic approach implemented with economically engineered solutions. As an Engineer I know that both the "angel" and the "devil" are in the details. I am also driven by a strong abhorrence to creating yet another empty, ugly, and harmful "Ism" for economics!

If Capitalism, Socialism, or Communism had been defined in a systematic way with details instead of vagueness, nobody in their right mind would have bought into any of these ideas! We must have been desperate for any solution? So I have a distinct desire to avoid the possibility of replacing "new chants" for the old chants or "new slogans" for the old ones. I'm proposing a scientific economic system.

So we need to abandon chants and slogans and turn to a scientific approach. This approach is based on fundamental first principles and axioms that we can scrutinize, debate, and agree to at the outset. So we follow a pattern much like we did with our own democratic political Constitution creating a parallel democratic economic constitution of axiomatic metaeconomics. The solidarity of our approach is obvious.

Furthermore instituting these principles and axioms under the charter and the authority of the ECA is our only short term goal. All the rest of these detail goals can in turn be accomplished by the ECA over whatever time frame and in whatever order the ECA finds diligently achievable. If we are not happy with their diligence or their progress we will demand more through our political representation and our new found economic representation. We must do this for our children!

After all it is **our** government and **our** economy! The rest of the details of the blueprint were presented to help you envision the vast future benefits and possibilities. We have suffered from bad economics for hundreds of years so we can afford to wait if necessary for most of these detail goals to come to fruition over the next working generation of 45 years or so. There is no need or intention to proceed forward more rapidly than stability, security, and safety dictate. The goals and methodologies of Humanism in general and specifically for HERA are simple and direct. We want economics as if people mattered! And I am hoping to convince you that the effort to accomplish these goals is manageable. So let me state our plan again in one small paragraph:

The primary goal of HERA is to establish an independent department of government called the ECA to professionally manage our national economy with cohesive technical control of monetary, fiscal, tax, and investment policy in a scientific manner. The ECA's primary mandate is to maximize democratic prosperity. This goal includes a mathematical definition specifying exactly what democratic prosperity is and exactly how it will be measured and managed. Other sub mandates are defined as well including provisions for ongoing national economic goals. There is nothing vague or uncertain about the goals, the methods, or the intentions. The guiding axioms and rights are clear, concise, and mathematically unambiguous.

This then is our mission statement and goal. The 37 goals are just some of our intended consequences. For the average citizen, we only need to be concerned with this mission statement. The ECA is like our "NASA". They will figure out how to get to our economic "moon". That is their scientific and engineering challenge. We only have to stand strong and ensure that the ECA is created and chartered with the mandate to go to the economic "moon". That is our political challenge!

The two phased legislative approach of the previous discussion will make the political effort much more manageable. Remember, our political democracy has already empowered us to solve this problem ourselves! We do not need a savior and we do not need permission to have a democratic economy! The key feasibility question repeated throughout this book is: when we vote on these economic reforms will we have the most votes or will they? We outnumber the 1%'ers a hundred to one and we outnumber the 85'ers even more. How could we not have the most votes? So this fear is brainwashed propaganda!

Can we democratically achieve our political challenge to institute the ECA? Hell yes we can! We already instituted the infrastructure and the monetary policy portion of our mission after the previous great crisis, the Great Depression. The Central Bank has operated successfully since then as an independent department of government. During the most recent crisis (2008 to 2018+) our Central Bank/Fed was the most, and sometimes **the only**, functional department of our government!

Moreover it was certainly the best suited to handle the task. The Central Bank stayed out of the political dysfunction and led our nation and the world through a difficult economic time. The fact that they took controversial actions in the face of difficulty is an indication that this type of structure will work well even during times of great crisis.

If the Central Bank had any shortcoming it was that they did not have full controls available. So they had to rely solely on monetary policy and invent mechanisms like Quantitative Easing. There is no doubt in my mind that they would not have even used QE had they had policy controls like we are proposing. A +/- 6.2% directly injectable payroll stimulus together with direct control over economic investment and taxation discussed in Title 23 would have been more successful with much less risk. Furthermore, if the ECA had long term control over tax and investment policy this crisis could have been avoided entirely!

As you can see the feasibility of achieving our mission statement is very doable. It is not political "rocket science" at all. Unfortunately we have been academically brainwashed by the propaganda of wealth economics to believe that we cannot and should not make demands of the pampered economy. We are told that we are its subjects and we must accept sacrifice as willing victims with the dictates of the economic privileged class. Otherwise our lives will be threatened with some obscure "economic eruption" and we will lose our jobs, our homes, and our families' wellbeing. So out of fear from deliberate, deceptive, and divisive threats we are motivated to comply with lies!

Instead the axioms of Humanism clarify exactly that the economy is **ours** and they show us exactly how to manage **our** economy to accomplish **our** economic goals with safety, security, stability, and success. We must stand and demand **our** political right to representation in **our** economy. This is difficult for most of us because we do not like to be demanding. But the time will come when it will be necessary for millions of us to go "campout" in Washington and our state capitols for a few weeks so that they get the idea that we are serious about democratic economic reform. Indeed the whole world will likely take up this cause in some fashion as an international quest.

If you cannot make the campout maybe you can save up a little so your college age children or grandchildren can have a fun "spring break" as a gift in your name? We will issue a demand heard around the world for all of humanity! We will demand that our economy must comply with the 6 axioms of international democratic economics and the Economic Bill of Rights to provide sustainable prosperity for the vast majority of everyone! Until that time comes, I am looking forward to seeing you there so that we can get this implemented and achieved.

The Corruption

The real difficulty facing us is not with the feasibility of the task at hand. The real issue facing us is the $1.7 trillion war chest of the 85 and their 1% friends that will be used to shout us down. Economists will be mobilized, legal firms will be retained, public relations firms will be hired, books will be written, the news media will be energized, documentaries will be everywhere, movies will be made, and our universities will be expected to earn their perpetual wealth donations.

We will be told in a thousand ways by a thousand paid "experts" that what we want and intend will not work and will destroy our economy if we try. The disinformation and intellectual manipulation will include a deluge of non-stop propaganda that will make Adolf Hitler giggle in hell! So the civil rights law of the balanced voice mandate discussed in Title 5, "Justice in Economics" and detailed in the "Phase I: ECA Formation Legislation" is key to our political survival and success.

There is no way we can fight back dollar for dollar. But we have a secret weapon, the power of the collective human spirit. We have endured hundreds of years of exploitation and we can endure this as well! Remember that we are not alone. The whole world is watching us no matter how silent they may seem. They are quietly praying for us to lead the way out of this economic darkness to a better world for all.

They know that we led the way to political democracy and they are hoping that we can lead the way to economic democracy as well. Of course we can! And if we don't; they will! Remember the equation 85 = 3,500,000,000? This equation is a statement of our worldwide strength not our weakness! The 3,500,000,000 represent only half of humanity and we will have support from the other half as well. Which side of the equation will you bet on? I am betting on the 7,000,000,000 - 85 human spirits against the $1.7 trillion of the 85. How about you?

The Conclusion

Well here we are back at the precipice that we began with in the Prologue. I hope that the vision of our economic "moon" is now full and clear for you. Now the focus of our attention must shift from this economic blueprint to you. This idea for economic prosperity for you, your children, and all future generations is so profound it probably seems overwhelming and unbelievable like a dream fantasy come true.

In summary, instead of a bankrupt retirement system, we could have a new retirement system that is 400% better with twice the benefit for half the cost with less risk, no taxes, and more security! In addition during our earning lifetimes we could have the 88% of our income that we already lost to corruption as explained in the New York Times article (Greenhouse, 2013) or the projected future loss of 129%. We could add to this the 20% increase discussed in Title 11, and the 23% increase resulting from the streamlining discussed in Titles 14-21.

The subtotal is at least 131% to as much as 172% increase in earnings prosperity over our working lifetime with little or no inflation! That means your income could have almost tripled with no increase in the cost of living and income would at least double again for our children and almost double yet again for our grandchildren. Yet we are not even counting the many other improvements discussed in this book!

Not counting the almost tripling of the minimum wage. Not counting the end to unemployment. Not counting the end to income taxes. Not counting the end to sovereign debt, perpetual wealth privilege, and poverty. Not counting the many other benefits discussed too numerous to summarize. Ongoing generations of our children could compound these gains with ongoing productivity improvements and economic goals into a "fourth dimension" of prosperity never before imagined!

FDR said it well! Only "fear of fear itself" could say "no" to such a promising and exciting future! Remember it is not just the USA we are talking about but the entire world! As reiterated many times: we don't need a savior and we don't need permission! The opportunity itself is so large that it is fearsome and $1.7 trillion will buy a lot more paid "experts" to exploit and exaggerate our fear with gloom and doom.

So **I am afraid**! I'm afraid that such a monumental opportunity could be lost to these lies and deceit. And that humanity will not rise up and throw off the yoke of this insane asylum for something much better. I'm afraid that humanity will be subjugated to yet another millennia or two of economic slavery! But I am not afraid, to be afraid, and that is the only fear that threatens us! How about you? Can you be afraid and yet stand to be counted? This vision is yours for the wishing! **Let's stand up together hand-in-hand and make this wish come true!**

Epilogue Discussions:

These ideas are embryonic yet they are simple and easy to understand. We have much to do before we can institute all these ideas. I can only envision these ideas to inspire your minds, excite your hearts, and satisfy your souls. I cannot achieve them for you. I spent my whole adult life struggling to grasp and formulate these intuitive ideas into an intellectually comprehensible economic system of human thought. Unfortunately I am now likely too old to see them into final fruition.

Only you can capture them in your hearts and savor them in your souls. However I can envision organizational details and a likely path we could follow to get started with our economic "moon". So I will complete this blueprint with hypothetical details to get started on a likely path, posture, rationale, and strategy that we could follow to accomplish these goals as soon as you are ready to pick up the torch.

Ok, What Can You Do To Help?

Before we explain how easy it is for you to help, let us clarify some of the things you need not and should not do. First you need not and should not change your voter registration unless you have some other reason to do this. Furthermore you need not and should not change your political party preference such as Democrat, Republican, Independent or specialty party. Keep your party affiliation as it is now.

The Prosperity Party (EHP) is an economic movement to achieve prosperity for all so that it is compatible with **all political parties**. I do not know of any political party that is against prosperity so keep your party preference the same as it is now. Moreover our Prosperity Party (EHP) is a non-electoral party so we will not have any candidates on the ballot. We are **not** a political party; we are an economic party. We are dedicated to getting Humanism, its prosperity paradigm, and

HERA endorsed by candidates and subsequently approved by Congress and the President at the earliest possible time achievable.

There is a lot you can do as an economic Humanist and the minimum action is very simple and easy to do. All you have to do is join the Prosperity Party (EHP) and take and keep your membership pledge. For many people this is all they will be able to do and that is certainly enough! If you could also pass the word on to your friends that would help even more! For those who want to do more check the membership box indicating you want to help volunteer and we will contact you.

If you are reading this document there is a very good chance you have already registered online. If not you should register online as soon as this website is available at economic-humanist-party.org (domain name reserved for the EHP). If you do not have internet access ask a friend to help and reimburse them for the fee or wait for a membership drive in your area when you can register by hand or get help by phone at 855-475-6800 (reserved for the EHP). We will be ready soon!

Online registration will require a registration fee by credit card, debit card, or transfer pay system. You can pay by cash, check or money order during local membership drives. The most important part of your registration is the membership pledge of solidarity. Here is the pledge:

I pledge that I will vote for whichever candidate endorses HERA in writing even if he or she is a candidate for my opposite party. If no candidate endorses HERA in writing I will be free to vote my conscience. Likewise if more than one candidate endorses HERA in writing I can also vote my conscience. **But if only one endorses, I am committed to vote for that one.** *I further pledge that if I find that I no longer can keep this pledge, I will deactivate my membership so that my membership records represent my true convictions!*

The key idea behind this pledge is that HERA is a legislative proposal much like a referendum where we as voters get to vote for a specific plan or idea rather than a candidate or a party. But our political system does not support referendums at the national level yet. So we vote instead for the plan by promising to vote for whoever supports the plan even though we are not changing political parties. This legislation is so important to us, our children, and grandchildren that we are willing to cross party lines and vote for a plan rather than vote for a personality!

This strong conviction is represented in our membership strength. It tells any candidate of either party that he or she must endorse HERA in writing, according to the specifications of the EHP, in order to get our votes. Furthermore if they do not endorse HERA in writing they risk losing votes that they would otherwise expect. That pledge gives you the voter power! Moreover this power is amplified because of the strength of the other members of the Prosperity Party who have joined with you to support the same cause and make the same pledge. This joint power is what we need to get this important legislation endorsed by candidates and then approved. Let's get started by registering now!

Political Strategy and Membership Goal Analysis

Our Prosperity Party (EHP) will be a non-electoral, non-political, economic party so we will **not** have any candidate on the ballot and we don't need one! Humanists who join our economic party will declare their political party affiliation as Democrat, Republican, Independent, or Specialty Party members who pledge that they will cross party lines if necessary to vote for the candidate that endorses HERA in a written statement specified by the EHP. This statement and endorsement will be general and directed towards the formation legislation of the Phase I effort discussed previously and documented in the epilogue below.

Phase I Timeline

This Phase I endorsement is intended to be general enough to be acceptable to Democrats, Republicans, Independents, and Specialty Parties. See "Phase I: ECA Formation Legislation" below. If more than one candidate provides the written endorsement of HERA the member is free to vote their conscience. Likewise if no candidate provides a written endorsement of HERA the member is free to vote their conscience. These endorsements will only apply to Congressional and Presidential candidates. You are free to vote your conscience for state and local candidates. During Phase II the EHP and our grassroots "street" support will pressure the ECA, our President, and Congress towards achieving the specific initial goals outlined in this blueprint.

Online registration will include the party pledge and the registration fee. A copy of this book, *From Profits To Prosperity* can be downloaded as well. Party membership can be deactivated at any time through the party website. Additional donations can be made in a similar manner. These donations will be used for political activities to gain approval of HERA at the Presidential and Congressional level. Before the first relevant national election, 2022, we expect to register between 5% and 20% of the voting population as members depending on the Congressional district. Our district strategy is explained below.

After the 2022 elections we will force the introduction of Phase I HERA in Congress. There is a good chance we will have sufficient votes in the House for a majority. The Senate will be more difficult because only $1/3^{rd}$ were up for election. But there is a good chance we will be successful on our first try. If not then we will gain more strength in the 2024 elections and repeat our effort following the 2024 elections and again if necessary in 2026. In just a few years we will be successful with approval of the Phase I authorization legislation!

Once the new ECA is created out of the old Central Bank (the Fed) they will execute the Phase II legislation to define HERA. During this Phase II period we will need our greatest support and activity to make sure HERA accomplishes our goals and is fully approved by Congress and the President. Once the Phase II legislation is finally approved, we will see results gradually and by 2028 the initial results will be obvious to each one of us and prosperity will continue to grow over the years. Remember we have suffered from bad economics for many hundreds of years or more. We can afford to wait as long as it takes to achieve fair economics for ourselves, our children, and our grandchildren!

District Goal Analysis

For the purpose of analysis let us assume the following statistics. Let us assume that 28% of the voting population is Republican, 32% is Democrat and 40% is independent. Further assume that the maximum 20% support will be proportioned as follows: 3% from the Republican, 6% from the Democratic, and 11% from the Independent registration for the total of 20% in the worst-case district. It is our intention that we will achieve EHP membership for a maximum of 20% of the voting population in the extreme districts. For analysis of this extreme case, let us suppose that in a particular district race, candidate "A" has 60% of the voting population and candidate "B" has only 40% of the available votes before considering HERA and the pledge. So "A" would expect to win by a landslide. The 20% of voters with EHP membership will on the average have the same 60/40 vote split so 60% of 20% = 12% in favor of "A" and 40% of 20% = 8% in favor of "B".

Now suppose "B" gets serious about winning the election and he decides to provide the written endorsement of HERA to the EHP. If he does not endorse he will certainly lose the election! Then the 8% who support "B" anyway will continue to support "B" but the 12% that support "A" will be required as they pledged, to switch their vote from "A" to "B". So "A" would drop 12% from 60% to 48% and "B" would increase by 12% from 40% to 52%. Now "B" is ahead by 52% to 48%. This assumes 100% pledge compliance. Suppose the pledge compliance was only 83%. Then 83% of 12% = 10%. So now "A" would drop by 10% to 50% and "B" will increase 10% from 40% to 50% and we have an even race instead of a landslide victory for "A".

This analysis was the basis for the 20% of voting population maximum district goal. Now suppose "B" who is not happy facing a sudden upset decides to endorse HERA as well. Then we have endorsements for HERA from both candidates and it no longer matters who wins the election. Most likely some of those who switched to "B" would now switch back to "A" and "A" could still win the election. Since we are not running a candidate we do not have to win the election to get an endorsement for HERA from the winner. We can win either way!

The first candidate to endorse HERA will be the only candidate to be endorsed by the Prosperity Party (EHP). The EHP will not contribute to any political campaign or candidate. Instead the EHP will spend on advertising that announces the first endorsement and support for that candidate because of their endorsement. A subsequent endorsement by a second candidate will not benefit from these promotional advantages.

Let us look at a less extreme more normal case. Suppose candidate "A" has 52% and "B" has 48% before considering HERA. This is a more normal case where the Democrat and Republican are more balanced. Now suppose the EHP has only 5% of the voting populace as pledged members. The breakdown is the same as the 52/48 split. So 52% of 5% is 2.6% for "A" and 48% of 5% is 2.4% for "B".

Now after endorsing HERA "B" would gain 2.6% from "A" and "A" would lose 2.6% so the totals would be 49.4% for "A" and 50.6% for "B". If the pledge compliance was only 83% the race would now be nearly even and slightly in favor of "B". So in this less extreme case the EHP only needs a membership of 5% of the voting population in order to persuade the winning candidate to fully endorse HERA.

A more complete analysis can be done later, but the idea of our district strategy is clear. We will analyze each Congressional district. Our goal will be to have 67% ($2/3^{rd}$ majority) of winning candidates endorse HERA in writing. In each district we will calculate what percentage of the voting population we need as members to achieve our national goal. We know from the above analysis that it will probably vary from 5% to 20% depending on the district. In any case it is a small percent.

This data will then become our goal for membership in each district. We will rely on grassroots membership drives to get our membership to the desired levels. Many districts will require little effort while the more extreme districts will require substantial effort. But these goals are very achievable from a political point of view. Notice that we do not need to have a candidate in the election. In fact not having a candidate allows us to have **more** power in the election because we do not need to win the election in order to achieve our goal. So we can do this and the sooner we get started the sooner we can achieve our goal.

A Call to Action

I have proposed an economic basis of first principles including a Bill of 10 Economic Rights and 6 key mathematical axioms that will guide us nationally and internationally to safe and secure economic reforms. I have applied these first principles to provide you with a detailed plan for specific reform legislation known as the Humanistic Economic

Reform Act or HERA. I have explained how HERA can be used as a template for worldwide economic reforms as well as in the USA.

Furthermore I have shown how we can expand the Federal Reserve's Central Bank monetary authority with delegated Congressional authority to add fiscal controls, tax controls, and investment controls to form the ECA to proactively enforce these principles and institute these reforms nationally. I have also shown how we can institute ongoing national goals that will continue prosperity improvements indefinitely into our future. Moreover I have explained how we can achieve fair trade and fair international economics as a new world order based on mutual metaeconomic principles and engineering.

In addition I have presented discussion concepts and details explaining and justifying the plan. Now I am asking you to set aside those new concepts and new details temporarily because they will become the responsibility of the ECA and the EHP. For your part all you have to do is join the Prosperity Party (EHP) and take and keep the solidarity membership pledge. Register as soon as the website is available.

This pledge will give the EHP and its international counterparts the power they need to achieve written endorsements for Phase I HERA from the Presidential and Congressional candidates. After you register, all you have to do is use the website to follow your Congressional district so you will know how to vote to keep your member pledge.

Make sure your Congressional district on file is correct for where you actually vote! There will likely be lots of last minute action so keep in close touch just before Election Day. We will report the current status of each Congressional district on our website. We will email, network, or text you on any last minute developments. If you do not have email, network, or text, check with a friend in your same Congressional district who does. This is all you have to do to achieve never ending prosperity for you and your children and I know we can do it together!

If you want to help further, you can pass these ideas on to your friends and urge them to join the Prosperity Party (EHP). If possible check the box that indicates you can volunteer. If you can do your part we will do ours and HERA will be approved by Congress and the President in just a few more elections by 2022 or so. It is truly worth waiting for!

Now it is time for you to stand and be counted. This vision is yours for the wishing! **Let's stand up together hand-in-hand and make this wish come true!**

Phase I: ECA Formation Legislation

This legislation will authorize the Federal Reserve System to change its name to the "Economic Control Authority" herein abbreviated as ECA. The intention of this enabling legislation is to authorize the existing Federal Reserve System to form shell organizations of no more than 6 new departments that will be used to specify proposed legislation to establish a new economic authority to achieve a democratic economy that embodies the following 6 proactive axioms:

1. The fundamental reason our economy exists is to serve humanity in facilitating the worker/consumer duality by achieving maximum prosperity for the vast majority of mankind.
2. Equal value wages must be paid for equal productivity of equal quality. $W = M \times P$.
3. Equal currencies can buy equal cost of living goods and services in their local economies.
4. The minimum wage paid must be equal or greater than the minimum cost of living to achieve life, liberty, and the pursuit of happiness.
5. Wages should increase at least to compensate for product price inflation, not caused by wage inflation, plus any increase in labor productivity. $W\% \geq Ip\% - Iw\% + P\%$.
6. We must ensure that the current depletion cost of natural resources worldwide truly represents their future replacement cost and that pollution costs truly represent their future elimination cost.

In addition the following Economic Bill of Rights will be used by the ECA for further guidance in proposing economic reforms consistent with our Constitution. These are inalienable implied rights that are believed to already be supported by our constitution's general rights.

1. The right to equal valued pay for equal valued work
2. The freedom from the oppression of an economic privileged class based on race, creed, gender, inheritance or other unearned or perpetual economic privileges
3. The freedom from economic exploitation especially unfair wages, unfair competition, unfair trade, unfair currency values, and other unfair or unequal economic treatments
4. The right to equal access to employment based on equal qualifications and abilities
5. The right to a living wage sufficient to achieve life, liberty, and the pursuit of happiness
6. The democratic collective right and responsibility to pursue and achieve economic prosperity for the common good of the majority
7. The right to sustainable life free from pollution and the right to share equally in the nation's natural resources with the responsibility to sustain them so all generations will preserve the same right
8. The freedom from taxation without representation achieved by financial or contractual burden passed forward perpetually from generation to generation
9. The right to affordable medical care and the opportunity to achieve and maintain good health
10. The right to an affordable education so that every human has the opportunity to develop to their full abilities

The above goals are unlikely to be achievable without eliminating the massive wealth and economic corruption that has infiltrated our political democracy. Consequently a new civil rights law for the balanced voice mandate will be needed that make it a felony offense to use personal or corporate wealth as a political privilege to advocate harm, obstruct, reduce or interfere with or exert unreasonable influence over the democratic rights of others especially "equal opportunity", "one man one vote", and the Economic Bill of Rights.

In addition to the general concept we need specific regulations limiting the annual sum of all local, state, and federal political contributions including specific lobbying and promotional costs. For institutions or businesses the sum of these costs cannot exceed the median contribution of the B90 group multiplied by the number of equivalent full-time employees or members. Thus the voice of any institution, group, corporation, or business is kept proportional to the voice of those citizens employed by or members of it keeping power balanced.

For wealthy individuals the total cannot exceed a median contribution of the T10 group multiplied by 10. Thus the voice of wealthy voters is proportional to the median of other wealthy individuals in their wealth class times ten. These restrictions ensure that the voice of the populace is kept in proportion to the voice of wealth power. These civil rights must be clarified prior to, or coincident with this formation legislation.

With these axioms and the Economic Bill of Rights as guidance, the ECA should propose new and modified legislation that will expand the control and responsibility of the ECA to accomplish the prosperity goals embodied in these axioms and rights including the current Federal Reserve inflation mandate and new sub mandates for full employment, employee participation, and annual productivity. In addition national economic goals should be proposed from time to time by the ECA and approved by Congress and the President to achieve and expand our national prosperity in an ongoing fashion.

Legislation authorization for the ECA board itself and its new departments will be submitted for approval one at a time to Congress and the President. Non-partisan committees will be set up by Congress for the ECA and each department to help with guidance for the preliminary approval. Once each political authorization is complete Congress will institute and approve final activation authorization and supply it to the President for final approval and enactment activation.

Publication Note:

As of the publication date we still need institutional supporters and party leadership positions filled to complete the party's legal formation, website, and phone support. Spread the word we need help! The author is reachable by using a *username* that is one word, lowercase, his full name (on the book title) at: *username*@ gmail.com and there is a blog available using the same *username* at: http://www.*username*.blogspot.com/

Bibliography

David Wiedemer, R. A. (2011). *Aftershock.* Hoboken NJ: John Wiley & Sons.

Schumacher, E. F. (1973). *Small is beautiful; economics as if people mattered.* New York, Harper & Row.

Domhoff, W. (2010). *Wealth, Income, and Power.* WhoRulesAmerica.net.

Excel file Tab Fig 2006. (2006). wealthandwant.com.

HuffPost Live. (2013). *CEO-To-Worker Pay Ratio Ballooned 1,000 percent Since 1950.* Huffington Post.

Benen, Steve (2014). *Perkins suggests poor should lose voting rights.* MSNBC The Rachel Maddow Show Blog. 02/14/14.

Rickards, J. (2011). *Currency Wars.* Penguin/Portfolio.

Wagstaff, K. (2013, August 6). What should the minimum wage be ? *The Week.*

Greenhouse, S. (2009, Feb. 10). *The Big Squeeze: Tough Times for the American Worker,* Knopf Doubleday Publishing Group.

Greenhouse, S. (2013, January 12). Our Economic Pickle. *New York Times Sunday Review.*

Shin, L. (2014, January 23). The 85 Richest People in the World Have as Much Wealth as the 3.5 Billion Poorest. *Forbes*.

Wikipedia. (2013). *China's Historical GDP figures for 1978-2013*. Wikipedia.

Hanks, T. (Director). (1992). *A League of Their Own* [Motion Picture].

Gross National Income, % of GDP 2001. (n.d.). Retrieved May 13, 2015, from Nation Master: http://www.nationmaster.com/country-info/stats/Economy/Gross-National-Income%2C-%25-of-GDP

McChesney, J. N. (2014). *Dollarocracy: How the Money and Media Election Complex is Destroying America*. Amazon.com.

Ryle, B. (2015, September 23). *Wages vs Corporate Profits: The Real Culprit*. Retrieved July 22, 2016, from Wealty Daily: www.wealthdaily.com

Butler, T. (2014, June 27). *COMEX - Why it's Corrupt*. Retrieved February 16, 2016, from SilverSeek.com: http://silverseek.com/commentary/comex-%E2%80%93-why-it%E2%80%99s-corrupt-13323

Davis, S. (2014, February 18). CBO report: Minimum wage hike could cost 500,000 jobs. USA Today.

O'Callaghan, J. (2016, January 19). Stephen Hawking Warns Humanity Could Destroy Itself In The Next 100 Years. Retrieved April 4, 2017 from ITL Science: http://www.iflscience.com/space/stephen-hawking-warns-humanity-could-destroy-itself-next-100-years/

Keynes, John Maynard (1931). *The Future, Essays in Persuasion*.

Made in the USA
Columbia, SC
27 July 2019